THE WOMEN'S WAR
VOICES FROM SEPTEMBER 11

THE WOMEN'S WAR
VOICES FROM SEPTEMBER 11

CHRISTOPHER HILTON

SUTTON PUBLISHING

First published in the United Kingdom in 2002 by
Sutton Publishing Limited · Phoenix Mill
Thrupp · Stroud · Gloucestershire · GL5 2BU

Copyright © Christopher Hilton, 2002

All rights reserved. No part of this publication may be reproduced, stored in a retrieval system, or transmitted, in any form, or by any means, electronic, mechanical, photocopying, recording or otherwise, without the prior permission of the publisher and copyright holder.

Christopher Hilton has asserted the moral right to be identified as the author of this work.

British Library Cataloguing in Publication Data
A catalogue record for this book is available from the British Library.

ISBN 0-7509-3021-7

Typesetting in 11/15½pt Sabon.
Typesetting and origination by
Sutton Publishing Limited.
Printed and bound in England by
J.H. Haynes & Co. Ltd, Sparkford.

Contents

	Introduction: 9/11/01	xiii
One	The Policewoman	1
Two	The Refusenik	16
Three	The Firefighter's Widow	33
Four	The Organiser	48
Five	The Businesswoman	61
Six	The Reporter	85
Seven	The Fiancée	107
Eight	The Naval Chief	128
Nine	The Coordinator	152
Ten	The Exile	173
Eleven	The Insurance Attorney	195
	Notes	222

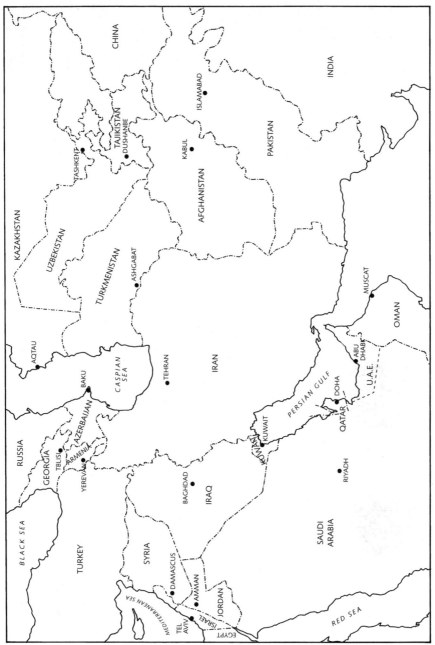

The Middle East from the Mediterranean, showing the position of Afghanistan.

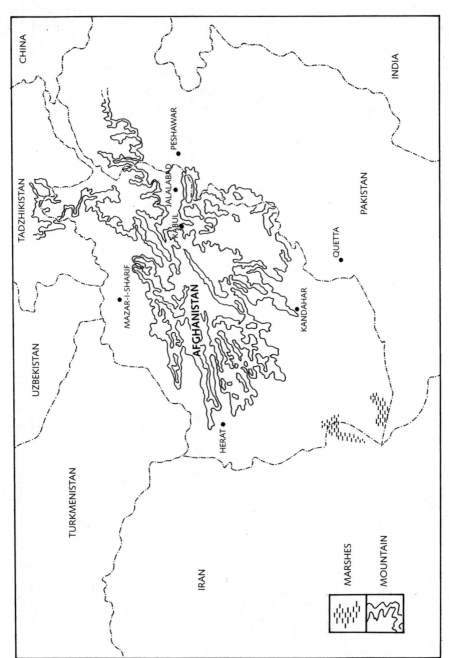

Afghanistan.

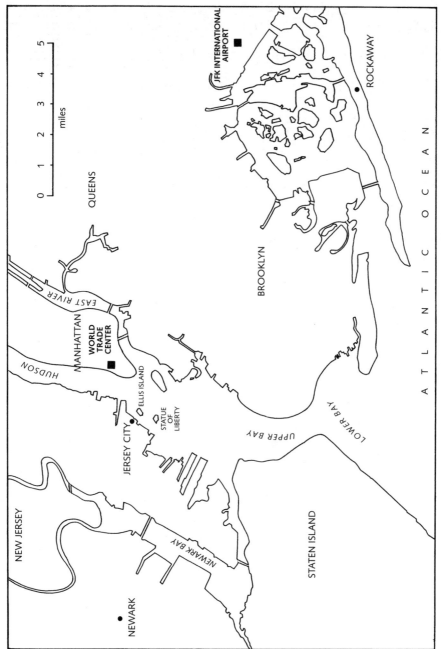

Greater New York.

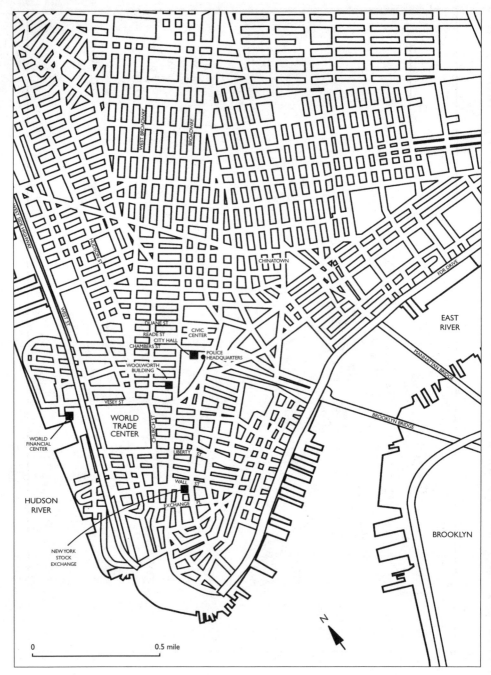

Lower Manhattan.

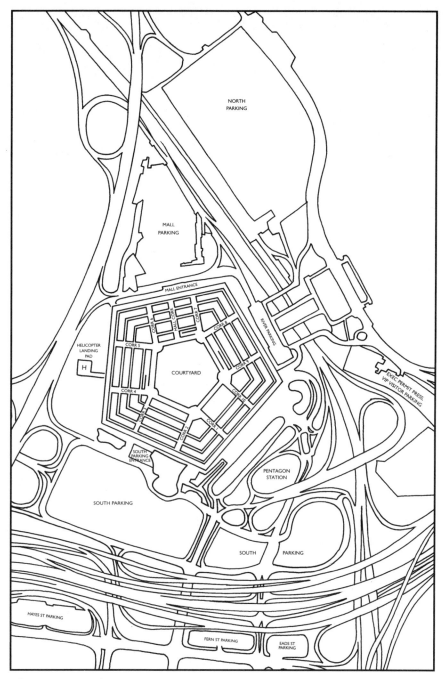

The Pentagon, Arlington, Virginia.

INTRODUCTION

9/11/01

It was an ordinary Tuesday. Lt Terri Tobin sat in her small office on the thirteenth floor of 1 Police Plaza, a dignified modern building in Lower Manhattan. The office had the bric-a-brac of modernity, shelves and files and paperwork and a computer. Her only window gave a view of a narrow corridor and, on the other side of it, a sink where the coffee cups were washed. Someone burst into the office at 8.48 or maybe 8.49 a.m.[1] talking fast: 'A plane just went into the World Trade Center.' Her mind reacted fast: *Must be a small plane, a Cessna or something, and the pilot's had a heart attack.*

A minute after that she was heading down towards the police garage for a car.

The World Trade Center stood a mile away but its Twin Towers – the north tower at 1,368 feet, the south at 1,362 – were so immense that they could be seen from here and everywhere else.[2]

Her mind, still reacting fast, thought *They'll be evacuating people eastwards* so she decided, rather than meet this flow of people as she tried to work her way west, she'd go round the tip of Manhattan and miss them. She got there at 8.54. She knows that because she saved the time on her beeper and 8.54 was 'when we were mobilised'.

By then the nightmare was already written in fire across the beautiful, pastel blue sky of late summer.

xiii

Introduction

Peshawar, Pakistan. Dusk wasn't far away in the first big town in Pakistan on the road from the capital of Afghanistan, Kabul. Tahmeena Faryal, a young woman who had dedicated her life to women's rights, was at home. It was 5.54 p.m., or thereabouts. Peshawar was a bustling town with bazaars where you could buy anything from videos to hair clips: everyone had something to sell. 'I saw it on television. We didn't have any electricity that night – in Pakistan, sometimes you don't – and we had to turn on our emergency generator. I'd heard that something had happened, along with some neighbours who'd heard the same thing. The first feeling I had was one of sadness because it was a terrible thing - on that first day it could have been 20,000 – 30,000 people dead. We didn't know. We were talking that night and we said the Taliban and bin Laden should be the first suspects.'

Brooklyn, New York. Marian Fontana was excited because this was her wedding anniversary and her husband Dave, a firefighter, would, when he finished his 24-hour shift, start a month's vacation. On the day before, their son Aidan had started school full-time which meant that Marian and Dave would have most of the day to themselves.

She was into theatre production and had received an invitation to try and get a grant. That was to be in the evening and when she'd said, 'No, no, no, it's our anniversary and I can't', he'd replied, 'I'll get off work and we'll go out during the day. Then you can go to this thing at night.' She found that very touching. They intended to visit the Whitney Museum in Manhattan. They rarely went to museums these days – hard er when the child had come along – and she had a friend working there who'd give them a special tour. Marian had rung Dave at 8.30 a.m., just before she left to deliver Aidan to school. Dave was happy to be on vacation and, like her, excited about the anniversary. She asked, 'Are you finished?' and he replied, 'I'm finished, I'm dressed and I'm ready to go.' That meant the next shift had arrived to relieve him. She said, 'I'll meet you in ten minutes' – at a coffee shop across the street. He said, 'Great, I'll be there.'

Introduction

Gothenburg, Sweden. Ulla Åsberg had been walking home in the solid and stolid port, and 'just as I opened the door my phone rang. I picked it up and my ex-husband said "put on the TV".' It was 2.54 p.m., or thereabouts. 'Then a lot of Afghan people phoned and said "have you heard the news?" I said. "It's just on the television now." My first thought was *it's Osama bin Laden*. I told my ex-husband *this is Osama behind this*. He said, "How can you be so sure?" and I replied, "I just know." In one way I couldn't be sure but in another way, inside myself, I could.'

She had spent a lifetime working in charity, two of them hard years in Kabul.

'Then I had to phone my kids. My son is in Lahore working as a volunteer and I knew he didn't have a TV, so this is what happened with me. Then I was stuck with the TV like everybody else and I sat there totally shocked.'

Peshawar, Pakistan. Dr Aqila Noori, like Åsberg a charity worker – for the same Swedish charity, as it happened – had spent the day in their offices and was now at home. 'I was just watching television. It was Pakistani television and we were not aware that anything had happened. They said, "Breaking news is coming" and they showed the pictures. We had a CNN connection and directly we changed it to CNN. My first reaction? I was too much surprised that such destruction would happen in the world because the people, they were too aggressive.'

Later, e-mails would come in to charity offices purporting to be from Americans saying, 'We will destroy you people, we will even destroy your children. You have killed innocent Americans.' The origin of these e-mails was invariably unknown and Dr Noori is 'sure they were from local people'. That would have been fundamentalist Pakistanis wanting to discredit the United States by pretending to be Americans.

Manhattan Island. Diane Kenna, a dedicated marathon runner, worked for stockbrokers Merrill Lynch in their building next to the

Introduction

Twin Towers, but the view from her desk was north-west and so she didn't ever see them through the window. She was on the seventh floor – the trading floor – and, at about 8.30 a.m., had gone outside for her second cup of coffee. She bought it from a little street-car vendor on the corner of the street. She took the coffee back in, and during the elevator journey up talked of work and jobs and stress with a colleague. She reached the trading floor: 600 or 700 people, mostly male, volatile and noisy. They all felt a vibration, a *whooosh* 'like a huge wind hit the building'. Trading rooms being what they are, as she says, there was some joking. People were saying 'Maybe it's a bomb, like '93, maybe we can go home for the day'. She decided she'd go back outside to see what had happened. The thought was that it might even have been that a taxi cab had crashed.

Manhattan Island. Marilynn K. Yee, an experienced *New York Times* photographer in her fifties, had just finished her first job of the day far uptown. She'd been covering mayoral candidate Mike Bloomberg voting in the primary election. She thought she'd drive down to Chinatown because the *Times* didn't carry that many pictures of ethnic groups and one of them voting had a good chance of being used.

She phoned the picture desk and they gave her a job, at noon: another political shot. She'd go there after Chinatown. She got into her car – an office Chevrolet - at around 8.35 and as the journey progressed she noticed the traffic wasn't really moving. A voice on the radio said a plane had hit the World Trade Center. She thought *what?* and tried to work out what could be happening. She assumed it was a light plane and the incident would be over long before she got there. Then the voice said that people were jumping from the tower. She phoned the picture desk again.

Estoril, Portugal. Christina Lamb, an experienced *Sunday Telegraph* foreign correspondent in her mid-thirties, was on a sabbatical.

Introduction

She had known Afghanistan for more than a decade but, now, she'd a book to write on the exploration of the Amazon – she had just come back from Brazil where she had spent a couple of months researching it.

Married to a Portuguese, they had a ground-floor apartment by a swimming pool. They went there so that she would have quiet for the writing and her two-year-old son Lourenço could learn some Portuguese. She'd spent a couple of days preparing the apartment because normally it was a holiday place. She needed, and bought, a desk. This Tuesday was Lourenço's first day at nursery school and by lunchtime he was back. She was ready to begin writing but, as journalists do, switched on the TV news. It was 2.54 p.m., or thereabouts. What she saw she found difficult to believe. Lourenço was just at the age when he liked planes and could say the word. He kept shouting 'Mummy, plane' because the image was being shown again and again.

The coverage was from CNN but with Portuguese commentators, and now they talked of an attack on London. Her mind moved immediately to Canary Wharf, the tower where her office was, and so similar to the Twin Towers: taller by far than anything else around it. She also thought *We are in Portugal and we are safe*.

That did not prevent her from reaching for the phone to ring the Foreign Desk. She knew it was the biggest thing that had ever happened in her life and she wanted to cover it.

Munich Airport, Germany. Valerie Powell, an experienced British nurse with the charity Merlin, had been working in Tajikistan with Afghan refugees and was returning to London via Munich. When she reached the airport she was struck by 'how quiet and empty it appeared as I went to check in for my onward flight. Looking downstairs to the restaurant area I noticed many people in front of the TV screen.' It was 2.54 p.m., or thereabouts. Curious, she went to see what was on. She remembers the absolute silence, not one person speaking. She couldn't understand the commentary because it

Introduction

was in German, but she didn't need to. She watched, horrified, until she had to board her London flight. She realised the implications of what she had seen. She knew she'd be going back to work with refugees.

The shoreline, New Jersey. Debbie Barrett was asleep in the house she shared with her fiancé Brian Cummins. He also had an apartment in Manhattan and had spent the Monday night there, as he did when he was working very late or had to be back at work very early. He'd called her that Monday night, they'd spoken for an hour and the final words were 'I love you'. She had a rule that he would not call her before 9 a.m. – 'I used to get mad because he'd call me at 6–6.30 when he got to work.'

He held a senior position with Cantor Fitzgerald and his office was on the 104th floor of the north tower.

It was somewhere between 8.46 and 9.0 a.m. – maybe even 8.54 – when the phone rang, waking her. It wasn't Brian but a friend who worked a few blocks away from the World Trade Center and who had been speaking on the phone to Cummins at the moment of impact. She heard him screaming, 'Brian's building's been hit, Brian's building's been hit. I don't know what's happened. Turn on your television.' He said his building was shaking and thought Wall Street was being bombed. As he spoke she could hear explosions.

'Debbie, I've got to go, we're under attack, we're being evacuated.' Within seconds the phone rang again and now Brian's brother was screaming, 'Turn on your television, turn on your television. Does Brian have his cell phone with him? What's his number, what's his number?'

Nobody knew the truth: it was a lifetime too late for that.

The Pentagon, Arlington, Virginia. Naval Chief Sheryl A. Alleger had arrived at her office on the Fifth Floor at 8.30 a.m. and carried out 'turn over' with her immediate supervisor. Soon after this the supervisor left to deliver some documents. Alleger settled to her

Introduction

day's work and the phone rang. It was a woman friend in the Air Force she'd been stationed with. 'I know you don't have a TV', the woman said. 'You need to go downstairs and watch CNN. Just go.' Alleger descended one floor and went to the Under Secretary's outer office. Three people stood there already watching.

CNN were broadcasting the aftermath of the first plane hitting. She watched live as the second plane hit. She'd remember Bush speaking and just then a phone rang. A colonel answered it, made no conversation, replaced the receiver and said: 'That was the Command Center and they are reporting an unconfirmed aircraft headed in this direction. We need to move.' Thirty seconds later it felt as if the whole Pentagon had been lifted and set back down again.

Faizabad, Afghanistan. Jacqui Tong, a 39-year-old Medical Coordinator with *Médecins Sans Frontières*, was emerging from her bedroom into the common room of the charity's house along an ordinary street. Dusk was coming in, as it was in Peshawar. Three of her team were there and one grabbed her arm, told her. They crouched over their high frequency radio tuned to the BBC World Service and she can still remember the eyes of the person she was looking into the whole time. He was completely stunned. She can still remember, too, that they knew who must have done it and they mouthed the name: 'It's bin Laden.' This was a calculation based on the fact that 'he would be capable of something like that'. Tong knew all about Osama bin Laden and the Taliban because this, her seventh tour for *MSF*, had taken her to Afghanistan.

London, England. Margaret Owen, a 69-year-old lawyer specialising in the plight of Third World widows, was in her local mini-market in Shepherd's Bush. It was 1.54 p.m., or thereabouts, on a crisp, dry afternoon. Her son Dan, wife and baby had flown back to the United States the day before, Dan to resume his job at the World Bank next to the Pentagon. The radio was on in the mini-market but the other six customers, and the Asian owners, paid no

Introduction

attention to what was coming out of it. Margaret Owen did and she was thinking *This isn't a very funny spoof – that a plane's gone into the World Trade Center. That's really peculiar, and not very funny.* Still nobody paid any attention, just kept on with their shopping. Now she thought *Is this a play? It's a bit early for the afternoon play on the BBC.* She walked back to her pretty terraced house and the phone rang. A great friend of Dan said, 'Put on your television.'

London, England. Seema Ghani, a 23-year-old Afghan exile, was working as a project manager with a big consultancy firm. The office was open-plan and 'all of a sudden one of my colleagues shouted from the other end that a plane just hit the Twin Towers in New York.' That would have been at about 1.54 p.m. Everyone gathered round his screen and he got the internet on it. They watched and listened. Phones began to ring in the quiet and people went to answer them. He shouted, 'Another one'. Ghani felt a sense of shock so profoundly that, although 'I knew my phone was ringing, I just couldn't bring myself to go and pick it up.' She heard a radio announcement that it seemed to be a terrorist attack. She had no way of knowing that it would end her exile: she'd go back to Kabul to run an orphanage.

Manhattan Island. Renée Mangalo, a New York defence attorney in her early thirties and – like Diane Kenna, although she had never heard of her – a dedicated marathon runner, lived in a Greenwich Village apartment she shared with a room-mate. There was the primary election and before work she was going to vote. She'd do that on Sixth Avenue, which had a direct view of the World Trade Center and the Twin Towers framed against this perfect morning. She noticed a 'big crowd' and she heard people saying, 'Oh my God, look at that.' She had absolutely no idea what had happened or, by definition, who had done it, but she could see a hole near the top of the north tower. The fire had not begun.

Introduction

She did not know much – if anything – of Osama bin Laden but she'd read a lot about the Taliban and the plight of women in Afghanistan under their rule because 'I was so distraught about it'. As a practising Catholic, a rule of her life was that people were not inherently evil but circumstances made them so. After this morning she'd never think that again.

She went in to vote and make a phone call to find out what the hell was going on. She'd ring her boyfriend Frank, who was in New York's Fire Department, because he'd certainly know. The fire brigade was bound to be involved, one way or another. As she made the call it was 8.54 a.m., or thereabouts. She never did get through and so she knew nothing yet; and neither did anybody else.

They were all going to find out, and some would be spared most of the anger and the fear and the grief.

Some wouldn't.

The context of this book embraces not only the United States and Europe but a tract of the Arab world: specifically Pakistan and even more specifically Afghanistan, that rugged and forbidding place which had been at war with itself and others for a couple of generations. We need an historical cameo to fill out the context. The Soviet Union, pouring its might in, was bled and beaten into retreat in 1988. The organisation known everywhere as the Taliban – which struck at the Twin Towers on 11 September 2001 – was created from Afghans who were Islamic fighters and Afghans who had been trained in religious schools in Pakistan. In 1994 they were appointed by the Pakistan government[3] as bodyguards for a convoy into Afghanistan. They protected it against looters, took over the city of Kandahar and by 1996 had Kabul, as well. They brought order to a war-exhausted and anarchic country but were determined to set up the purest Islamic state in the world. Among other things, that meant removing basic rights from women.

In 1989 Osama bin Laden, a Saudi from a very wealthy family, founded a group called *al-Qa'eda* with the stated aim of driving the

Introduction

United States military out of the Saudi Arabian peninsula. The group had tentacles worldwide, with training camps and guesthouses[4] in Pakistan, Somalia, Kenya and Afghanistan. *Al-Qa'eda* provided money for the Taliban, and bin Laden came to live in Afghanistan as a 'guest'.

Al-Qa'eda resolved to fight a holy war against the ultimate evil, the United States. One attempt had already been made, in 1993, to blow up the World Trade Center but it went wrong. *Al-Qa'eda* would come back, and, at 8.46 a.m. on 11 September, they did.

The book is not choreographed; it has gender but no agenda. It comprises in-depth interviews with a broad spectrum of women touched, mentally and physically, by a war like all other wars: men launched it and (almost without exception) men prosecuted it. No doubt in time men will sit in judgment on it, and those who fought it, too.

Ground Zero has many levels.

The participants represent different aspects and were chosen without preliminary research. I knew none of the people before I began and some I came across entirely by chance – Kenna and Mangalo, for example because they were fleetingly mentioned in an article on the New York City Marathon. I had no idea what they'd tell me. Others, like Lt Tobin and Chief Alleger, were kindly found by their respective press offices. Again I had no idea what they'd tell me until I sat down with them.

I wanted ordinary people and, cumulatively, I wanted them to say *this is what it was like, this is what it is like*. It is a book about experiences, not conclusions. Those must wait for another day.

I have tried to be unobtrusive. The questions I asked were open and I let the answers evolve in any direction they were going. I did, however, ask each participant two specific questions. *If there were more women leaders would there be fewer wars?* and *What would you have done after 11 September?* Those answers evolved, too.

At the end of most chapters I have put in a subsection entitled *Silences and Other Voices* which has allowed me to include shorter

Introduction

interviews and explore a wide variety of related material. It goes into some unexpected corners and some painful wounds.

I have been astonished, and I do not wield that word carelessly, by the willingness of strangers to open their hearts to me and let me reproduce what came from those hearts. I therefore salute immediately the main participants, who you have met briefly already. In order, Lt Terri Tobin, Tahmeena Faryal, Marian Fontana, Ulla Åsberg, Diane Kenna, Christina Lamb, Debbie Barrett, Chief Alleger, Jacqui Tong, Seema Ghani and Renée Mangalo.

I owe a special debt to Flora Myer because it was in conversation with her that the idea was born. My original thought was to tell stories of eleven people touched by the war but, ruminating, she said eleven women might be more interesting because, as with so many aspects of life, here they were on the receiving end again. E.L. Gordon, an old journalistic friend, scanned what seemed the entire North American media output and directed me to whatever was relevant.

I thank those who made, I trust, *Silences and Other Voices* relevant and revealing, primarily Marilynn K. Yee because she was honest about the implications of trying to cover tragedy with a certain dispassion and took the trouble to search out photographs from her superb portfolio. The book is richer for having them in. Jennifer Middleton, Staff Attorney of Lambda Legal Defense and Education Fund, explained the legalities which might touch every unmarried couple, and Dr Aqila Noori of the Swedish Committee charity gave me an update on the situation in Afghanistan. Lucy Aita spoke about the vagaries of human nature. A doctor, who could not give her real name in case of reprisals against her family still in Afghanistan, laughed her way through choosing to be known as Miss X, Miss K of Kabul or Miss Afghan – and chose to be Miss Afghan.

Some were conduits to the interviews and deserve thanks, also: James Kliffen of *Médecins Sans Frontières*; David Martin of Merlin who set up an e-mail interview with their nurse Valerie Powell in the field – and special thanks to her for responding in such detail; Ron

Introduction

A. Steiner of the US Navy's media department in the Pentagon – a ferociously efficient (and agreeable) man; Carmen Melendez of the NYPD; Karen Bartlett, formerly of the Fabian Society; Dennis Roddy of the *Pittsburgh Post-Gazette*, who did his best; Dianne C. Baumert-Moyik, president, Baumert PR and Design, Inc; Angela Keen of the *Sunday Telegraph*, London, Foreign Desk – and I am particularly grateful to Robin Gedye, that newspaper's Foreign Editor, for giving permission to use material from three of Christina Lamb's feature articles.

I must add a particular word of thanks to Amelia Nice, Advocacy officer of WOMANKIND (Raising the Status of Women across the World) who became an instant and enthusiastic supporter of the book, and helped me enormously with contacts. One of them was Margaret Owen, founder of Empowering Women in Development and Widows for Peace and Reconstruction, who gave chilling insights.

ONE

The Policewoman

I was literally blown out of my shoes and thrown at least thirty feet, where I landed face down on a small grassy area. All I heard was people screaming – for help, for God – and then it became pitch black. I was struck in the back of my head. I heard the helmet I was wearing split in half.

Lieutenant Terri Tobin of the New York Police Department was born into the job. You can't put it any other way and even she says it's genetic. 'My father was an officer with the NYPD. I am one of five children and four out of the five of us became law enforcement officers. My sister got off the hook because . . . she married an officer. I do think it is genetic, although living day in day out with someone like my father, who truly loved what he did, came across as the best advertisement for the NYPD.'

Tobin, a native New Yorker, is single and 'just turned 40' in December 2001. She'd been in the police for nineteen years and at the time the 'focus' of her work was media relations. She was, however, widely experienced. 'There are over 6,000 women in the NYPD and they do the same job as men for the same pay. It's all civil service. We are trained to use guns, and gender does not change that training. I have never shot anybody, thank God. Sure, I have waved the gun at people and been present at gunfights. I have never fired my weapon and I think that is true of 95 per cent of all NYPD officers. They do a twenty-year career without firing their weapon other than for training purposes. Murders tend to make the headlines when they happen but they are a very rare occurrence.'

And she sat in her office at 1 Police Plaza, amid the bric-a-brac. She was wearing 'civilian attire – I had on a skirt and blouse. My shoes weren't high heels, they were flat like a loafer.'

She was about to move from media relations to frontline duty inside nine minutes. It was 8.46 on 11 September and someone burst in. She grabbed a pair of sneakers, because the World Trade Center covered 16 acres and she 'knew that I was going to have to be running around, so it seemed like the most efficient thing to do'.

She set off urgently for the police garage and a departmental car, which was assigned to her. She put the sneakers in the trunk and drove, with a sergeant on the passenger seat next to her. 'There were two people walking up the ramp to the garage from our photo unit so I stopped. Obviously I knew where they were going. I said, "hop in, I'll take you over".'

The police headquarters was on the east side of Lower Manhattan, the World Trade Center on the west. Its evacuation would be to the east, and since some 50,000 people worked in the Twin Towers, they'd be blocking her passage through. She went *south*, to follow the tip of Manhattan and go round the evacuation.

'In my mind, as I was leaving, I thought it was a Cessna and the pilot had had a heart attack. I never thought of a commercial airline except when I was on FDR Drive by the base of the Brooklyn Bridge and I saw the amount of paper that was floating. It was like a ticker tape parade.' She could see the north tower and 'I started thinking *there is a huge hole in that building*. I know that I was there by 8.54 because I saved the time on my beeper. That's when we were mobilised.'

Lieutenant Tobin has carefully set down her experiences from this moment on[1] and I propose to quote it in its entirety.

The Policewoman

On September 11th my colleagues and I responded to the World Trade Center. Arriving shortly after the first plane had hit, the north tower had flames shooting out and the ground was covered with shattered glass. The NYPD had mobilized us to Church and Vesey Street, where the Command Staff dispersed us to posts.

The First Deputy Commissioner, Joe Dunne, grabbed me and told me to get an ESU [Emergency Service Unit] helmet and put it on. The second plane hit the south tower, and a huge explosion along with shooting flames and flying debris shook the ground. It was at this point I became aware of people jumping out of the north tower; some people jumped holding hands while others jumped individually. I can't imagine what a hell it must have been for them being inside the towers at this point; some people were on fire as they jumped from the windows.

I went into the north tower to assist the uniformed personnel who were evacuating people. I was also sent in to make sure that the pathway out of the building was clear and that no unauthorized people were in what we refer to as the 'frozen zone'. The officers there were doing a great job, and no matter where you looked there was an officer directing people to safety. I crossed over to the south tower and saw a photographer taking photos of people coming down the escalator. As he was impeding the process and shouldn't have been there, I escorted him out of the building to Church and Liberty.

As I had parked close to that location I thought, 'it's going to be a long day, I should change into my sneakers'. I walked underneath the overhang of the south tower and got close enough to pop the trunk of my car, when I heard a very loud rumbling noise behind me. I turned and started to walk back to the south tower. Then all of a sudden people started running toward me, screaming that the building was coming down. When I looked up, the building had already begun to pancake.

Due to the force of the explosion, I was literally blown out of my shoes and thrown at least thirty feet to the west side of West Street and Liberty, where I landed face down on the small grassy area in front of One World Financial Center. All I heard was people screaming – for help, for God – and then it just became pitch black. As I was laying on the ground, and debris was falling all around and on top of me, I was struck in the back of my head. I heard the helmet I was wearing split in half and fall off my head.

There was blood flowing down the back of my neck and when I reached back, I felt a huge piece of cement embedded in my skull. I thought for a moment that I was unconscious because it was totally black and totally quiet, but I was aware of how hard it was to breathe. At one point, I pulled my shirt up to cover my nose and mouth. The time sequences are very difficult to recall but, as the black smoke started to clear, I was able to make out a silhouette of a firefighter on my right who called out, 'are you okay?'. I said, 'yes' and he yelled back not to move and to keep my nose and mouth covered.

I was hearing someone scream and moan to my left, so I reached out and felt fingers which I grabbed. I shouted to the person that I was a Lieutenant with the NYPD and there was a firefighter to my right and we would help them. I told them to stay down and repeated the same instructions the firefighter had yelled to me. There were very loud explosions in the darkness and I thought we were being bombed. The air was very heavy and my eyes were burning as well as my throat.

As the blackness began to lift, I told the person whose hand I was holding that I was going to try to see if I could get up, but wouldn't let go of their hand. I was able to get the top half of my body out of the rubble. As I knelt, I realized that the hand had come up too easily and when I looked down I was holding a hand and an arm with no one attached to it. I tried climbing over to the area, but there was no body to be found. Kneeling, I discovered I was enmeshed in building cables and it took me a while to get untangled. When I was able to get to my feet, I turned to where my car was parked and it was engulfed in flames, along with an ambulance and fire truck. I joined with the firefighter who had been on my right and two EMS [Emergency Medical Service] workers. The EMS workers had saline solution and we washed out our eyes and spit out the black soot that was in our mouths and throats. I thought I had spit out a piece of cement, only to find out later it was my wisdom tooth.

The EMS workers then wrapped my head in gauze to stop the bleeding from my head. It was eerily silent, but as we were able to listen closely we heard people calling out for help. As we could decipher where they were calling from we moved as a group toward the voices and began digging through the rubble to get the people out. We knew that the people at our location were other rescue workers, as all civilians were directed in the opposite direction.

Shortly after, people started screaming bloody murder that the second tower was coming down and to get out of the area. I started to run toward the water[2] but, unknown to me at the time, I had a fractured ankle and before I knew it a second cloud of debris was upon me.

I was hit hard in the back and fell but, as the blackness started to engulf me again, I got up and was able to run into a nearby building. It turned out to be an apartment building that had lost its power. I followed the emergency lights into the interior of the building. When I got to the elevator shafts and saw that they were stopped on the first floor I opened the door to the stairwell and there were at least a hundred frightened and panicked people lined all the way up.

I told them to filter out of the stairwell and enter the lobby but stay away from the glass windows. After they were all down I went back to the door I had entered. The white ash, which later I found out was pulverized cement, filled the air. Through the haze I saw two NYPD members, belonging to our Technical Assistance Response Unit (TARU) out on the street. I went out and called them. They came over immediately and they told me that we were evacuating people by boat to Jersey. It was at this point that one of the officers told me there was a shard of glass through my blouse and sticking out of my back, between my shoulder blades.

One officer said he would go to the boat with me and the other said he would begin evacuating the building. Once at the dock, there were two boats being loaded and an additional two Harbor Units were pulling in. The Captain of the Harbor Unit called over two EMS workers who told me they were going to cut my blouse off so they could pull the shard of glass out. As they did this, they poured peroxide over the wound and wrapped me in gauze. Once wrapped up, they immediately put me on a Harbor Launch which took me to Ellis Island.

There I was then taken by ambulance to a medical center in New Jersey. I was met by a triage team[3] who took me into the emergency room, where they immediately did a chest x-ray and sent me up to surgery. Because of the blunt trauma to my head, the surgeon could not give me anesthesia but she was able to cut the cement out and stitched me across the back of my head. She then tended to my back where she stitched me between the shoulder blades.

An x-ray of my ankle showed it was fractured but due to the lacerations and open wounds in the area they were unable to cast it. The doctors told me I had suffered a severe concussion and recommended that I not be alone for forty-eight hours. The doctors also told me how lucky I was to be alive and I couldn't agree more.

This remarkable human testimony was complete unto itself in one sense, but in another, seemed to demand amplification.

The Policewoman

Lieutenant Tobin, taking the overview six months later, is sure that a 'guardian angel' was watching over her. 'First, I get a helmet on. There was a report of a third plane in the area – an F16 [fighter plane] which, on the ground, we obviously didn't know until it passed. Only then did we have an idea of what it was. I jumped on the ESU truck and I got one of their helmets. It's made so that bullets can't go through it – much heavier than the one I had in my trunk. If I hadn't had that helmet on when that slab of cement came crashing through, I would have been decapitated. Then to come across a photographer and if I didn't have to remove him I would have been in the lobby when that building came down, no chance of escape. So then I'm outside the building. Then the force of the explosion actually blew me up – the rush of air lifted me out of my shoes. Then to land on a patch of grass in Manhattan, and they're kinda few and far between on the landscape of the city . . .'

In the film last night,[4] *one of the things that struck me was the thud of the bodies. Did you hear that? I know you saw them . . .*

'It was horrendous. You didn't realise until they got closer that they were actually human beings: the buildings were so tall and the volume of debris that was falling . . .'

Could you see them hit the ground?

'[softly] Oh yeah.'

Is that easy to live with now?

'[softly again] Oh no. [Pause] Oh no. [voice rising] and I can't imagine the hell that they were in to make that choice. I don't fault them, obviously, but what an evil choice: jumping 90 floors to my death or do I stay here and burn? I think that's a very hard feeling to live with as an officer. We are not used to being helpless – and to be there watching those bodies come down and be helpless, that's not a word or a feeling that we experience too often.'

And some holding hands.

'[softly] yes.'

One of the most striking things about your description was that even in the most extreme moments of your discomfort, when you cannot possibly have known whether you'd be alive or dead in the next 60 seconds, you were still trying to help people.

'That's exactly what we're trained to do.'

But you're not trained to cope with the Twin Towers coming down. Nobody on earth is trained for anything like that.

'If you were in my position, and you get up out of the rubble, you look at fire engines burning, an ambulance burning, my own car in flames and it feels like I was in the middle of a war zone. I *was* in the middle of a war zone, it's an accurate description. Someone here said to me "why didn't you get out after the first tower fell? At least you wouldn't have gotten the glass injury if you had left." I think it was a half an hour between the first tower coming down and the second tower coming down [north tower at 9.28, the south tower at 9.58]. My question back to the person is "how could you in good conscience leave when you know that there are people in that rubble?" You'd be running away from the whole of your life. You stay and you dig and you do whatever you can to get people out. You don't walk away and you don't run away.'

Did you feel it was really happening?

'It was really surreal, although I must say I didn't think those buildings would come down, and getting knocked on the head threw off my thought process. I remember when I got up – I had no shoes on, my clothes were torn – that I looked at my hands and I don't have my car keys. I turn around and I look at my car. It's on fire. Then the thought process went *I guess I don't need my car keys*. It was trying to make a connection between all of it.

'It's bizarre but we have these pagers, they are called Operation Pagers. I was getting beeped every two minutes by the people who made it back to this office. I caught some of them and they said "Terri, please call the office." At that point, I am at Ground Zero, I'm just at the site. Obviously it took a while to get extricated from the rubble and then I was focused on getting these people out. At a certain point I became aware of the beeps and they're coming in every two minutes. The last beep said to me "Terri, if we don't hear from you we are listing you as missing." I had a cell [mobile] phone with me but when the tower came down so did the cell site so I had no way of communicating with the office to say "I'm alive" and to check on the people I had responded with, because at this point I had no idea.'

The arm and the hand. How do you take something like that?

'I think having the hand put it into perspective for me. Injured as I was, I was extremely lucky. Nothing to complain about.

'At first I was taken to Ellis Island and a National Park Ranger[5] came over to me. He said, "is there anyone I can call?" I said, "yes, my boss." He said, "before you start, I can't reach [area codes] 212, 718 or 917" and for me that eliminates 90 per cent of my world, but I have a sister that lives on Long Island and I gave the number and her name. He asked, "what is the message?" I said, "just tell her I'm alive." So he's saying to her, "I'm calling from Ellis Island," but he doesn't say I'm there with him, only that somehow I've got in touch with him and asked him to call her on Long Island. My sister is saying, "I think she's at training in Brooklyn" – she had no clue that I had actually been at the World Trade Center.

'She called my sister-in-law and she reached my brother, who is also an NYPD officer. He was off duty that day. My sister-in-law said, "listen, I've just had this strange call. A National Park Ranger on Ellis Island rang to say Terri is shaken up but she's OK." My brother put two and two together and he is aware that injured people needing hospitalisation are going to Ellis Island. He has been like an angel in my life, my brother. He makes his way over to the medical centre but I'd been taken to a medical centre in New Jersey. He finds out, he tracks me down and he walks in the door.

'I'm laying there and, to be honest with you, there was this sense – not only in New York but New Jersey – that thousands of people who'd need medical attention were going to rise up out of the rubble. One of the great shocks was that no one came.

'When I got to the hospital the doctor said, "we have good news and bad news." They'd done an x-ray. I said, "well, what's the good news?" They said, "a surgeon is here and we're going to take you up to an operating room – it's actually a recovery room but we're going to operate on you there. The bad news is, because you've had such a blunt head trauma, we can't give you any anaesthesia." They never know when they're putting you under whether it's because of the anaesthesia or whether you are sleeping because you have internal bleeding. They never take that chance. I said, "OK," they stitched the back of my head and I was wrapped in this immense turban.'

Did you feel pain when they took this concrete out?

'Well, she said, "I am going to try and give you a local," and started injecting with needles and I said, "you know what? Your needles are hurting more than the actual stitches so why don't you not give me the local and just do what you need to do." Likewise with my back. And because I had all these open cuts and lacerations on my feet – I was in bare feet – they couldn't cast my ankle.

'It wasn't until I got to the hospital in New Jersey that I even knew the Pentagon was hit. It might have been just because of my hearing [nerve damage, as we shall see], but I thought there was someone in Pakistan who had done it. It wasn't registering and when I got back to the office it wasn't about Palestinians, either. Bizarre.

'I am laying there and in walks my brother. I said to the doctor, "is there anything you want to do?" and she said, "you've got to have a CAT scan[6] and an M.R.I" – that takes pictures of the interior of your head. "And you can't be alone for several days, obviously." I said, "listen, my brother is here, I've got a ride back to New York, I'm outta here." I had no clothes, I had nothing, so they gave me a pair of green surgeon's pants, a pair of bootees and a blue paper top, the disposable ones like you wear in hospital.

The Policewoman

'Obviously I'd had my gun with me when I got to hospital and it had been taken away so my brother went and retrieved it for me. We were getting into the car. Another officer, a Lieutenant, was there because he'd escorted another Lieutenant – who'd been injured – over to the hospital. He said, "are you going back to Manhattan?" I said, "yes" and he said "could you drive me back to the World Trade Center." He jumps in the car, we drive back to the World Trade Center, let him out and see if there is anything we can do there.

'It's about four o'clock in the afternoon. My brother said, "where to now?" and I said, "Kevin, I need to go back to my office to let them know I am alive and well." I came walking in and in the time since I left New Jersey to the time I got here someone from the hospital was able to get through – an officer from the local police department there – so they knew that I was alive. I said, "Kevin, go. The phones are ringing off the hook here." At this point I was running on adrenalin – I did not sleep for 48 hours.

'I worked for a couple of hours answering the phones trying to help people and someone started saying, "you know, your eyes look really bad – one is blown up . . . the other one is like your whole eye is the pupil. Something is wrong." It was from breathing in all that stuff. Two other people in the office needed medical attention as well – their eyes and noses were so pained – so I guess about seven or eight o'clock that night the three of us went off to a hospital on Long Island and they did a CAT scan. They had their eyes washed out. I was told, "Your skull is dented but it's not fractured, we'll leave the bandages in place". There was an issue because they had given me prescriptions in New Jersey and could I get them in New York, that kind of stuff.

'I had a sister living on Long Island and I went to her house. I stayed there for several weeks – not that I slept a lot. The other part of it was my ankle being in bad shape so I couldn't get around.'

It's amazing that you had been able to move around after the tower came down virtually on top of you . . .

'There was no pain, and as a result I probably caused more damage. And the glass in my back that I didn't even know about: that is the wonderful response of the body to shock. It would be unbearable if it didn't.

'I finally laid down and that was tough, too, because I couldn't lay on my back – I was bandaged across the stitches – and I couldn't lay with my head back because that's wrapped in the turban and I couldn't lay on my right side because I couldn't move my foot: I was in this awkward position in bed. That's when I discovered that I had damage to my left ear, nerve damage. When I originally went for testing, I thought *OK, I'll have significant hearing loss in my left ear but I'll pop a hearing aid in there* but it was explained to me that there's nothing they can do about nerve damage. It's not like a regular hearing loss.

'I was out for about eight weeks. The person that I work with called me and said, "Terri, is there any way you can come back?" I went to the police surgeons and they were insistent "you're still out." I said, "Listen, I really gotta go back." And the doctor said, "OK, you really wanna go back, then go back." One of the reasons was that I was so aware of how hard my colleagues were working – maybe I wasn't physically capable of being out in the field but if I could physically be here, maybe someone could get a day off to see their family and then it was worth it. Each day that I worked, if that gave one person one day off it was worth it.

'I came back and we're dealing with the anthrax scares and then a week or two later I'm sitting in my office at 9 o'clock in the morning, a detective comes in and says, "where do you live?" I had had a beach party over the summer for the office [and he must have attended]. I said my house was on 128 and Newport and he said "a commercial plane just went down on 129 and Newport."

'I got in my car and went out to Rockaway.[7] There were engine parts in my driveway and in my back yard. The house directly across the street from me was demolished by one of the engines. The other

The Policewoman

side of me, the gas station, got the engine and one block down was where it came down like a missile and took out homes.'

Somebody's been looking after you.

'Without a doubt. Absolutely. I'm a practising Roman Catholic[8] so I do believe that. The first eight weeks were taking care of my physical needs, then I come back and a plane crashes. We had a memorial for my cousin in October [2001]. We got a call right before Thanksgiving that they found his body. My cousin was a firefighter from Ladder 20 and as a matter of fact he was on the film last night, the CBS 2-hour special [mentioned above]. They sent us an advance copy of the tape because he's on it, him going in, and that's the last footage of him because he never made it out – but finding his body was some closure. I mean, we put a casket in the ground. Obviously at the time they found him he was pretty mummified.

'Is life back to normal [March 2002, six months to the day afterwards]? Last Sunday they found another two bodies, two of our officers. Life is not back to normal and until the recovery effort is over at Ground Zero I don't think life goes back to normal.'

Have you had nightmares about it?

'Not yet. People have said to me, "are you having trouble sleeping?" or "are you having nightmares?" Did I have problems sleeping! We were working 90-hour weeks. When I put my head on the pillow I was out.'

Do you think the events of 9/11 have had more effect on the women than men?

'I don't think that there's a gender difference in the reaction to it. I can be very honest. It wasn't like I was struck or not struck by the women officers there. You look at an officer you see blue. You don't see male or female. After nineteen years it's a distinction that I don't make. That day responding, it wasn't like rescue workers doing anything other than trying to get people out. It didn't make a difference whether you were male or female, white or black or Hispanic or anything else.'

The Women's War

At the end of each interview for the book, as you will see, I posed the same two questions. I was curious because these were all women answering. Men of course started the war (bin Laden, the Taliban) and other men (Bush, Blair, Powell, Cheney, Rumsfeld) were prosecuting it. Here is what Tobin replied to the questions which, by book's end, you will be familiar with.

If there were more women leaders would there be fewer wars?

'I think if we were all more compassionate people, regardless of male or female, that would make a difference. I'm not sure if it has to do with gender.'

What would you have done after 11 September?

'I don't know. I think that Bush was smart in waiting and not responding immediately. In the 48 hours afterwards I was just glued to the television – almost information overload – and my feeling was that within those first 48 hours we were going to do something horrific, like annihilate Afghanistan. I'm glad we didn't.'

But as a woman if you'd been in the White House, what would you have done?

'A group of extremists is responsible for this. I think the war on terrorism is going to happen behind closed doors and we're not going to know about it. I think that's the way it needs to happen.'

Would you have bombed Afghanistan?

'Probably not.'

What would you have done?

'Probably sent in operatives to infiltrate and seek out. The bombing does touch the innocent and somewhere along the line someone's got to take the higher route and not spread this hatred, to respond to evil with evilness.'

SILENCES, AND OTHER VOICES

It's a crisp, cold day on 11 March, and the clocks are moving towards 8.46 a.m., six months to the minute since the north tower

The Policewoman

was hit. I'm outside Police Plaza waiting to go in and interview Lieutenant Tobin. The entrance to the police headquarters is along a broad path lined by leafless trees. To this, shortly before 8.46, come the police in their uniforms and wearing their medals. There is an easy camaraderie about them, as if – just an impression – they can do parade ground formations if demanded but are used to working to more personal discipline. A few bystanders have gathered beyond a distant barrier and stare, mute. They line up in a squad, the name of every policeman who died is read out and they turn towards where the Twin Towers stood to observe a minute's silence. The wind is rising, bitter, and it makes the eyes water so that, all at once, it is impossible to tell whether people are crying or it's the wind.

The silence is tangible, the hum of the city subdued at this moment. Just then a siren wails out of sight, travelling fast to what must be some emergency and the two worlds are united: the silence of the past, the eternal rush to the future.

'There's a solemnity about today,' Tobin will say. She is the sort of person you instinctively trust immediately, open and friendly and taking service of the community as a calling as much as a career, just as the genetics dictate. She has a merry way about her and an openness that, even when she is discussing the most distressing moments, is touching. Like so many Americans, she is unafraid of telling it how it was. Her office has just the right blend of order and comfort to be homely [homey to her]. That did not alter my impression that I was in the presence of a person of stature.

'Someone asked me the question how have things changed,' she would say. 'Well I can honestly say that any organisation's greatest assets are the people that work for it. I know and I knew how great the people I work with day in and day out. They are hands down the finest people that I have ever met in my life. On September 11th I think the world saw that.'

TWO

The Refusenik

I went back under the Taliban, I went back to Kabul. I had to wear a burqa and that was the first time. It was quite difficult to wear – difficult to breathe and difficult to walk . . . I had to cope with the feeling that I no longer had any identity.

'All I can say about my personal details would be rough details. I can say I am in my mid-twenties. I have brothers and sisters but I can't be specific about the numbers. I have been living in Pakistan for a long time, actually most of my life – longer in Pakistan than Afghanistan.'

Tahmeena Faryal is not her real name and there is no photograph of her in this book. She doesn't particularly object to photographs, she says, but they have to be of the back of her head so that she cannot be identified. She has eyes which dance and a slow, deliberate – sometimes reluctant – smile, and a photograph only from the back is in itself a kind of violation. Picture her instead: a elfin face purified by convictions. The eyes which dance settle upon yours and don't dance anymore when she wants to emphasise a particular point hewn from the convictions. It happens all the time.

The Refusenik

If she feels in constant and very real danger she rides that with a creed which you feel more and more strongly the longer you speak to her: the cause takes precedence over her fate.

For her, and for her family, everything changed when the Soviet Union invaded Afghanistan in 1979 and installed what she calls 'the puppet government'.

'I was born in Kabul and my family, like other Afghan families, opposed the invasion. Even through children they tried to find out the way our families were talking. I remember it in our school, I remember they asked me in order to find out whether my father was one of those who supported the Soviet invasion or not. I was told by my family what to say if I was asked that question.'

What would such a question be?

'The government would want you to join an organisation – they had a lot of organisations, for women, for youths, for children. They'd send kids to Russia to teach them things that were definitely not the most appropriate for children to learn. Even in a country like Afghanistan they are not acceptable and still not accepted in Afghanistan. So they'd ask me, "do you want to join this organisation?" and my parents had told me to say no. I'd be asked "why?" – these people would say they'd give me this and that, all beautiful clothes. "Why don't you come?" The kids had to be smart enough to give them the reason in a way which did not say, "well, my parents don't want this at all." You couldn't say that.'

What would you say?

'"I have to study here, I have no time to get involved." You'd use reasons like that.

'We decided not to stay in Afghanistan and we came to Pakistan. I was ten years old. I would always be able to remember Kabul, of course, because it was the place where I went to school and I remember my friends. There was not the discrimination that came under the fundamentalists but there was a lot of discrimination. At the time I didn't feel it – I was just a child – but my mother was a RAWA member.'

Here is the central axis of Ms Faryal's life. The Revolutionary Women of Afghanistan is revolutionary only in the sense that reaching women's rights involves fight and revolution.

'A lot of discrimination was also passive. Obviously my mother could feel it despite the claims that the Soviets and the puppet regime had brought women's liberation. One of the ways of giving a human face to the invasion was the image of liberating the women of Afghanistan and westernising the country.

'It was difficult to travel to Pakistan, as it is difficult nowadays. Anyone coming to Pakistan meant they opposed the Soviet invasion and the puppet regime. At that time everyone opposing them was considered Mujahideen [the Afghan force which fought the Soviets]. My father had already gone six or seven months before. We had to be very careful. We didn't say goodbye to any of our neighbours or relatives, except grandparents. We were quite sure about them: they wouldn't say anything to anyone.'

She speaks softly, sometimes close to a whisper but that's not being cautious against eavesdroppers, that's the natural timbre of her voice. She speaks of this leaving – the 'little family house and its yard, most people in Afghanistan have a house with a fairly big yard' – as if, long ago, it had been absorbed into her normality and is no longer tragedy, just history.

'We didn't carry anything with us. We left the house and we told our neighbours we were going to another province for a wedding. We didn't say goodbye. Obviously I didn't go alone, I went with my family and it didn't matter whether I understood why or not.'

What pushes a family to leave everything?

'Opposing the government, because my parents could not accept the Soviet invasion and the policies of the Soviet-backed regime. Most of the people who disappeared or were killed, there was nothing against them. They just did not want Afghanistan to be occupied by a foreign country. That is the only reason they were killed. Others had to live underground.

The Refusenik

'We travelled by car. Actually we did not come by the mountains. Most of the people who had migrated, especially in the first days, came by the mountains because it wasn't possible to cross the border. We got a letter from one of our relatives to say that we were going to Pakistan to attend a wedding – that relative worked in the government. We travelled in something bigger than a taxi, more like a small bus, and it had been paid for. We were not the only people coming, there were some others. First we went from Kabul to Jalalabad, spent the night in Jalalabad and the next day we went from Jalalabad to Pakistan in a different bus.'

So you are now in Pakistan, aged 10, and you speak Persian which they don't.

'I didn't speak any Urdu, the national language of Pakistan. I spoke and speak a little bit Pashtun,[1] yes, but I'm not that fluent although I can understand it. But language-wise it wasn't that difficult being in Pakistan. The first days, yes, the language was another problem, going outside and everyone speaking a language which was not Persian – although there are similarities between Urdu and Persian: but it wasn't language that had made us leave. For my mother it was even more difficult because obviously she had lived much longer in Afghanistan than I had. Later my grandparents moved to Pakistan as well, when the fundamentalists came.

'Being a RAWA member, my mother knew that they had activities in Pakistan, including schools. When we first came we stayed with some of our relatives and then my mother found out more about this school, which was in another city. It was a boarding school and I was extremely privileged to be able to go. We had boys' schools as well.'

Is that how you started to become politically aware?

'Well, as a child I could see the suppression and the oppression of people, particularly being in a family that opposed the Soviet invasion, but everything took shape when I went to the RAWA school.'

But you weren't anticipating that the Soviets would simply go away and be replaced by the Taliban?

'Well, a bit – not me personally but the organisation. Well, not exactly the Taliban because the Taliban was quite a new phenomenon and not as visible as the other fundamentalists [the Northern Alliance] who had power from 1992 to 1996. It was only after this that the Taliban came to power. In fact Meena, who founded RAWA and who was killed in 1987, mentioned this in an interview she gave in France.[2] She said that if the fundamentalists take the power after the Soviets, we will have worse days than the Khomeini[3] regime in Iran, and that exactly happened.'

You must have heard the Soviets were leaving, then there was the Northern Alliance, then the Taliban. Did you have contact with home, with Kabul?

'Not me personally, but RAWA had a lot of contacts and we have many members right now in Afghanistan. Basically now I don't have any personal life. Like many members who went to our school, I just became RAWA. Everything in my life became RAWA. I do have most of my immediate family members in Pakistan. My parents are in Pakistan and they are in contact with those family members who are in Afghanistan. I could get the news of them through my parents but personally I don't have any contact with them. With other members of RAWA, yes.'

What made you oppose the fundamentalists so strongly?

'Their behaviour towards women, towards democracy, towards humanity, towards civilisation, towards education. That's not normal in the Twentieth or Twenty First Century. People might have thought Afghans were not created to be rulers, because most of the population was uneducated, but that's really not the case.

'[In fact, however] we had the Taliban thirty, forty years before but they were just religious students. Nobody could imagine that one day these people would be the rulers and they would have the power to impose, for example, the burqa on us on top of imposing all the other restrictions that they did. The real tragedy for women began when the Northern Alliance took power in 1992. They even raped seventeen-year-old mothers. They were the ones who destroyed the museum of Afghanistan which was one of the best in the world – and the hospitals, the schools. They were the ones who burnt books and libraries. They didn't leave anything for the Taliban to destroy except the statues.[4] That's why some people are so scared of these people in the interim government now [winter–spring 2002].

'I went back under the Taliban, I went back to Kabul. I went there with some other RAWA members in a bus. I had to wear a burqa and that was the first time. It was quite difficult to wear – difficult to breathe and difficult to walk, a heavy garment on top of you with only little meshes and no way to see properly but, more than these "technical" difficulties, I had to cope with the fact that it was imposed on me because I'm a woman. I had to cope with the feeling that I no longer had any identity. Supposedly the Taliban made you wear it to give you protection, but as a woman's activist I don't need that – and, as a person who is aware of the rights of women and the nature of fundamentalism, it was the opposite of protection.'

Why did you need protection? From whom?

'From men. The reason was that the women should not attract male attention to themselves.'

Why doesn't that work the other way round? Why aren't the men completely covered so that the women aren't attracted to them?

'For most of human history it's been the women [who need protection], not only in Afghanistan but all over the world. The safety of the burqa was that men didn't know what was underneath.'

Did you feel angry wearing it?

'I was extremely outraged, of course. I was there only for ten days or fifteen days and other women had to wear it every day for years and if they showed a little bit of their face because they could not breathe they could be beaten or put into prison. That was even more difficult for me to accept, in that I wasn't just thinking about myself. Yes, I was allowed to walk about with a man.' [See *Silences and Other Voices*, page 29].

*Do you feel that, in a way, it **is** men trying to protect women: the man knows the woman is physically weaker and wants to protect her from attack? Or it is simply a way of exercising control?*

'Their thinking is men cannot be controlled and what is the answer to that? Burqa! I guess the good point about this is that they accept men cannot be controlled and they cannot control themselves, and that's why women have to be covered, and are not laughing, and are not wearing colourful clothes – but that's what these men don't say!

'In Pakistan women are not covered like that. Even in male-oriented countries like Pakistan men feel they have the right to look at women: it's ok for us as men not to control ourselves – but women have to be able to, or be controlled. In the West, in the countries I have travelled to, women can't be controlled. It is related to education, to culture, to mentality.'

When you went back to Kabul, did you recognise the place?

'Well, no. It was totally destroyed although I didn't remember much because of leaving when I was ten. The first thing that brought my tears was the destruction. I had seen photographs of this but they did not prepare me for seeing the actual destruction.'

And when you arrived in Kabul, did you know where you were?

'I knew we had arrived because the bus driver said "Kabul!"'

Your first impression?

'The women in burqas begging on the street, especially one old woman. I could see by her hands that she was old, in her sixties, asking for money from mostly men, because they were walking by. No one gave her any money, they didn't have any money to give her.'

She exposed her hands?

'Yes, and, like many other things women did, because otherwise you starve to death. I mean, women ran underground classes' [dangerous and forbidden].

Did you recognise the religious police when you walked along the street?

The Refusenik

'I didn't see any of their cars – which I wanted to see – although several times I heard that a car had come. I remember one day I was with RAWA members eating ice cream in a corner that was allocated for women. They were exposing their faces and we were told that the special police were coming so we had to cover our faces and leave.'

You've said that you saw 11 September on television and you felt The Taliban and bin Laden should be the first suspects. Why?

'Because the people of Afghanistan had been receiving 11 September for years. It was understandable to us, and especially to those people living in Afghanistan: they would have been surprised that it *hadn't* been the Tablian and bin Laden. Another thing. RAWA had made another prediction which came true. We warned the United States, we warned all these other countries that if you keep on supporting the fundamentalists one day they will be a danger not only for the people of Afghanistan or the region. They can be a danger to the countries who are supporting them.'

There's an expression in English: my enemy's enemy is my friend.

'Exactly, but . . . it was so sad. We didn't predict 11 September or anything like that, but we wondered why the rest of the world had not realised or, if they had realised, why they had shied away from taking action. We thought this especially after they did take action and the bombing campaign began.

'Afghanistan was the forgotten tragedy for years and it became the centre of attention only after 11 September. The bombing campaign started under the name of liberating Afghanistan's women. Was the world unaware of that before? Where were they? The world knew it, the world heard it. That's the point. Why not a step before? Because the colour of the Afghan's blood is different from other countries? Steps were taken by people only when they had been damaged themselves.

'It seemed to need a tragedy to make it happen – like Kuwait [the Gulf War]. For some reason I was comparing it with the Second

World War, and 50 million dead. It didn't seem right that 50 million would have to die to finish Nazidom . . .'

Since September 11 has the plight of Afghan women improved?

'Not in a radical way at all. Obviously the departure of Taliban from Kabul and other cities was a kind of victory for the people – they are definitely happy about that – but still women wear the burqa although they don't have to. The question is not whether there is or is not a law about it but why they prefer it. The answer is because there is no safety and there is no security. Women have experienced the Northern Alliance soldiers and commanders and leaders until 1996 and they cannot easily be deceived by the Northern Alliance saying "OK, we defeated the Taliban and we are different than them, take off your burqas. From now on you will be safe and secure." Obviously no one can be convinced about this.'

Are you a Muslim?

'Er . . . yes, culturally.'

Why are you smiling?

'Culturally – yes.'

If there were more women leaders would there be fewer wars?

'I don't think that the problem in today's world is because there are not any women leaders – men have been given the opportunity to lead the world because they have been mainly the dominant part of society. Women can also be violent although I guess maybe it's more the case with men. As a feminist, I don't say that that can be the answer to the problems of the world.'

After 11 September, what would you have done?

'We had been asking for practical action before 11 September, and before they started bombing, to finish fundamentalism. That is still our goal. Fundamentalism should be finished in Afghanistan and all over the world, but to finish it does not mean physically. That is not the solution. It means not to give them any kind of financial, military or political support. That's the only way.'

Why do you think 11 September happened?

The Refusenik

'Because they have that nature. They were trained as terrorists against the Soviet invasion and in their nature they were, and are, anti-civilisation, anti-democracy, anti-humanity. And these people who came from Saudi Arabia and Yemen and elsewhere to Afghanistan, they are traitors to their own countries. How can they be loyal to another country?'

My interview was in the afternoon and that evening Ms Faryal gave a lecture courtesy of The Fabian Society at the London School of Economics, admission free. Outside, squalls became drizzle and became squalls again and the dark pavements round the Aldwych – on the rim of theatreland and, as it happens, near the BBC World Service – glistened. A weary workforce, heads down, tramped home. Pakistan seemed utterly remote, and Kabul further away than that. It was a sense heightened by the LSE reception area where students of both sexes, and from around the world, mingled quite naturally. You could sense their vitality and hear their laughter as shifting currents of them came and went. You could hear English spoken in many accents, and fast, irreverent banter man to man, woman to woman, man to woman, woman to man. It was the normality of youth with no obvious inhibitions.

Some 200 people gathered in the auditorium and, scanning them, they were hard to place: the gender split seemed about fifty-fifty. Some women were in headscarves but none wore veils. Some were from the Middle East and some of the men, too. The others? Who knew?

Ms Faryal began up there on a stage with a lectern in front of her, some notes on it. Two ornate carpets had been laid over the lip of the stage. RAWA, she would explain, has 'handicraft centres in which women, mostly widows, make things like carpets and whenever RAWA members travel they take the carpets. A carpet may need three months to make.'

Even with a microphone her voice was quiet, the words reaching discreetly into it for a little amplification. She did not give a performance in any theatrical sense, using the devices of surprise and indignation to rouse her audience. She was uninterested in that. She laid out her case as coldly as she had laid it out to me, often using exactly the same phrases.

'It is a question from the people of Afghanistan: why was the world silent before 11 September? The people of Afghanistan were forgotten. Was it because the blood of the people of Afghanistan had a different colour from the rest of the world and the United States? Why?'

She worked through the story of it, the Soviet invasion replaced by the Northern Alliance replaced by the Taliban.

The Western media coverage had concentrated, she said, on 'the Taliban and women's issues, and of women's issues the main point was the burqa. The burqa – or veil – had never been the main problem for women in Afghanistan. It is the symbol of oppression, but what is more important is the suffering' – the everyday suffering which lay beyond this symbol. 'We had burqa before. RAWA opposed burqa because it became something that was forced on women and it was not a matter of choice anymore.'

At various moments she said:

'Most of the Taliban were orphans of the Soviet war. They were in religious schools in Pakistan and were taught that women were objects, with which you can do whatever you want.'

'You cannot call Afghanistan a normal society. It does not have any infrastructure, economic or cultural. Most of the population suffered psychologically, especially women, according to the statistics by a US-based organisation on human rights. Ninety per cent of Afghan women, especially in the major cities, suffer from these problems. Most of the women who used to work as teachers and doctors and engineers and lawyers became, after 1992 and the arrival of the fundamentalists, unemployed. Some are beggars, some are prostitutes because that's the only way to survive or prevent their children dying in front of their eyes or committing suicide.

The Refusenik

These were some of the options for most of the women who lost their jobs. We don't know how long such a life could have gone on if there hadn't been 11 September.'

'We are the first ones who felt the great pain of 11 September because we had had that experience time and time again – but we don't think, as a women's organisation, that eliminating terrorists or fundamentalists physically would be the way to get rid of the ideology.'

'Right now in Pakistan there are more than 7,000 religious schools, each with hundreds or thousands of students and all of them will be future Taliban. As long as there is no stoppage – particularly financial – more and more of them are going to be trained.'

'None of them [fundamentalist governments] have their strength and their power because they have popularity, it's because they are supported by other countries for political purposes.'

'We are aware that more than 3,000 people have been killed in Afghanistan [since the bombing campaign began] and one can say, in a sense, the response to terrorism was terrorism in order to kill Osama bin Laden or Mullah Omar[5]. We condemn each and every civilian casualty.'

'People think that because the people of Afghanistan are uneducated they do not know the word democracy and there is no need for democracy. But we believe it is the only solution, the only cure.'

'After an appearance on the Oprah Winfrey Show, in just one night we had more than 300,000 visitors to our web site and RAWA was flooded with e-mails. The same was the case after 11 September. Before we had the web site people didn't know of our existence.'

She showed a twenty-minute film of RAWA's charity work, particularly feeding women in the refugee camps and clothing orphans in Kabul. A line of girls filed obediently up to the back of an open truck and, as their turn came, an X was drawn with a felt pen on the palm of their hand (to show they'd had their turn.) The girls were given warm jumpers and one of them, a little creature with a lost, permanently stunned gaze, was helped on with hers and suddenly, all in the moment, she became just a little girl like little girls everywhere.

The boys were given socks and trainers and one of them had a cluster of raw blisters on his foot, like barnacles. He must have been walking over stones on all these broken streets for a year, two, three. Soft hands pulled a sock on, then a trainer. It must have been painful because he didn't move: too small, perhaps, and squeezing the blisters. Soft hands fitted a larger size and he could move without pain. He stood, not comprehending this moment.

The camera worked a journey slowly alongside the line of girls and the line of boys, capturing each face of those who waited as if to say *this is humanity at its most vulnerable and its most abandoned, aside from starvation this is as basic as it gets, and we're putting it in your face.*

The auditorium was absolutely silent.

Some of the footage in the documentary had been included in a television programme called *Beneath the Veil*, shown in the United States, Britain and I assume large tracts of the world. It was of an execution and had been taken by a RAWA member with a hidden camera who, if caught, 'could have been executed right in the same place.' It was in the football stadium and a crowd had gathered, on the terraces, exactly as they would have done for a match.

Three women in their light blue burqas were brought in an open pick-up truck and one walked to a designated point, knelt, hunched herself, might have been reaching in this last instant for the foetal position. A man came forward and held what seemed to be a gun at her head but for some reason he retracted it, backed off and another pushed a rifle barrel against the head, fired. She fell forward and one of the other two women went to her, tried to arrange the burqa over the body, or make it into a shroud, or something.

The auditorium was absolutely silent.

The woman was called Zarmeena and, evidently, her children had been in the crowd calling loudly for her. 'Several minutes' before the

The Refusenik

execution her husband's family 'announced to the Taliban that they forgave Zarmeena. But the Taliban said it was impossible to stop the execution because they had already announced it to thousands of people.'[6]

What she had been accused of doing, or whether she had ever been tried, or what manner of trial she had had, was never specified and seemed perfectly remote from the body which lay and these soft hands trying to rearrange the burqa.

Ms. Faryal took questions although there was no microphone for the audience, so that men's voices sounded aggressive ('speak up!') and women's largely inaudible ('sorry, can't hear you'). The questions were asked in batches of three and answered in batches of three, too, giving the whole thing a dismembered, distant feel. The questions were mostly disguised statements and her answers were always undisguised versions of what she had been saying all the time.

A woman who was almost certainly from North Africa – she wore a headscarf but spoke with a French accent, suggesting Tunisia/Algeria/Morocco – moved into a long harangue about why all this seemed to apply in Afghanistan but it didn't seem to apply to all women, and so forth. One of the male voices called out "you can't say that about Islam" and the auditorium murmured "yes we can. We're here to say what we want and hear what we want. That's *why* we're here." Leaning lightly on the lectern, Ms Faryal whispered into her microphone: 'In all our statements we have announced our solidarity with women all over the world . . .'

SILENCES AND OTHER VOICES

'In most of Afghanistan, especially in the rural parts, women did not have the opportunity to get an education,' Ms Faryal says. 'They were not aware of their rights as human beings and as women.'

That is the background to the restrictions which the Taliban put in place. Those restrictions have been set out almost dispassionately

The Women's War

by RAWA on their website[7] in numbered paragraphs. I am grateful to RAWA for permission to reproduce them in full because, although some have been widely publicised, the cumulative effect has not. Note that RAWA were carrying them when the Taliban still had power, hence the present tense in some paragraphs.

These are the silences and these are the other voices which could not be heard.

1 Complete ban on women's work outside the home, which also applies to female teachers, engineers and most professions. Only a few female doctors and nurses are allowed to work in some hospitals in Kabul.
2 Complete ban on women's activity outside the home unless accompanied by a *mahram* (close male relative such as a father, brother or husband).
3 Ban on women dealing with male shopkeepers.
4 Ban on women being treated by male doctors.
5 Ban on women studying at schools, universities or any other educational institution. (The Taliban have converted girls' schools into religious seminaries.)
6 Requirement that women wear a long veil (a burqa), which covers them from head to toe.
7 Whipping, beating and verbal abuse of women not clothed in accordance with Taliban rules, or of women unaccompanied by a *mahram*.
8 Whipping of women in public for having non-covered ankles.
9 Whipping of women in public accused of having sex outside marriage (a number of lovers are stoned to death under this rule).
10 Ban on the use of cosmetics. (Many women with painted nails have had fingers cut off.)
11 Ban on women shaking hands with non-*mahram* males.
12 Ban on women laughing loudly. (No stranger should hear a woman's voice.)

The Refusenik

13 Ban on women wearing high-heeled shoes, which would produce sound while walking. (A man must not hear a woman's footsteps.)
14 Ban on women riding in a taxi without a *mahram*.
15 Ban on women's presence in radio, television or public gatherings of any kind.
16 Ban on women playing sports or entering a sports center or club.
17 Ban on women riding bicycles or motorcycles, even with their *mahrams*.
18 Ban on women wearing brightly coloured clothes. In Taliban terms, these are 'sexually attractive colours'.
19 Ban on women gathering for festive occasions or for any recreational purpose.
20 Ban on women washing clothes next to rivers or in a public place.
21 Modification of all place names including the word 'woman.' For example, 'women's garden' has been re-named 'spring garden.'
22 Ban on women appearing on the balconies of their apartments or houses.
23 Compulsory painting of all windows, so women can not be seen from outside their homes.
24 Ban on male tailors taking women's measurements or sewing women's clothes.
25 Ban on female public baths.
26 Ban on males and females travelling on the same bus. Public buses have been designated 'males only' (or 'females only').
27 Ban on flared (wide) pant-legs, even under a burqa.
28 Ban on the photographing or filming of women.
29 Ban on women's pictures printed in newspapers and books, or hung on the walls of houses and shops.

Of course, as RAWA point out, these were specific to women, who also fell under the general prohibition against listening to music, watching films, television and videos, keeping pigeons . . .

'And so on.'

The Women's War

In direct contrast, in March 2002 Ingeborg Breines, UNESCO's Representative in Islamabad, had a consultation with a group of Afghan women in Kabul. This is a list of their priorities in order of importance.

1. Peace and security. The women urged immediate disarmament and said they were very concerned about their safety and that of their children, especially with the presence of so many guns.
2. Education, especially education of children and of women/girls who were married but prohibited from attending school. With marriage age as low as 10 this means a huge population of women are out of education.
3. Access to health facilities, in particular maternal and child health care.
4. Access to employment – to be allowed to open bank accounts and to work.
5. 25 per cent of Loya Jirga [the country's ruling body, still coming into existence in mid-summer 2002] to be women, and to be included in the democratic process at all levels.
6. Identity documents and cards: only 1 to 2 per cent of women have ID cards, allowing them to travel and vote. Lack of identity documents prevents them getting a passport but was also felt by the women to be a denial of their identity and therefore a blow to their confidence and self esteem.
7. Access to the media so their voices can be heard.
8. The development of women in Afghanistan should be in the context of Islam.[8]

THREE

The Firefighter's Widow

I got on the bus to go back to the hotel and there was a beautiful rainbow from one end of the sky to the other. One of the firemen I'm closest to got very sombre. I asked 'what is the matter?' and he said 'nothing, nothing, nothing.' It turned out he'd just had the phone call from New York that they had found Dave's body.

Marian Fontana, thirty-five and from Staten Island, won't ever forget her first date with Dave, the man she'd marry. In the first place, she fancied someone else – a Bohemian-looking artist – and found Dave too shy to be interesting. In the second place, an unforeseen problem arose. Dave turned out to be the Bohemian artist . . .

'We met in college, a university on Long Island. It was my freshman year[1] and I lived in the arts dorm. I was a music major[2] and he was an art major and sculptor. He lived there and I lived there and we met. For him, he said it was love at first sight. [Laughter] I am much more rational than that, I think [laughter].

'The campus was a little disappointing: the guys drove sports cars and all dressed the same and all looked the same. They weren't really my type and I saw a guy that was just *so* different. He had on a

33

beret, a long trench coat and boots. I was immediately attracted to him and intrigued by who he was. He was fixing his car in the parking lot. He was with a friend and they handed me an invitation to a party, so I was all excited.

'We get to the party and I don't see him there so I'm very disappointed. There was a man in the dorm who was asking me out. He was kind of preppy,[3] wearing a Rugby shirt[4] – not my type. I politely say "no" and he starts hanging out more and more and we go out on a date. He was very shy and I thought *I can't go out with him – too shy and he doesn't have a sense of humour*. Then he got sillier as the night went on.

'At one point he lay down on the road in front of me and he said "what am I?" I was very perplexed and I said "I don't know." He said I'm a speed bump!' [Sleeping Policeman, if you're a Brit].Then we get closer to the dorm and he grabbed me from behind, grabbed my breasts, and said "what am I?" and again I said "I don't know." He said "I'm a bra!" He kept doing all these very silly things which completely endeared me to him. Then on our second date he wears this beret and this trench coat and these boots. I went *oh my God* . . .

'We dated for ten years. I like to be very well-thought out about my choices. We were so young – I was eighteen, I'm in my freshman year at college and I want to have fun with my friends. I didn't want to settle down and I wasn't even thinking about that. I thought he would just be a college boyfriend, you know, and ten years later I was still in love with him – more in love with him. He was a sculpture major – hence the beret and so on. Great. I loved that!

'He graduated before I did because he was a little older and all my friends had graduated. I'd decided to transfer colleges and I took a year off. I travelled through Europe with Dave for about two months. Then we came back and he got a job working in a neon shop, making signs. I went to a college in the area and I got him a job building sets in the theatre department.

'He was not your typical fireman. A lot of them are not college educated, and he was very artistic. He was a funny mix – he could straddle two different worlds very easily, he felt a part of both of them and I liked that about him. He took the tests to join the fire service straight after he graduated from college. He wanted that right away, wanted a job that would be a steady, paying thing where he could also have time to sculpt. He was a lifeguard at the local beach – Jones Beach – and had been for twelve years. A lot of the guys there became firemen. He always had this life saving, helping others aspect to him. It's hard to describe your own husband but he was very generous in spirit about that kind of thing. He was a person who would always hold the door open for somebody. He was very aware of people around him, which made life frustrating for him sometimes because most people aren't like that [chuckle].

'We got married in 1993 and our son Aidan was born in 1996. A daughter? No, we were working on that.

'I live in Brooklyn. It's become upper class [laughter]. It started out middle class and now all the brownstones[5] – Victorian era buildings – are a million dollars. It's a very pretty neighbourhood, very family oriented. We moved here because when my husband joined the fire service he was assigned to a firehouse in the neighbourhood, in Park Slope, Brooklyn. It's by a park designed by the same guy that did Central Park.

'We used to say that we were yuppies living on a blue collar salary. Firemen make very little money and I was always a struggling artist. I did theatre and writing and, of course, didn't make much money at it. We struggled along and we were lucky enough to have landlords who never raised our rent, so we were able to stay here. All my friends are here and I'm so glad we didn't move. It's a real family neighbourhood and socially conscious.

'When my husband and I lived in Manhattan I didn't know my neighbours and we lived there for five years. My husband was the one who convinced me to live here. I'm such a snob, I thought

I could never live in Brooklyn! I came out and we looked at one apartment, ground floor with a postage size back garden. We fell in love with it and we've been here ever since [chuckle]. I know my bagel guys, I know the restaurant guys, the principals at school. My husband called me Pope of the Slope because I know everybody! I also taught in the neighbourhood and that helped.

'9/11 was our wedding anniversary and Dave was starting a month-long vacation. I wanted to be with him all day but we received in the mail a thing about grants for performing artists. He saw it and he said, "you have to go to this workshop to get some money to do your show." I said, "no, no, no, it's our anniversary and I can't." He said, "I'll get off work and we'll go out during the day. Then you can go to this thing at night." I said, "OK, that's really sweet of you." That was our plan. We were going to the Whitney Museum, a small museum in Manhattan. I have a friend who works there who was to give us a special tour. We hardly ever went to museums and Dave missed that because, once we had a kid, it was harder to do that sort of thing.

'That week Aidan was starting school for the full day for the first time so we were really looking forward to having the whole day to ourselves. On 9/11 I was bringing Aidan to school for his second full day. Dave had done a 24-hour shift, so he'd been at the firehouse since the previous morning. I called him at 8.30 just prior to delivering Aidan to school, and when I asked him, "how are you doing?" he said, "I'm so excited to be done and be on vacation." I said, "are you finished?" – because sometimes they have to wait for someone to relieve them. He said, "I'm finished, I'm dressed and I'm ready to go." I said, "great." He couldn't get changed into his ordinary clothes until he was relieved, so I knew somebody had come in. I said, "I'll meet you in ten minutes" – it was at a coffee shop across the street from Aidan's school – and he said, "I'll be there".

'I dropped Aidan off and as I was heading out I bumped into a friend who was going to Africa. I ended up talking to her for longer than you'd expect. I said, "I've got to run, I'm meeting Dave and I'm late." I went over to the coffee shop he wasn't there. It surprised me. I sat and waited, and I started hearing people talking and pointing. I saw a big straight line of smoke coming across to Brooklyn. The day was crystal blue and this line resembled a really black jet stream. I heard "a plane" and "the tower". At first I was completely annoyed because every time there was a big fire in the city Dave would get stuck there for a bunch of hours and it was going to screw up our day. I knew he'd go if there was a big fire. Then I thought *well, maybe he just went home because I was late.*'

At this point she encountered a friend, Lori, who asked if she'd heard that a plane had crashed into one of the Twin Towers.

Marian: 'yeah.'

Lori: 'is Dave there?'

Marian: 'oh, no, he's probably at home.'

Lori: 'let me come with you.'

Marian: 'no, no.'

Lori: 'please let me come with you.'

Marian: 'OK, but I'm sure there's nothing really to worry about. I'm sure he's home.'

They walked to the apartment but he wasn't there. Fontana 'turned on the TV and saw the second plane. It felt like Armageddon. The first plane I thought was an accident. A small plane hit the Empire State Building in the '40s and it was no big deal. I thought it was just a small plane again now, I had no idea of the severity of it all and then when I saw the second plane I said *oh my God*. They were talking about the Pentagon and they were flashing round all these planes that had been grounded. Then there was another crash, in Pennsylvania. It felt like *this is it, this is the end of the world.*

'People started calling. Another girlfriend asked, "is Dave down there?" and I said, "I don't know, I think so." She said, "what would he be doing?" and I said, "he'd be running up the building, up the stairs," and right when I said that the whole building collapsed. I knew he was there, I knew he was in there. I dropped the phone. I can't really tell why I knew, I just felt a severing. I dropped to my knees and Lori was equally freaking out. I kept repeating, "oh my God, oh my God, he'd dead." She said, "you don't know that." I said, "I *know* he was there".'

A very close family friend, Jason, rang to find out what was happening.

Marian: 'can you come down? I think Dave's died.'

Jason: 'no, he didn't. Don't say that, Marian, you know him.'

By now she was hysterical. Jason hung up and made his way to the apartment as fast as he could. She said to him, 'you have to help me. I can't do this alone.'

The fact that she knew – whether by feminine intuition or whatever – ought, in the rational world, to have spared her the hours and days of diminishing hope which others had to endure. 'It was awful because I convinced myself that I wasn't a good wife unless I had some hope and I talked myself out of it and all my in-laws who came the next day were absolutely convinced, not a doubt in their minds, that he was still alive. So how could you sit in a home with everyone around you saying 'no, no, he is alive"? Well, he was so strong and big and stubborn.'

Stubborn? Dave's brother said that he could not get an image of Dave out of his mind. They'd worked at the beach together and one day Dave said something which wasn't properly heard so he said it again. An obnoxious boss said 'you know what your problem is, Fontana? You repeat yourself.' For the entire remainder of the day Dave followed the boss round repeating everything. He was, Marian recounts with some relish, 'relentless' and *that*, she adds, was exactly her husband's character.

Could a man of such strengths really be dead?

The brother said, 'I know him and I know he would never give up.' Marian said, 'I don't think it is an issue of giving up, not when a building comes down on top of you. It was hard, too, because the fireman came that evening and said "Marian, there's voids, there's gaps in the concrete, air pockets. He could be in there." So of course I then dismissed my intuition as being wrong – wrong in having no hope and no faith.

'Thus proceeded the tortuous ensuing weeks where I dropped to my knees in every church in my neighbourhood and this is the borough of churches, by the way. I went into churches and I didn't even know their denomination, I went to temples. I prayed my heart out and I did not stop crying and did not stop praying. It was really tortuous because every day it would be "they found five guys" but they'd turn out to be rescue workers who'd got there later. It got worse and worse with every hour. One of my sister-in-laws won't accept it, she says "still I can't".

Did you ever discover what happened to him?

'No – well, I know, I know. I know he was in the south tower and I know he was pretty high up.'

How do you know that?

'Just instinct. I don't have any proof. All my instincts are that he was about half way up.'

Marian now found 'the entire neighbourhood going over to the Squad[6] for information. I am the only wife of those who are missing that lives in the neighbourhood of the firehouse. I was going over there constantly whenever I got overwhelmed in my home – because my small apartment was still literally filled with people wall to wall and it got very overwhelming. I'd go down to the firehouse and I found it very comforting being with the firemen. They were just great because they talked about Dave and of course they knew the work environment. *That* was very comforting.

'The moment of acceptance came, I guess, when they officially turned it from a recovery to stopping looking for bodies and began taking what was left of the buildings down. Then I didn't have much of a choice but to accept it. If you see the film of those two towers coming down there was no possibility of any kind, really, anyway. It would have been instantaneous – that is what I hoped, no suffering of any kind.

'My husband always said, "yes, but this is what we do". That is why there were so many men from our company who died and weren't even on duty. They went in. There were firemen who came from their homes and died. The level of dedication that those guys have: this is what they love, and a fire is what they sit around waiting for. The unfortunate thing is that they could have handled it if it had been a fire, but it wasn't a fire. They were trained in high rise fires. My husband was part of a Special Operations Command, a rescue company different from your regular ladder engine company. You're transferred there to be trained more, to be skilled. They get all sorts of extra training and they don't get paid anything extra. They prepare for terrorist attacks. Giuliani[7] had dumped tons of money into SOC. It trained them in how to handle hazardous material, in terrorist attacks, building collapses, rope rescues, all sorts of stuff: extra training that they thought might be needed – but nobody saw *this*, nobody saw 20,000 gallons of aeroplane fuel catch fire. It wasn't a fire [in the ordinary sense] and there wasn't anything they could do, nothing at all.

'About two weeks after it all happened, the guys at the firehouse called me. I am a pretty outspoken person, if you haven't already figured that out for yourself. They called me and they were very upset. A chief from headquarters had just come over to tell them that the squad was going to be shut down and the men dispersed into Manhattan. Why? Because Special Operations – that small, highly trained group of guys – lost ninety-eight killed on September 11. It took a very hard hit.

'They were going to shut down the firehouse and I fought that because that was my home now. We haven't cleaned out their lockers, nothing. I still haven't cleaned out Dave's locker. The morale of the men was so low already and they said to me "can you do something?" I said, "absolutely." I was so angry that I was up all night and I could feel my heart beating. I started calling my friends in the neighbourhood and I typed a flyer to hang around the place – I was going to hold a rally.

'Because the people in my neighbourhood are so incredible, by the time I took Aidan to school next morning they had already plastered the flyers about a rally. There were mothers in front of the school getting petitions signed, there were hundreds of people in front of the fire house already and, by the time I went to that first rally, there were at least a thousand people and every news crew in the city at the firehouse. Fortunately this was the day before the primary election, which was originally on the 11th but they rearranged to this date. We had every politician in the city there and none of them was going to say "we want it closed".

'I got up and made a speech about how important it was that it stayed open, this was our home and vital to the neighbourhood for a lot of reasons. The argument put up *against* was that it wasn't accessible to Manhattan – but my husband got there in minutes. By 5.0 o'clock that day the Commissioner[8] had sent a fax saying "we are going to keep this station open" and I sent a fax back saying "that's not good enough – I want the men kept together." By 7.30, when we held the second rally, there were even more people and that had the effect "OK, we'll keep the men together."

'I thought that that was that, and it felt good to channel my anger and do something productive. I didn't realise it started a political career which I had had no idea would be in my future. Shortly thereafter I started to hear from the guys that the retrieval effort had turned into a construction zone, that basically they had opened up a dump in Staten Island to ship debris to and bodies were being found there. My ears popped open but I thought maybe it was a rumour.

'Then they took the firemen away from Ground Zero: 125 firemen at the site and they took 100 off, supposedly for safety reasons. The guys were devastated – and upset – because there is an amazing ethic ingrained into the history of the fire department: *you never leave a fire without your men, ever*. To take them off the pile was such a punch in the stomach of an already hurt group of men. They said, "we are going to protest tomorrow," and I said, "let me come with you." They said, "absolutely not, you've already done enough for us." I regret not going.

'It was a peaceful protest. I decided that if I wasn't going to go I would send all the news connections to cover it that I had made from the rally. This was to make sure the protest was acknowledged. A journalist I had become friendly with was in the neighbourhood, and his friends were firemen that died. I called him and asked, "can you cover this?" and he said, "absolutely." He went. Next thing I know, on the news I see firemen and police clashing. I called the guys and they said, "Marian, it wasn't like that." I called the journalist and he said "Marian, it was peaceful, it was reverent, it was sombre. All they wanted to do was walk to Ground Zero and say a prayer for their brothers and leave. It *was* a peaceful protest."

'They weren't allowed into Ground Zero. A barrier was put up and the young policemen who had been working side by side with the firemen wanted to let them through and the top brass said no. A lot of union guys were arrested and it became a crazy witch hunt. They were playing the video and saying they were going to prosecute all these firemen. It was completely ridiculous. *I* was so upset because, for the first time in history, firemen were getting the reverence they should always have gotten and now this stupid thing happened.

'That's when I decided I had to do something, so I started calling every politician that I had met. I called the Deputy Commissioner[9] who lives in the neighbourhood. I said, "things are getting tense, the families are getting upset and you're not giving us any information. You're going to have a riot on your hands." Meanwhile, I am going to funeral after funeral after funeral, and all the wives and family members are getting more and more upset because there is this lack of information about what's happening.

The Firefighter's Widow

'I said to the Deputy Commissioner, "if you don't act soon there's going to be people on Giuliani's steps with pictures of their dead husbands and I don't think that's going to be pretty." She said, "you're right. I have a meeting tonight and the Mayor will be there. I'll get the Commissioner to come – you bring a few of the wives."

'That's what I did. I formed an ad hoc group of women and we went over to an apartment in my neighbourhood. For three hours we talked about [how] they had to have the men back on Ground Zero and they had to drop the charges. I was really adamant. Giuliani was hemming and hawing. His argument was that it wasn't safe. Giuliani's big thing was a fireman almost got hit with a grappler and you can't have the men standing near there. Finally he said, "I see now, you're right, I made a mistake." The next day the men were back on.

'Essentially the news people would not stop calling, I was on every television show. It was really overwhelming. Meanwhile, the people helping me started to form an organisation. They were doing everything to make sure we were organised in case anything happened again. The organisation is called "The 9/11 Widows and Victims Families' Association". In the beginning it was the widows and then I realised I had to incorporate and include everyone.

'I went undercover to the dump and I found firefighter's boots on the ground in the mud, and that was really upsetting. That began another whole aspect. I was meeting weekly with the Mayor and I became friendly with a civilian group. Together we started going to these meetings and becoming a watchdog for Ground Zero. We've been doing it ever since. I'm also working on mental health issues with the firemen, I'm trying to get them to have some counselling before the retrieval ends, because when it does they won't have a way to use their anger and energy.

'I went to Hawaii in December. I was torn about going but I really needed a holiday: I was fielding about sixty-five phone calls a day and I had had no time with my son. It was absolutely a whirlwind and I had to get away. While I was away they found my husband. That was December 6.

'It was really hard, but he was the last one to be found from the squad so I feel really blessed. From hoping he was alive to hoping they would find the body to hoping he would be in one piece to hoping that I would even get a finger: this is how it changed as I realised the magnitude of what had happened, and realising that thousands of people were not going to have anything.

'I fought really hard to make sure that if [generally] there was something to be found, it would be found with dignity and respect. That was another reason for starting the group and I am really sad that I wasn't able to provide that for everyone.

'I was going to interrupt the holiday and thank God there were some guys from my husband's company there on the trip with me. They said, "if you want to go home we'll go home with you." That was so sweet because it was the middle of the week, we had just had a ten-hour plane ride to get there and my son was having fun for the first time since September 11th. He loves the beach. He was just like my husband – my husband was a beach bum! He surfed, the ocean was his home and Aidan is the same way.

'That day was an amazing day because we went out to an abandoned beach with a group of firefighters from Hawaii who owned a surf school. They were to teach us how to surf. I didn't want to do it because I was quite depressed when I got out there. The guys said, "c'mon, Dave surfed, you've got to learn how to surf." I said, "no, no, I don't want to." Anyway, they signed me up. My sister was there and we all went out, a whole bunch of us, and I decided I was going to do this. My husband and I went to Hawaii for our honeymoon, he wanted me to surf and I was too chicken so now I thought *I am going to do this for him*. I surfed. I loved it, it was beautiful! It was the first time I'd felt relaxed in months.

'Then the guys that were helping me said, "what about your son, what about him surfing?" I said, "all right." He had to be a good swimmer and he is not quite a good swimmer yet but the guys said, "no, no, we'll take him. It will be good for him." My son had come along and he'd wanted too as soon as he saw the surf boards, but most kids his age are too young. One of the guys pulled him out into the ocean and showed him how to do it. They had one guy standing to catch him in case he fell.

'He popped up right away and he rode a wave all the way in and everybody on the shore stood up and started clapping. I was crying and laughing and I was so amazed – I could just feel David everywhere that day. I got on the bus to go back to the hotel and there was beautiful rainbow from one end of the sky to the other. One of the firemen I'm closest to was on the trip and he got very sombre. I asked "what is the matter?" and he said, "nothing, nothing, nothing." It turned out he'd just had the phone call from New York that they had found Dave's body. They came to my room when we got back, three of them, and they told me.

'It was very hard to change the whole vacation but in some ways that day was somehow . . . perfect, one of those days which was meant to be.

'They found Dave almost in one piece and it gave me hope that all the wives would have the same comfort. Only four have been found.

'I had already had a big funeral, which was overwhelming. I mean, everyone who was at that funeral says it was a day that transformed them forever. All the planets were in line that day, if I can put it like that – a *beautiful* service, just a *beautiful* service. People said it was the most amazing thing they had ever witnessed. Everything happened in a very reverent, *beautiful* way that was such a honouring to his memory. Unbelievable: the streets were lined five deep with firemen from all over the country and all over the world. The church – a huge, *beautiful* old Gothic church where we had baptised our son – was so packed they had to turn people away.

'My friend Mila, who has a voice of an angel, sang – Dave always loved her voice. Everyone was sobbing. My mother-in-law eulogised.

I didn't think I'd be able to because I felt like I was going to throw up the whole time but in the end I did through some divine way. I'd had two understudies, my sister and my cousin, ready to go if I didn't think I'd be able to do it. I was so grateful that I could, and I did, and that it touched so many people. This was on his birthday, October 17th. This is before they found him: most people had their funerals before bodies were found.

'I guess I wanted him home so when they found him I had already picked a grave for him. The funeral director thought I was insane because I had his ashes divided up into five and I plan on scattering them on all of his favourite places. One will be in Prospect Park, the park near my house where he proposed to me; one will be in Ireland, where we were going to retire – a little town called Ballycotton where we spent the best day of our lives; one will be at Jones Beach where he lifeguarded for twelve years and was very happy; one I'm going to keep at home, and one I'm going to bury. I had a very small graveside service because that other one was so overwhelming I couldn't do that again – very tiny, with just my immediate family and firemen from the squad. Twenty minutes and then we went to a great restaurant and we drank ourselves silly. I made speeches to the guys and we gave them Christmas presents.'

If there were more women leaders would there be fewer wars?

'Hmmm. I think so. I think . . . fewer wars? . . . that's interesting. There's a part of me that says we certainly have to protect ourselves. I feel that if the country had protected itself in the first place this never would have happened. There are firemen I know who knew, before it ever happened, that a plane could crash into that building, and the fact that these smart people running our country didn't, disturbs me. Yeah, I do think there would be fewer wars. Women are good at negotiating calmly. That's the tactics I used [in the struggles with officialdom]. I didn't act crazy, I didn't yell, I just calmly made sense.

'I saw a lot of wives screaming at the Mayor and I saw how ineffective that was. I know from being with someone for seventeen years that screaming at people does not get you heard, and what does is making your point with intelligence and in a well thought out manner, backing it up with research and facts and passion and speaking from the heart. I think women are probably better at that, yes.'

What would you have done after 11 September?

'If I'd been Bush? Heaven forbid! [long laughter]. I would certainly seek out bin Laden, send in special forces to seek him out. I don't know if I would declare war on the whole country. That seems more of a move to appease a lot of angry, grieving people. I would have to look at all the facts, all the ramifications, how many people would be killed and would it be worth the cost. I would have to look at the whole picture. How long have they been doing things like this? How does this affect our country? How does this make us look to the world? Can you beat them this way or will it be another Vietnam, and we're in there forever accomplishing nothing but wasting money and lives? Those questions.'

FOUR

The Organiser

I got all dressed up, not in a burqa but very smart – high heels, red lips – and I went to the Ministry of Education, whoosh. They didn't know how to face me because, to them, at 60 I was too old to be alive. Usually their women die between the ages of 37 and 42.

Different levels to Ground Zero: this is the official one, couched in that language. 'The Swedish Committee for Afghanistan[1] in August [2001] began supporting two more schools with 456 girls in Afghanistan. Totally the SCA supports schools with 29,000 girls in Afghanistan. The number of girls in the SCA schools is over 25 per cent, which is a higher percentage than the total in pre-war Afghanistan.' The SCA does not specify which war and somehow it doesn't seem to matter.

This is the human level, couched in that language, of confronting the Taliban. 'They wouldn't look at me but they wouldn't neglect me. This Minister of Education just stared down on the floor and he answered me but he didn't look. I felt quite amused because I knew if I turned my head around – so he'd think I couldn't see him – he peeked upwards. Well, anyway, I threatened him. I said, "OK, if you won't open these four schools I will close down all the 500 boy's schools."

The Organiser

Just as I was going to leave the room he called me back and he said, "let me think about it." I said, "well, I give you three days, mister. And I want a paper from you that is signed and stamped by you."

The speaker is Ulla Åsberg, now over sixty and retired to Gothenburg (although an SCA Board member). Before that 'in Kabul I was the regional director. It involved everything: we had clinics, I had rural engineering – which meant we built all our schools – so I had a bunch of engineers, and then we had agriculture and education and health and logistics.'

It's an interesting thought that you were the exact proof that the Taliban were wrong because as a woman you were running all these things. You disproved the idea that women couldn't do these things.

'I think they were afraid of that. I was too old. I used to joke with the Swedes and say that I'm too old for sex in their eyes so I'm not dangerous in that way. I was an old woman, I spoke the language [in their eyes], I had sons who Allah had given me, and I had been working for poor people both in India and Pakistan. When one Taliban governor up in Konar province[2] heard my life story he turned around to me and said, "Madam, please. You are standing with both feet in the grave but you don't have the guts to fall in! So before you decide to fall, please convert to Islam because you will go straight up to Allah." I couldn't say what I thought, I had to be diplomatic. I did say "thank you for this. I will take it under deep consideration and I have already bought the Koran but I don't know the way of Allah."

Ms Åsberg is a formidable combination of welfare worker, organiser, diplomat, negotiator and *lady*. She sets out the background of the SCA. 'In 1979 the Russians marched in and there were a lot of young Swedish people then who wanted Russia out of Afghanistan. They got involved. I think it all started emotionally – and a little bit politically, of course. There was a lot of politics in this. Then a group of them went out to Pakistan and settled in Peshawar. Via Peshawar they were going with donkeys into Afghanistan because everything was blocked. They took medicine, they saw the children and they started a school there. Everything had to be done via Peshawar and now the organisation has grown to the point where we have 500 schools – I mean real schools, with buildings.

'Under the Taliban we had to keep a very low profile, especially on women's education and girl's education because The Taliban stopped all that. So what we did – and this was good work together with the communities, because the mothers and fathers wanted their daughters to get education – we started home schools. During the Taliban we shifted the girls out of the boy's schools, or their own schools, and then we made home schools instead: a home in a village would take care of that.

'It was in private houses and it was secret, it was underground. The Talbian did find out about it in some places and they stopped it.'

It's not like as western society with rules which apply to everybody.

'It was necessary to negotiate, sometimes day by day, and I took part in that. I didn't find it difficult. I'm used to a Muslim country, you know, after being for such a long time in Pakistan. I always had my interpreter with me and a bodyguard. I was never alone.'

You were running the schools underground and the girls must have understood that they musn't say anything.

'Yes. It did happen that confidences were betrayed. During my period I had to face this closing down of schools and it was one of my biggest problems. The governor in such-and-such a province found out in so-and-so district that there were four girl's schools so he shut them so, yes, these four girls schools were shut down in that province and also schools in many other provinces – Afghanistan consists of twenty-six provinces and we work in nineteen. It depended on who was the governor. It could be a broadminded chap and we even had some governors sending their own daughters.

'When the four were closed down I told the school consultant to go and talk at provincial level first and if he couldn't manage then I'd go to the minister. I had to go.

The Organiser

'I got all dressed up, not in a burqa but very smart and high heels and red lips – you know me when I'm dressed up! – and I went to the Ministry of Education, whoosh. They didn't know how to face me because, to them, I was too old to be alive you see. At sixty I am too old for them in every sense because usually their women die between the ages of thirty-seven and forty-two – the average is forty. They didn't know what to do with me and *that* meant there could be no arguments or disputes – and I could open them again.'

We heard that only some schools remained and these were underground. The pupils took the Koran and if the police burst in they pretended to be studying it.

'That could be true of other organisations and we had the Koran, too, because you have to cover religion as a subject, but we also had them in science and languages and maths.'

How old were the girls?

'Now this is one thing: it was not always straightforward. In some provinces the governor was quite open minded and he'd say, "OK, I allow the girl's schools but only up to third grade" – out of the six. They'd start at first grade but when they reached the third such governors felt "girls don't need more education". That was when the girls were about ten or eleven, and then their education stopped.

'We said to ourselves, "we don't want to start a fight here because we risk being thrown out of the country" and it was done in other ways. For example I came to one girl's school in a village in the province of Nangarhar[3]. I saw so many girls – there were too many, knowing that they were only up to third grade. "How many children do you have in each class?" I asked the principal. She said, "we have only twenty-five because that is what you have told us, but we have up to six grades." I said, "how do you manage that?" and she said, "oh, we keep it underground." I said, "I have done my homework and I know this school only has three teachers because you don't have a budget for more." I am very budget minded. This lady said, "we have managed to fix that also. When we get our

The Women's War

salaries we put it all in one pot and then we divide it into six" – for the six teachers they had. *That* is solidarity.

'I lived in Jalalabad for six months and then in Kabul from '99 to 2000 – two years. I couldn't get out in the evening because, after eight o'clock, you had to be indoors and there was not a lot of social life, you know, anyway. The burqa? No, no, I only had the Patan[4]. The white ladies didn't need a burqa. I was happy I didn't need to wear it, of course, because the burqa is not nice. What I was worried about was that Mullah Omar came with edicts every now and then – "you must do this and you must do that" – and no music, nothing.'

But you are a sophisticated Swedish lady, Sweden is famous for its political correctness and its equality and suddenly here you are in the Middle Ages. How did you adjust to that?

'Well, you must remember I spent forty years in total in Asia. I was born in India and I have seen the remote areas there and in Pakistan, so I wasn't that shocked. The only thing I *was* shocked by, when I came to Kabul that last time [in 1999], was what had happened to it. I used to go there in the late 1960s and early '70s to have a good time – Kabul was famous, a beautiful city where you could buy wine and dance in small discotheques: a really good time. I hadn't seen it since and it looked like Berlin after the Second World War: destroyed. Everyone looked sad on the streets, no one was happy, no one was allowed to sing, no one was allowed to laugh. We had a department called the Police of Vice and Virtue and they used to go and whip women if they laughed.'

What takes men to that?

'They must have been brought up in that way, and also these guys, the Taliban, they'd gone to the Koran schools where they are taught to believe that this is the way women are to be treated. It is total brainwashing. They don't know. They think they are doing good for Allah.'

But why would that involve denying girls medicine?

'I don't know.'

The Organiser

Why would Allah want girls who can't read and write?

'Women are to be kept low, women are supposed to be at home feeding the children and feeding their husband and giving birth to many sons. That's it. Women don't need to be educated for that. Why do women need to read?'

Ms Åsberg could read, all right, and think on her feet too.

'I judge The Taliban and the ministries in Kabul found this lady quite exciting. One day when I came home from my office I saw two pick-up trucks outside my gate and on them were Taliban sitting with their Kalashnikovs. Next morning when I left, there they were sitting again. And the next day. I was wondering: why are they watching me? and so I went and bought some toffees, English toffees, very expensive, all smuggled.

'When I got back that evening I told my driver to stop and let me go and say hello to these young poor boys who had to sit and watch me. I did that and gave them some of the toffees. They got so shaken up because they are not allowed to look at a woman! And they're not allowed to speak, so they couldn't say thank you. Well, one of them, he spoke a little English – I don't know if he got beaten up afterwards. I said, "thank you very much, it's so sweet of you watching over an old lady to make sure no one comes and hits me. I have to buy you more toffees." He said, "oh, thank you for that."'

What sort of a standard of education were you able to give the girls?

'Well, anything is better than nothing and I would say it's not super. I found out in many schools that the boys – especially the boys in third or fourth grade – couldn't read. They learnt it by heart and that's absolutely the same in India and Pakistan, because we don't change the method – which we should.'

Do you think there will be equality or something approaching it?

'I think something approaching it. The Swedish Committee is working hard on that now and working on upraising the teacher's quality also. Hopefully that is easier, but we don't know because at the moment it's terrible [in terms of a central government and law and order]. Nobody knows who's doing what now, it's just like the wild west – which is almost more disturbing.'

Did you find among the schoolteachers and the female pupils there was a resentment of what happened under the Taliban or was it just an acceptance?

'A kind of acceptance. They had to, in order to survive.'

If you have a ten-year-old girl, does she accept that the world looks like this and you have to learn things underground?

'That's why I said a kind of acceptance. No, she doesn't accept it, but what can she do about it? She can't do anything, she just nods her head in the typical Asian way and says, "I have to live with it." If you ask her, "what do you want to become if you had the opportunity?" let's say 80 per cent of the girls would reply "doctor" and the rest would say "teacher" or "engineer". That's it, but they know it's no use having dreams. I found that very sad, very hurting.'

As a woman, that's a violation of what you are.

'Yes, absolutely.'

We understood that women were simply denied hospital treatment.

'I was there when Mullah Omar spoke on the radio and "those women who are working should stop and go home directly." What I did together with the other NGOs,[5] and the UN, we went to meet the Minister of Planning. He said, "well, women don't need to work, they should be at home taking care of their families. That's it. No more discussion." I had to go around and tell all my doctors and it was a difficult trip because we usually worked in the rural areas. I had to go and send them home until further notice. Yes, of course, they were very sad and I said, "I am sad, too, this is terrible." That night I sat with all my documents – because we do document everything, you know. How many women patients, how many children in all our 300 clinics? I'll never forget that figure I got. It was 56,563 women and children who would not get treatment although they were sick. That was the main thing.

The Organiser

'This was July 2000 and next day I went around and checked Kabul's hospital. They were all full of soldiers – even the children's hospital. The children were thrown out and there were only soldiers lying wounded, Pakistanis, Indians, some from Saudi Arabia – from all over – and that was that. The third day I went to the Minister of Health and said to him "I have got a very big problem and you are the only person who can help me with this, and this problem concerns you and your country. You *can* help me." I turned it around. *I* had the problem and *he* was my helper. They are not used to that, you know. Then he looked up, actually. "You need my help?" I replied, "yes, I do, and I would be very grateful if you could give me some sort of solution on this."

'I explained, "I have sent all my doctors home, all my aid workers, all my health workers that are female and I know that in one month we see 56,563 women and children. Now these mothers of the sons of Afghanistan" – I said it exactly so – "if they are sick, how can they look after their children? And how can they look after their sons? I need your help. I need them to come back and you are the one who can help me with that." He said, "I don't know what I can do." You know what he said then? "Well, why don't you send them to our hospitals?" I said, "I can't do that. You see I am a very strictly moral woman, I can not send my women to your hospitals which are full of men. That is against my morals. I would never do that."

'It was why I'd been to the hospitals, so I would get that answer and be able to give it to him. I had put him in a very, very difficult position and he said, "I will give you a reply in three days." Again three days. Three days must have been the time they took. Then I said, "I want it in black and white with signature and stamp" – again. I needed that for my own security.'

. . . and three days later?

'I got it! And also the rest of the NGOs could send their women back to hospitals or their clinics.'

As far as I am aware, this was not reported in the West.

'No, no, it wasn't. Probably just as well, because we had faced a lot of trouble that summer and I was there throughout. One rule after the other came.'

If women are ill and don't get treatment they may die.

'Yes.'

And they may have little children to look after.

'Yes.'

It is extraordinary that anybody could want that.

'Hmmm.'

Isn't it?

'Yes.'

*You have lived for so long in such places but was **that** still a shock?*

'Yes, it was. I didn't think it would go so far. I thought somehow they would use their brains. "We need our mothers, we need our wives. If they are sick who's going to take care of the husbands? Who is going to take care of their sons?"'

We have read here that in the Cuban base where they have taken al-Qa'eda, there were one or two doctors and nurses who were women.

'Oh!'

Oh yes, because this is America and the al-Qa'eda people felt a tremendous insult in being treated by women.

'Yes, and this is one thing we had in our clinics. The building was shaped in a U, and one side was for women and one side was for men. On the women's side we only had women doctors and the men doctors on the other side. Even if the female doctor was sick or she had a day off, or something like that, the male doctor would not see her. He didn't dare to. It was terrible but we made it work, a little bit at least.'

If there were more women leaders would there be fewers war?

'Yes, because we think of our children, we think more of the home and the children. We are more domestic.'

What would you have done after 11 September?

The Organiser

'When I got to Sweden I started a Swedish Women's Afghan group in Gothenburg and we have grown quite strong. We went out on the streets and made speeches. Twice a week I have been out talking about the girl-children and the women and I have collected £100,000 for girl's schools. If I'd been forty maybe I'd have done something else but this is what was easiest for me and easiest for me here.'

Actually, I meant what would you have done if you'd been President Bush?

'I don't think I would have started bombing, no, but negotiating with the Taliban, we know that that is hopeless.'

So what do you do?

'I don't have an answer.'

Why do you think 11 September happened?

'Oh, that's the capitalistic thing. The whole Muslim world they are just fed up with the United States and Bush putting their noses into everything and trying to control the world. It's not only *al-Qa'eda*, we have a lot of these terrorist groups: 'we' – the Afghans and the Muslims. I am not Muslim myself.'

SILENCES AND OTHER VOICES

Dr Aqila Noori is health coordinator for the Swedish Committee and, incidentally, their first female head of unit. She took over in October 2001, and in February 2002 visited Kabul as part of a trip to Afghanistan. She is an Afghan 'from Vardak province, two hours [west] from the centre of Kabul'.

What is the situation like now?

'It's a little bit better but the women are still wearing this veil. They can't remove it.'

Why?

'I heard – it's a rumour, it's not confirmed – that they poured an acidic solution on the face of a woman and everyone was scared.'[7]

In that sense nothing much has changed.
'No, no.'
Has it changed in Kabul?
'No – well, I noticed a few ladies without any burqa. Just a few.'
How long do you think that will take to change?
'When there is perfect peace and security, then they will be able to remove it.'
Do they want to remove it?
'Yes, why not? They want this, everyone wants this.'
It's just that this seems a very sensible way of protecting yourself.
'Yes, yes, this is the main source of them protecting themselves.'
. . . particularly from men who haven't seen women for many years.
'Yes, yes, that's another reason. They are scared that maybe someone will injure them – because it's possible.'
What's your situation in terms of nurses and doctors?
'Women are working again, they are all working. Almost all our health facilities have female workers – it was the same before. We have lost some of our staff because of the low salary scale, not because of other reasons. The situation is almost the same as it was under the Taliban.'
We understood that women couldn't get treatment in hospital.
'No, they were not restricted about health. Education, yes. The Taliban were flexible about health but there were strict restrictions on education because they didn't want females to go to school, so the mothers had to decide that they'd get education.'
But a female nurse could not treat a man.
'Yes, but sometimes this did happen, sometimes a female surgeon performed an appendectomy [removal of the appendix] on men. A man would know it – he wasn't under anaesthetic first – but he was in a terrible condition and as a result he accepted it. There were not many examples but there were a few.'
Do you see women ever getting equality?

The Organiser

'We are in the initial phases, the start of every activity. The rest will take some time. No one has any objection now about equality or equal access and the present people have good thinking. I can say the women are damaged psychologically and that will take a long time: one year for them to readjust themselves to the new environment. That's why so few have removed the burqa. They are also waiting for security to come because there is not any security now – outside of Kabul city. People can do whatever they want.'

What was Kabul like this time?

'There are a lot of people, too much rush of the people, everyone is trying to find accommodation. A lot of foreigners. Everyone professional is trying to get to Kabul to take a job because it's easy to get a job now. The embassies were offering so many jobs for people who know English and computers, and that included women. The Arab Emirates Embassy has asked for three special females – two accountants and one computers. They asked our office for female staff to join them.'

You as an Afghan woman, how do you feel?

'I am hopeful that, *Inshallah*, peace will come, stability will come, education will come and, *Inshallah*, all will be educated, but still that will take time for everyone because the twenty years of war has disturbed everyone's mentalities. It will take this time to come to a normal state again.'

Extracts from the Swedish Committee's Newsletter, Vol. 7, No. 3 (Winter 2002, reproduced with permission).

> The activities in Afghanistan continue normally despite the turmoil caused by the recent fighting and the downfall of the Taliban in the SCA areas of operation.
>
> 'The SCA assists 12,000 internally displaced people with drinking water, mother and child healthcare, and education for boys and girls in the Hisar Shahi camp outside Jalalabad in eastern Afghanistan.

The Women's War

An SCA mobile Mother and Child Healthcare clinic is providing healthcare to the women and children of the camp. 1 female doctor, 2 female and 1 male nurses are coming to the camp every day from Jalalabad. The health team receives daily some 40–50 patients. The SCA also give trained traditional birth attendants in the camp refresher courses.

There are some 2,400 boys and girls in primary school age in the Hisar Shahi camp. When the SCA began its emergency work in the camp there were 16 teachers teaching 400 students at the government primary school in the camp, but the teachers had not been paid for the last 8 months.

In addition to the existing 13 sections in the school, the SCA will be able to provide all the children of primary school age with education and has budgeted for some 60 teachers and 60 temporary classrooms if needed to supplement the existing school. The support includes all the school material needed, the teachers salaries and supervision and monitoring from SCA school consultants.

The SCA in August began supporting 2 more schools with 456 girls in Afghanistan. The Ashki Daund school in Jaghori district, Ghazni province, has 426 girls up to grade 6. The other school is the boys and girls school in the village Omna Zwaka, Paktika province, with 30 girls in grade 1 and 125 boys in grade 1 to 6. Totally the SCA supports schools with 29,000 girls in Afghanistan. The number of girls in the SCA schools is over 25 per cent, which is a higher percentage than the total in pre-war Afghanistan.

FIVE

The Businesswoman

Looking up, I would see the person and I tried to say a prayer for them before they would actually die. And you couldn't even finish the words before the next person would fall or jump.

Diane Kenna is thirty-seven and was born in Brooklyn, 'which is where my family still lives now'. She's at Merrill Lynch as a 'vice president in their global debt market. We work on structuring and documenting bond issues and debt issues for foreign governments and foreign corporations. We work with a lot of governments that are looking to raise money in the US.' She'd been doing this for seven years in September 2001. Before it she went to a business school and was in advertising for five years – selling copywriting to magazines and newspapers. She knew of the Taliban and some of the abuses from petitions going around on the Internet.

'I have had a reasonably well paid life although I still can't afford my own apartment! I rent one in Manhattan, a small one-bedroom on the ground floor. I am, I would say, comfortable. My average day consists of getting in to work about 7.30 or so. If I haven't met some friends for a run in the park in the morning I'll try to run after work. Central Park is near my apartment and I'll meet my friends at

5.00 a.m. I'm on a running team in New York so I'm always training for races and marathons. I'd run between six and ten miles.

'I'm lucky because I live on the west side, so very often I'll run to or from work [see following paragraph]. We had a gym here at work where I could shower. I'd leave clothes the night before, run in and then shower and change for work. Sometimes after work I'd change into my running clothes again and run home. It's about six or seven miles to my apartment. I get home [in] almost the same amount of time as the subway takes so I save my dollar fifty that way and when I can I run to or from work.

'I had run the night before, actually. I prefer running home. It's a nicer feeling running away from work, a good feeling at the end of a stressful day. You run up the West Side Highway [which runs past the World Trade Center and on up Manhattan, following the shoreline – see map on page ix]. You turned around and you could see my workplace before you cut over the West Side Highway for home. On the night of September 10th I ran home with a buddy. We met at my office and we ran up the West Side Highway and it was pouring, pouring rain. It must have been around 9.0 and I commented to him "you can't even see the Twin Towers it's raining so hard."

'On the morning of the 11th I took the subway. I had an early meeting and Tuesday morning I'm always cranky. I remember walking across the West Side Highway feeling like I was the only one that had to be in work so early, but I saw other people heading into the Twin Towers. I went to work, went to the meeting, went outside for my second cup of coffee about 8.30 and came back. I go to a little streetcar vendor on the corner of West Street and Vesey Street. I took the coffee back in. I remember meeting a colleague of mine in the elevator and we were complaining about work and jobs and life and stress that morning.

'At the time I was helping out at one of the trading desks so I was on loan for about six months. I was on the seventh floor and it had the north west view: you couldn't see the Twin Towers. The trading floor is about 600–700 people, mostly male, usually very active, volatile, noisy and that morning it felt like a vibration, like a huge wind, hit the building. It wasn't like things were moving on desks, more a *whooosh*.

'There was confusion as to what had happened, nobody had any news. Trading rooms being what they are, there was some joking and people were making comments. "Maybe it's another bomb like '93, maybe we go home now." We didn't think it was anything serious, a minor taxi cab accident or a light plane fell outside, something like that. In keeping with that atmosphere I kind of joked as well. I said I'd go outside and "get to the bottom of this. I'll find out. I'll give you the scoop". I came out the building and looked up and saw this was not a joke. One tower was on fire. I didn't know it was a plane that had caused it but I do remember thinking *surely there's some death or injury there*.

'I went back into the building to tell them it was serious and people were probably hurt. I was walking across the trading floor and I guess at that point they must have known a plane had hit because they were focused on the news monitors. We had news monitors all the way along the trading floor, TVs that follow the news all day long. I'm half way across the trading floor and you have to imagine that this is 700 people staring at these TV screens. That's when the news cameras caught the second plane hitting. I won't say it was chaotic, but a scream – a shriek like *wow* – went out from the floor and there was no looking to management, there was no questioning: everybody was getting out of the building. You didn't have to wait for the memo. It was *get out*.

'I'm still thinking *OK, something's happened but I'll be back here this afternoon so what do I need now? We're coming back*. This is where being a runner comes back into play because I had a pile of work documents on my desk. I had my running sneakers wrapped in a T-shirt and that's what I took out with me. You just grab whatever you can on the way out. I went upstairs to make sure a colleague, a woman secretary called Linda I had been very friendly with, was out because she sits in a corner of the building where she is isolated.

'I'm going against traffic now because everybody is going the other way. There was no panic and every time you felt people were moving too quickly there was someone there to calm them down. "Take it easy, take it easy." I went to the right floor, Linda was gone. It felt empty to me because most of the people had gone – nobody around. I thought my mum, who's 78 years old, will be watching this on TV and let me just tell her I'm leaving the building. I think I'm being very calm and collected at this point. I rang my mother in Brooklyn and as soon as I heard her voice – that's when I got weepy and emotional. I'm trying to say to her "I'm leaving the building, don't worry." She can't hear very well and she's saying "what? What? What building?" She hasn't turned the television on and she doesn't know what I am talking about. She's saying "who is this?" She's a bit confused and I thought *my God, I shouldn't have even called.*

'I go outside the building again to where I'd gone to have a look before, and now the scene is . . . frightening. The smoke from the second building was tremendous.

'You know that morbid curiosity when you see an accident? I could not pull myself away from it. I kept staring and staring. There were some other people around me and I was aware that police were pulling people away but I'm staring and staring. I have tears falling down my cheeks.

'I could see one tower – the north tower – because from where I was standing you could only ever see that. Then I guess my Catholic upbringing came out because people started to jump and it was very clear that many, many people were going to die that day, but there are about a dozen or so images I have in my mind. Somehow I feel I saw twelve of them. Looking up I would see the person and I tried to say a prayer for them before they would actually die and you couldn't even finish the words before the next person would fall or jump. I guess I must have been crying and putting my hands up.

The Businesswoman

A colleague came and said "move, Diane". I shouldn't have been watching and I knew I shouldn't have been watching, but I could not pull myself away. It became as if it was my obligation to pray for each of these souls.

'Then larger debris started falling and we had to leave. I had the little bag over my shoulder. We started moving and at that point from the north tower you could see people leaning in the windows, hanging on to the windows and you still felt they were going to be rescued, it was only going to be a matter of time. They were waving a sheet. I can't imagine where they would have found a sheet but it looked like one. They were saying *here's where we are, firefighters come get us.* I am looking at them and I am seeing the fire rage on the floors right above and below them, and I'm thinking *get out.*

'I can't see their eyes but it felt like I was looking into their eyes. They were a hundred storeys up and I am not seeing their eyes but I feel like I am looking into them. They would have seen me waving but not trying to look into their eyes.

'And I get to live. They work on that side of the street, they die, I work on this side of the street, I live. It's a strange feeling and something you feel guilty about. When people called to ask if I was all right I'd say "fine, I was across the street. I wasn't on that side of the street". You look up at a window on that side of the street – just across it – and you see somebody waving to try and save their life. I never feared for my life that day. I was concerned, I had no clue what was going on but I never felt *I am going to die today* and those people I looked up at knew they were. They looked down at me, I looked up at them and I thought *I get to live.* I say that to myself once a day.

'I could see one gentleman who was the most graceful – what can I say? It was beautiful. He would be seeing the Statue of Liberty. It has stuck in my head: blue sky and he was like absailing, he could see the sky and the river and the Statue. Beautiful, yes, when you contrast it with the clawing of the air, the screaming.

'I don't want the memories to go away. I have certain idiosyncrasies. I make myself read every biography [obituary] I see in the paper.[1] When I am leaving work on Friday I sort of bow my head towards the direction of where the Towers were. I don't want to forget and I want to honour those people because they could have been me and I would be diminishing them by forgetting, although to the people who lost loved ones I feel shallow. What can I do or say?

'We started running up the West Side Highway to try and get away – the same route I had run home fourteen hours before. That's when I see all the fire trucks and the ambulances. They'd closed the highway to traffic. My religion comes up again and I start praying for the rescue workers. "Bless you boys, God bless, good luck." I wasn't thinking that they are not going to return home today. You could see them coming in their own cars, you could see them putting on uniforms, borrowing hats from each other, anything they could do to get in that building where they belonged. It was only about fifteen minutes later when the first building came down.

'After seeing all these people who had headed that way, and knowing that they'd probably been rushing towards the building, it was common sense that they would have reached it and gotten in. I was nearly ½ a mile away, far enough that I wasn't hit by the dust and debris. We saw the first building come down, yes, but by the time the second one came down we were much further away. I remember people around me fell to their knees and collapsed – in disbelief, I guess.

'In 1993 I was in Arizona in a town called Glendale. There were about 100,000 people in the town and I remember that was when the bomb hit the World Trade Center. I was there in Arizona and they couldn't believe that those buildings could contain as many people as lived in their town. *They could not comprehend that.* I'll never forget it and when I saw the two buildings collapse that number drifted into my mind because I remembered the conversations I'd had with Glendale people. I knew roughly how many people could possibly have been there.

The Businesswoman

'We watched the dust engulf the buildings and go out towards the river. I think it was going east and west. I still had a suit on but I changed into my sneakers and I walked briskly. We had no idea what was going on even though we were seeing it – the people who knew were those watching it all on TV. We had no cell phones. You'd bump into colleagues and people from different companies and everybody asked, "what's going on?" Nobody knew. It looked from our vantage point like it was a bomb in the building. We thought they had entered the building and planted bombs inside. It was an implosion – so that rumour was spreading – and we heard a bomb at the State Department. That became a rumour. Then the Pentagon – that was a rumour that turned out to be true. There was this mass confusion, this "what's going on, what's going on?" All you saw as you walked along was people trying their cell phones and getting no signal.

'An Australian colleague of mine had one of those little e-mail devices. He sent an e-mail to his friend in Australia to call my mum in Brooklyn to let her know I was OK, because the last thing she'd heard from me was three hours ago when I'd made the call inside the building. She'd have switched the TV on and seen my building engulfed although she'd not really understood my call. In fact, she'd rung my sister and said "I don't know, Diane said something about the building". That was three hours of me worried about her and them very worried about me.

'I continued to walk home and just about 5 miles into the walk my first cell phone call came in, from a friend in Germany because outside the US the lines were working better. He had also been trying to reach friends and relatives in New York to find out if I was OK. The calls from Germany had a better connection than any of the local New York phones. So – I got my mom through Australia and my friends through Germany!

'I went to a friend's house, who worked in the World Trade Center in Tower 2 [the south tower] to see if he was home yet.

There was a police car at the entrance to his building and the baby sitter was there with his son but not him. They didn't know what was going on and I didn't want to be the one to tell them what was going on, especially if he was OK. I just said, "call me when he gets home." He was OK . . .

'Then people came by my apartment, people who were displaced from their homes. My brother-in-law couldn't get home and it all became a sort of revolving door: who needs to stay where, who needs to use the phone, things like that. We were trying to figure out where everybody was, hours and hours of accounting for people. "Have you heard from that one? Is this one OK?" I have a lot of friends who are firemen and cops so I was trying to track down each of them. It was non-stop phone calls 'til about eight or nine o'clock that night.

'With two of my friends I went over to a running buddy's apartment. He was fine. His wife was working in the recovery effort so he was alone, and nobody should be alone that night. I don't think we spoke. We had the TV on but with no volume. There were three of us and I'm sure we went through five or six bottles of wine without speaking. Not a big hug or kiss, we're not friends like that, but there was a pat on the shoulder, *you OK? I'm OK. We're here and we're together.* We were in that comfortable silence you have with long-time friends. Then it's one o'clock in the morning. We'd been drinking this wine and of course now there was the feeling of being invincible, of recklessness. I remember bike riding through Central Park at one in the morning after drinking the wine: you wanted to feel alive, you felt like nothing could harm you now. Myself and one of the guys, we were riding up and down. It was completely stupid. Would I ever in my life ride my bike through Central Park at one in the morning? It was a crazy reaction to the day but that's what I did. Nothing could touch me. Then I slept, I guess.

'My running team has about thirty active members and we hadn't accounted for all of them. It's very, very professional in the sense of policemen, lawyers, bankers, everything. We all met in Central Park and there was this group touch, pat each other, yes we're all here. We love to run and I run almost every day of my life. It defines my life so basically – the races and travel I do takes just about all of my money. I thought I would enjoy that run but you feel guilty, you feel strange. I felt so healthy and Central Park looked so beautiful: the days around September 11 were some of the most beautiful Fall days I ever remember. You felt . . . well, it goes back the whole time to that "I get to live" thing. Running is an expression of being alive, of working your body hard. Again, nobody was really saying a whole lot. We were all thinking the same things.

'When do you feel that alive? When you're running in Central Park on a beautiful day you think *this is what life is* but that day I was asking "why am I here and others aren't? What am I going to do about that?"[2]

'About six of us – everybody was out of work! – cycled to Chelsea Pier[3] to try to give blood. We cycled because we didn't know how the subway was running. They weren't taking any more blood donations and there were at least 150 ambulances lined up with nothing to do. That was an image which disturbed me. Ambulances had come from all over the tri-state area[4] because they thought "OK, now we'll just get the people out", and there wasn't anyone.

'Everybody in the city was asking, "what do we do now?", and after we'd tried to give blood there was a feeling of helplessness. It was my mom's birthday and I rode my bike to Brooklyn to have a family lunch with my mother. I rode over the Brooklyn Bridge and there was a lot of smoke, fires still going on, dust all over the place, but as I rode into Brooklyn all the flags were out. I still don't know who did this or why they did it but all I see is all the American flags hanging out and it gave me a sense of pride – *this is OK, we're going to be OK.*

'You know those newspaper vending machines? I went and got the paper from the day before and scanned through it to possibly see what did we do somewhere that provoked this. I was trying to grab for anything that might fill me in. There were stories about touring the defence centres in Iraq – but, really, there was nothing.

'It's curious. The next couple of days I heard from wonderful friends all over the world and they kept calling me to ask if I was OK and I felt *but it wasn't me, I wasn't in that building*. There was this hierarchy of who was hurt, and it went: were you downtown? Were you in the building? Were you near the building? Did you lose your office space? Did you lose your life? Did you lose your mother? And the further away the hierarchy got it became "don't worry about me, I was only across the street somewhere. Don't worry about me, I got out of our building".

'The company was very good with a disaster recovery plan. The trading operations went across the river in Jersey City, and we had a daisy chain of phone numbers to call: you phone so they can phone so they can phone. We had a lot of conference calls telling everybody where to go the following week. Then we were sent out to Princeton, which is about two hours south, for the next couple of weeks. In a way that was awkward because you didn't want to get back to business just yet, you didn't want to be a functioning organisation, you wanted to be crippled and harmed and hurt like everybody was – although it was wonderful, also, that we could pick up the pieces.

'There was no access to our building, no coming back to it and nobody knew what it would look like. Starbucks[5] was the temporary morgue area.

'Where we now were you had to make do with what you had and what you could remember, you had to rely on clients and colleagues. It's very difficult but everybody was very resourceful. It made me want to clean my office out and throw away a lot of files when I did get back because you realise you can pretty much function without them.

'We got back in on December 17. It was kind of creepy. The company did a wonderful job with Welcome Back and they screened out any windows that might look down on disturbing parts of Ground Zero. I thought it would be worse. It was actually good to see everyone again because we had been so scattered for so long. You got to look each other in the eyes and say "well, we're going to be OK". You also feel guilty. [softly] You feel guilty.

'You make decisions. I think everybody looks at their life – I know I certainly have – and you re-evaluate. What are your priorities? These 3,000 people were just doing what they did and if you read some of the wonderful biographies of them they were just trying to get through the work week to spend more time with their family and friends like normal people, like we're all trying to do. Will I work a fifteen hour day any more? I'll stick to eleven or twelve.

'And you make other decisions. At the time I was considering maybe moving to another position [within the company] but it would involve much more work and much more time at the office. If you'd asked me in August 2001 I would have been gung-ho, career-motivated, I can do it, I want to do it, got to keep my job first in my life. You ask me post-September 11 and I may say "no, thank you very much. I'm comfortable with the hours I know and the life I know and enjoying the things I like."

'We were at a memorial service [in March 2002] for one of the firefighters and someone said the ones who died would want us to *use my years*. I always say to myself, of every single person that I saw at those windows that day: *use their years*.

'I don't think I have a story to tell because I have to recognise that day-to-day my life is a wonderful life, and it was on September 10 and it will be September 11 next year. I am very, very fortunate and I know that and I always try to live each day to the fullest. I emphasise that. Even when the alarm goes off on a Tuesday – the worst day of the week – and I don't want to go to work I think *I get to go. I don't have to – I get to.*'

You watched the CBS documentary by the French brothers?

'Very moving. The most incredible footage. A couple of friends had come over, big movie buffs, and that was the point of the evening. We were watching the Screen Actors Guild Awards in Hollywood and I switched over from that. I just couldn't switch back. You know, how trivial are the Awards? We had our glass of wine out and once we had switched you couldn't even think of going back.'

If there were more women leaders would there be fewer wars?

'I don't think it's a gender thing, I think the devil makes work for idle hands. It's an empowerment issue.'

What would you have done after 11 September?

'We all felt we needed to see Bush soon. I know they had to protect him and keep him hidden and moving about but there was a sense, a desire, a hunger for leadership. I am not politically minded. I don't have respect or contempt for leaders but I wanted someone to tell me what happened, someone to reassure me. Here in New York we had that a little bit with our Mayor.'

What I mean was, when you'd got over that phase, what would you have done as a woman? Would you have bombed Afghanistan?

'Hmmm. [long pause] I don't think it's as a woman, I think it's as a leader. [long pause] It's not a country thing. To say would you have bombed Afghanistan? – it's not Afghanistan that we're fighting against, it's terrorism, but I'm no leader of armed forces. I've benefited from the protection the armed forces give me and I've never really thought how I would react as a leader of them.'

Did you feel uncomfortable as a woman?

'I did with some of the immediate calls for "bomb the bastards" – the reflex, let's just go in there. I felt there needed to be some time to evaluate and discuss.'

But you didn't have any qualms once the strategy had been worked out?

Lt Terri Tobin. (*Courtesy of NYPD*)

The Fontana family – Dave, Marian and son Aidan – at the place Dave loved, the beach. (*Courtesy of Marian Fontana*)

Ulla Åsberg in the field.
(*Courtesy of Ulla Åsberg*)

Marilynn K. Yee, self-portrait.
(*Courtesy of Marilynn K. Yee*)

Happier times. Diane Kenna (centre), and the warmth of the marathon. (*Courtesy of Diane Kenna*)

The absolute ferocity of the Twin Towers blast – taken just before Marilynn K. Yee ducked her head into a doorway. (*Courtesy of Marilynn K. Yee/New York Times*)

(Courtesy of Marilynn K. Yee/New York Times)

Altered landscape, 9/11. (*Courtesy of Marilynn K. Yee/New York Times*)

Landscape detail, 9/11. (Courtesy of Marilynn K. Yee/New York Times)

Suddenly everybody was on the front line doing whatever they could. (*Courtesy of Marilynn K. Yee/New York Times*)

A woman in an office building opposite St Patrick's Cathedral watches the memorial service for a fireman, Assistant Chief Donald Burns, 9 October 2001. (*Courtesy of Marilynn K. Yee/New York Times*)

The Businesswoman

'To be honest, I guess I distanced myself from that aspect of it all. It's not necessarily a woman's point of view, but I feel better fighting for something than against something. I don't think I'm going to go in there and wipe out the bastards. You say "I'm going to go in there and fight for the freedom of the people there and get them out from under the Taliban: equality for women". So is it making me sleep better at night being at war with them? Certainly. I feel like we're fighting for a cause rather than against an enemy.'

I met Ms Kenna* at her offices in New York, knowing nothing of her except her job and that she was a marathon runner, both gleaned from a press clipping on the New York City Marathon. We had spoken by phone across the Atlantic, that's all. We walked past where she had seen the people jumping and had some lunch in a pleasant eaterie. I did the interview while we ate. Emerging, we were walking back – she walks fast, incidentally – and I wondered if she had ever been to Britain.

'I'm a Liverpool supporter!'

'Pardon!?!'

'I support Liverpool!'**

She was clearly enjoying surprising me (I suspect she'd been saving this up) and equally enjoyed my bemusement. She is small, neat and has eyes which dance with delight. The tale followed, that

---

* Diane Kenna ran the New York City Marathon, to try and raise money through Foot Locker, which specialises in running kit. Foot Locker was donating to a firehouse. She also ran in the London Marathon and finished it in 3 hours 10 minutes, and that's quick.

** That evening in April 2002 she'd invited her Liverpool friends to a London pub called The Champion and we all met there. She seemed fresh, lively, full of energy and it was a very sobering thought to think that just a few hours before she had truly powered the marathon. She was thoroughly at home with the Scousers and they clearly delighted in seeing her again, delighted in her company and *could even understand what they were saying*. And I'd asked her if she'd ever been to Britain!

she'd lived a while in Cheshire and had friends in Liverpool. She'd even been to a Celtic–Rangers soccer match, itself a form of fundamentalist struggle and not an occasion for persons of a nervous disposition.

When we reached her office she invited me up to the fortieth floor. From there, across the street, the sixteen acres of Ground Zero spread like a vast building site, the dump trucks and excavators crawling across it. She pointed out the entrance to the subway station she'd used every day, and where the shops had been, and did it without visible emotion. You can only carry it publicly for so long.

Then she became the businesswoman, eager to get back to her office – and was gone.

SILENCES AND OTHER VOICES

A professional paradox: while Kenna was moving doggedly away from the scene of the tragedy Marilynn K. Yee, who worked as a photographer for the *New York Times*, was trying to get as near as she could to it. Members of the media have no official standing in society, unlike the policemen and firefighters who had taken charge.

This can be sensitive, because the media has no *right* of access to such places and may be regarded as simply getting in the way. We saw an example of that – and incidentally the ultimate paradox – in chapter one with Lieutenant Tobin and a photographer: 'As he was impeding the process and shouldn't have been there, I escorted him out of the building.' Doing that, of course, saved her life but that's not the point I'm making. She had every *right* to move him and he had to obey, even though he was doing his job, it was the only way he could do that job and, beyond dispute, it was in the public interest that he did it.

Marilynn K. Yee was doing her job, too, and faced exactly what the photographer at the Twin Towers faced. She had a certain emotional detachment from the unfolding tragedy because, by definition, you cannot function for a sustained period under pressure and do a professional job if emotion is running your judgements. If you are on an operating table, a semi-hysterical surgeon is what you do not need. At 8.46 on 11 September the southern tip of Manhattan became Yee's operating table.

Yee, a married Manhattan resident with a 14-year-old daughter – Alexandra – was fifty-two. By a further paradox, she'd been one of the first photographers on the scene at the first World Trade Center bombing in 1993.

'I was born in Sioux City, Iowa. In my high school years everybody kept saying "you have to be something, you have to do something to earn a living." I didn't have the patience to be a teacher and I get sick at the sight of blood. Science and myself is like *I wish I could find a cure for cancer or the common cold*, but dealing with chemistry or the physical sciences reduces me to just saying *what?!* I was not good at math and figures so that left out accounting.

'I was good in art. I always had to have something that I could adapt or change or whatever, some sort of an image in front of me in order to create something. I guess in hindsight I was thinking of photography. To be a photographer, you really have to have images in front of you in order to take the picture. The reason I chose photography, too, is that I was shy, painfully shy yet I wanted to be extraordinary. We all want to be different and I did want to be different, do something different from everybody else, I guess.

'I thought photography would be interesting because one of the photographers from the *Sacramento-Bee* [a daily newspaper] in California came and spoke and described what he did. It sounded very interesting.

'I didn't want to be shy. I wanted to save the world, I wanted to change the world! When you're young you still think "ah, if I take pictures maybe enough people will say *enough of war, enough of poverty*" and that would lead to change, but it hasn't happened and it doesn't happen. At least you've tried to do something."

But surely that happened on 11 September?

'I took the pictures. I don't know how much of an effect one has. Hopefully you try to help people deal with it – or whatever.

'There are many, many women photographers now but no so many then, because I've been in the business for 30 years. I got on the *New York Times* in 1977. I worked on the *Ventura County Star* [also a Californian daily]. They said they were going to have an opening for a photographer in six months, and after eight months I left – but I took pictures. I went back to Sacramento and strung[6] for UPI. My first real job was with the *St Louis Post-Dispatch*, then the *Los Angeles Times*, then the *New York Times*.

'I was usually the first woman hired at the newspapers. There weren't that many, and not that many Asian photographers, either. In general I was hired as the second photographer. They hired a man and then me, a token ethnic woman! It's a very limited field – there were not many openings for staff photographers because they were always a smaller population on a paper than reporters or editors.

'I did everything, sports, hard news, accidents, whatever comes along on your shift.

'9/11 was actually a primary day in New York City. I was asked to cover Bloomberg, who was not the Mayor yet.[7] He was voting and we were supposed to be uptown at a school in the 70s or 80s and Fifth Avenue where he'd cast his vote. I had to film that. There were several other photographers there. We hung around and took pictures of him, and another photographer and I walked with him. He was going to his office – down around 57th, I think – and we'd follow him, take some more shots. His PR person said, "well, you can't really take any pictures of him in his office," so we said, "OK". We went back to where we'd been and this was pretty close to 8.30, I guess. I get in the car and check in.[8] They tell me that they have another assignment for me – another voting picture somewhere.

The Businesswoman

I thought I would go down to Chinatown because usually the paper doesn't do that many kinds of ethnic groups and I wanted to try and show something. A picture which is a little bit different always has a better chance.

'Then they said I had a 12 o'clock job – another politician shot. I got into my car at around 8.35 and started downtown. After a time I noticed the traffic wasn't really moving that much. I was listening to the news and they said the World Trade Center was hit, a plane had hit it. *What?* I was trying to figure that out. I decided to go over to FDR Drive[9] because it was a pretty direct route to Chinatown – and the World Trade Center.

'I started heading west because of the traffic and called the office again. They told me to go to the Empire State Building; they wanted me to get up high somewhere to take pictures of the Trade Center burning. I called my husband's office – he's an immigration judge – because you could see the World Trade Center from there. I asked him if he could see what was happening and he said he could. By that time I'd heard that it was a big plane. I'd originally thought it had just been one of these little private planes and by the time I got down there it would probably be over with. By then, too, word was coming through that people were jumping. I went to the Empire State Building, parked the car and got out. This was about 9.0-ish.

'The second plane had hit, there was burning and you could see smoke. I still couldn't see the World Trade Center, but I saw people looking at the smoke in the sky. I wasn't allowed into the Empire State Building. People weren't, as a security precaution. I jumped in the car again and started making my way downtown. I was still five miles away. There were reports on the radio that people were watching the two towers burning from Hudson Street and 10th and 11th. The radio station had a reporter that lived nearby and he was on his rooftop describing people jumping from the buildings.

'I drove down to Hudson and could see the tops sticking up and the towers were burning. I did some shots there. I don't think there was a point where I really thought that this was a massive story and not just an accident. My main thought was trying to get down there to get pictures and seeing how the best way was to do it. The radio was saying it was a terrorist attack. I was listening and thinking *what should I do?'*

You had to switch off your humanity and go onto professional autopilot.

'You do. If someone had been injured in front of me I would have stopped to try and help – or do something – but there was no way of rescuing the Twin Towers and, anyway, my main priority was to get there: if I did, fine, if I get turned away, fine. It's still your job to try and get about and do what you can.

'When my husband saw the pictures I took he said I was stupid. "Here it is, everyone trying to run away from it and you're headed towards it." He's an immigration judge with the Justice Department and he was deeply affected by it. Once he saw the second building being hit he said to the whole of his floor "everybody is leaving now. OUT." He went to Chinatown and got some food – because he knew it was going to be a long, lousy journey walking home. I think he still is deeply affected by it. To me it's a bit like a personal conflict because you have a home, a family and then a job – and in that you try to do what you can. I shot what I could.

'By now the first tower has fallen and there's only one tower left. I didn't see the first tower go but I heard a gasp. I turned round and got people's reaction, then I turned back and got some of the tower going down, but not much of it.

'I made my way down to Duane Street or Reade Street and West Broadway, which is about four-five blocks away from the World Trade Center. There were too many people in the street, all walking the other way, for me to be able to continue. The easiest way was to park the car somewhere. I parked the car and it was good I parked where I did because I was able to retrieve it later and get to some other places.

'Actually when I started walking, there weren't too many people on West Broadway. I noticed a cop in a doorway and that's when I saw the cloud debris. I got down there at 10.29 when the second tower collapsed. I didn't really see that because I was still on my way. There weren't that many people but some cars were burning. The next block was where the base of the World Trade Center was. I saw the cloud of debris coming – this all happened very quickly, I mean extremely fast. I had a wide angle lens with me and that makes things seem further away than they are. I took as many pictures as I could and turned into the doorway.

'I was wearing a hat and I closed my eyes and stood there. I was covered in dust, I was coughing and keeping my mouth shut. Once that went by everything turned black. In the next shot I took you can see this blackness. It lasted something like five minutes and it seemed like a long time. It was *so* dark, *so* black. You couldn't see anything, *you really could not see anything*. I tried opening my eyes and – black.

'You're not thinking about being frightened, you're thinking *what happened?* Once the darkness was lifting I opened my eyes as much as I could and took pictures of the scene. I bumped into a series of policemen, the head guy grabbed me and said "lady, out of here, NOW." He started pulling me along. They had just lost many of their co-workers and he was berating me. "Are you stupid? What are you doing here?" He was upset. After a couple of blocks he calmed down and he apologised. "Nothing personal." I said he didn't have to apologise, I did realise that he had lost his friends and he was trying to do his job, I was trying to do mine.

'Eventually I lost him and came back. That's when I found one of my co-workers. She was one of the first photographers there and she got some great shots. We hugged and said, "are you OK?" We went into a bank, I think it was the City Bank, because it was being used as an emergency area. They had people handing out water around there, a cop was injured and some people were being moved. A man had, I guess, an asthma attack and the firemen took him up to an ambulance.

'I shot stuff there in the bank – the firemen coming in – and at that point, since the two towers had gone down, more cops were saying "you can't go to that area". I went as far as I could and then got kicked out. I hung around with some other photographers, people walking with masks coming past me. There were not that many coming past. A lot of firemen and police started to come down Broadway, the trucks were parked around City Hall and these firemen were using a wheel barrow and whatever they could to carry their equipment. The stuff was pretty heavy: oxygen tanks and emergency supplies. A worker was handing out water to all these firemen. I tried to join them and walk down, but . . .

'I don't think I was aware of the full scale of it. You're still trying to think like a photographer: *what have I covered, what should I really do? So the other photographer's here, let me maybe try going to a different area.* I made my way uptown because on Broadway cops were stopping you. I went back where I had come from, the west area and cops still kept kicking me up further north and away. I took some more shots and went back into the office. Basically I'd been shooting whatever I could. Actually I haven't really thought about what time I got back to the office. Three or four, maybe. I'd done my best. Then I went home.'

How did you feel when you got home?

'Unreal. Unreal, unreal.'

What did you do when you got home, switch the TV on?

'I took off all my clothes and had a shower. Everything was just sort of stuck on me. You try not to think about it, but your shoes have been walking in the ashes and basically the ashes are body parts, bodies that had been incinerated in the towers. The ash

The Businesswoman

covered everything, even your hair – I was wearing a hat, luckily, but it got into everything.'

Did you throw the clothes away?

'No, actually I didn't [self-conscious semi-laugh]. I just washed everything and still wear 'em. That sort of thing bothers me and . . . it doesn't bother me, I guess. In a way it does but I am very practical, too. I washed them and you try not to think about it – but you do. The reality is that there was the remains of a lot of bodies that were killed, a lot of building debris. And you'd been breathing things that were not good for you, like the gasolene tanks [on the planes]. I felt OK physically. I went to see a doctor and everything was OK. The thing was, if you blew your nose the stuff was black.'

Did you come to work the next day?

'Yes, I did. My first job was to meet the Coast Guard. I was supposed to get a ride up and down [to photograph the skyline]. They let me off and I tried to make my way into Ground Zero to take some pictures but the cops threw me out again. I don't mind getting kicked out but only if all photograhers are getting kicked out. In that case I'll gladly leave, but if there's another photographer it's "if he's there, I'm there".'

Do you think it makes a difference to you, being a woman, in terms of what you photograph and how you photograph it?

'It would be different to a man because we are raised differently. It's the way you're raised and how you see things. I photograph things much differently to another woman, too, I think. It's because of your upbringing. Some people may be a little bolder when we have to cover things. They may go straight to the front when, say, the President is speaking. What I try to do is go back and around people so I don't bring any notice to myself. I try not to upset the event. I just try to record it, not be a part of it.'

There is an ethical question and it's one which reporters don't face so sharply in circumstances like 9/11: intrusion. I would have to go and speak to someone to find out about them but you can just take their picture.

'People can tell me to get lost. What I would do is take a picture – in normal day-to-day picture taking – of say a mother and ask her if she minded, then ask her for details for the caption.'

But this is not a normal situation at all.

'Normally I'd have introduced myself and gotten their names but I was in no position to do that now, so what you try to do is get as many pictures as you can to show what was happening. [In the film 9/11 there are] shots of the firemen milling around because they don't know what's going on, and nobody else knows what's going on, but the TV cameras are there. It's the same thing when you are covering something.

'Plus you have no communication with the outside world so you're asking *what is going on?* When I was in my car on the way there I knew more than when I got out of it – I could listen to the radio. The moment you step from the car you're on your own. You might chance to meet another photographer and ask what they know but the rest is what you can see.'

You couldn't ask permission of people stumbling out of the debris and the wreckage.

'But it's still a public street.'

I'm thinking more of the morals than the law.

'Well, I would never take pictures of a body that has been decapitated or something like that.'

If you had been able to get pictures of the people who jumped, would you have taken those?

'Yes, but I don't know if I would have used them. I would not have taken pictures of them after they landed, I wouldn't have done that. One of my friends, he's an AP photographer, was at a fashion show and got the last train, got off at Chambers Street [five blocks from the World Trade Center]. As he reached the Trade Center he got people jumping. The *Times* carried his shot of a

The Businesswoman

man in a straight position, head first going down parallel to the building. You could see the features but it was not really tight on the face. You can imagine the fear. What is worse, to burn to death or jump?

'The photographer covered it for two days and then said "no more". I didn't ever see things like that. I didn't see bodies in the street, I didn't see body parts. What I saw was the injured coming past me and they weren't really injured. It's affecting me now, just because of my imagination.'

Were you watching the 9/11 film last night in professional mode?

'No – well, half-and-half. It was like "could I have gotten those pictures? Where should I have gone to get that? How did that person get that picture?" – but, you know, you are still affected by it. No matter how professional you are, you still cry. You still cringe. I recorded it and when I was watching my daughter came by. I stopped it. I didn't want her to see it.'

There had been a warning about strong language.

'Yes, and she said to that "we're New Yorkers!"'

Since 9/11 how have you dealt with it?

'It hasn't affected me that much, in that I didn't know anybody killed and I didn't see the gore. You do your best and thank God for what He has given me.'

If there were more women leaders would there be fewer wars?

'I think so. We women have more of an understanding of how to compromise and how to make things work better – but you'd still have a lot of empowered men in the military. You could be the head of state but I don't think you have a lot of power.'

What if you had women generals as well?

'I think they would realise the necessity of war, but I don't think they would go do it. If you have enough, I don't think you have to prove yourselves the biggest, roughest, toughest man there is. Women generals wouldn't feel the need to do that at all.'

What would you have done after 11 September?

'Almost the same thing, I guess, as we have done because negotiating with the Taliban is not an option. You can't do it. They are terrorists for many reasons: they think they're doing it for humanity, for writing their laws, for God etc. They're not. They've been hurt in some way and they're doing it for themselves.'

So you agreed with the bombing of the Taliban?

'I might have done a few things differently, but only a few. There is evil and there is good, people have a basic sense of rightness and wrongness. These Taliban people, well, they have pushed things to the extreme. Take the women: that's *your* mother, that's *your* sister, that's *your* grandmother, that's *your* daughter, that's part of *your* family, it's *your* other half. How did *you* come into this world? It takes two, it takes a man and a woman, period. Hopefully you have a mother and a father who teach you right from wrong, who teach you about your background, your history as a people and as a nation, who you are as a person. It just didn't happen there.'

SIX

The Reporter

The Taliban made it clear that they had banned all foreigners and expelled all foreigners. They kept issuing these edicts, like if you were caught with a satellite phone you'd be hung. But I was planning to go.

For Christina Lamb from south London, Pakistan was an enchanted place she discovered by accident, and, in a way which now seems inevitable, it led to a love affair with Afghanistan. As a journalist on the *Sunday Telegraph*, she has been able to separate the love affair with reporting aspects of reality well enough to win an award of genuine prestige.[1] In conversation this reveals itself in an intriguing way. She can talk descriptively about witnessing the horror of a civilian population being shelled and bombed, but retreats far into modesty if you mention the award. Like the photographer Marilynn K. Yee, she doesn't stop being human when she does her job but she's had to arrange aspects of that to accommodate some very strange situations.

She's thirty-six and married to a Portuguese man. They have a 2½-year-old son Lourenço.

'I always wanted to write – books – and travel. When I left university I thought working on a newspaper would be the best way to make some money and see the world. The idea was to do it for a short time and make enough money to stop, then write *the* novel – but I got addicted to it and I've never stopped.

'When I left university I spent the summer as an intern on the *Financial Times* Foreign Desk, and one day we had an invitation to a lunch which the Foreign Editor couldn't go to. He looked round for somebody and I was the most junior. It was a lunch for south Asian politicians – quite senior people. Benazir Bhutto[2] wasn't there, but the secretary general of her party was so I got talking to him and he said, "would you like to meet her?" – she was living in exile in London. I said, "yes, I'd love to." He arranged that, I went and we got on very well.

'It was also when she announced she was going to marry and we ran that in the *FT*. It was my first big piece. At that time the Pakistani press was banned from reporting her, so the foreign press was her only way of getting out her message.

'After that we kept in touch. I went off training at *Central TV*, and it was very male orientated – very sexist – and quite difficult. I'd get sent on the worst kind of jobs, anything to do with babies and knitting. I was renting a room and working long hours, so I virtually never saw daylight – the Central office was underground! One day I got home in the evening and on the mat was an invitation written in gold script to Benazir's wedding *in Pakistan*. I took two weeks off work and went to Karachi. She'd invited me as a friend so I went to all the women-only parts of the wedding and it gave me an incredible insight into Pakistan. I'd never been there before. I'd been to India. I just fell completely in love with the whole thing, the smells, the colours, it was all so intense. So I came back and decided to go and live in Pakistan!

'Because I'd spent the summer with the *FT* and got on very well with them they said "we have someone in Pakistan but we'll pay for what we publish. It didn't occur to me to talk to anyone else, I just went".

The Reporter

She calculated that with the war underway in Afghanistan it was a place where she was getting 'two ongoing stories' in one. Her eye settled upon Peshawar, (see map on page viii) a place she knew nothing about 'except having read Kipling. I took what was known as the Flying Coach – mini busses that go between Islamabad and Peshawar. They used to go on to Kabul. It was completely mad. I had this huge suitcase containing all my worldly belongings. It was much too big and I couldn't carry it. I arrived in the old city of Peshawar at about sunset. I got off the Flying Coach – I was the only foreigner and the only woman – and thought *what the hell am I going to do?* Peshawar had old bazaars and people selling everything. It used to be a beautiful place and these days it's far more Afghan than it was then, it's really an extension of Afghanistan and it's not as friendly as it was. I would be less happy about arriving there on my own now that I was at the time, and that's nothing to do with being older, more than Peshawar is different, there are more of the so-called fundamentalists.

'Anyway, I ended up getting in a rickshaw to a hotel called Green's, which was where all the arms dealers used to stay. It *was* completely mad.

'This was the beginning of 1988 and the Russians were still in Afghanistan. They were negotiating to leave but they hadn't started leaving. For almost two years I lived mostly in Peshawar and then Islamabad, and I was going back and forth to Afghanistan. Peshawar is a big Asian crossroads, so it's where merchants have always passed through. In those days, because of the war in Afghanistan it was full of spies from all sides, even unlikely ones – like Italian spies. Then there were aid workers and all kinds of other people. You never knew quite what anyone was. There were so many aid agencies and a lot of them gathered intelligence, there were a lot of journalists who weren't really journalists – they were ex-army people who'd gone out. Everybody was there trying to get in. There were lots of spokespeople who could arrange it for you, even diplomats.'

How did you feel as a woman going in there?

'In an odd way this was more of an issue with other journalists than with the Mujahideen themselves. A lot of the journalists were Vietnam vets and this was an ideological thing for them as well as a story.⁵ I used to get into terrible arguments with them because I wasn't that impressed by the Mujahideen. On one level I could see they *were* very romantic figures – medieval clothing and fighting with their Kalashnikovs against one of the world's most powerful armies – but on another level they were incredibly disorganised, they were all fighting each other and exaggerating all the time. They'd say, "we shot down eleven helicopters yesterday," and – no helicopters.

'To go there at twenty-one always having lived in England and then – I never met women. I went to tribal areas and I met men. Women were always somewhere else. Sometimes because I was a woman they'd say "do you want to come and meet our women?" I always felt very uncomfortable because I was taken into the woman's area behind a curtain and all the women would come out and they'd all touch me – because they'd never seen anything like me before. I must admit that I still find it uncomfortable when I am taken into this purdah area.

'Sometimes they were educated women and they even spoke English. It was shocking to me to see women the same age as me, I'd been able to travel all over the world and they were also educated but must have been brought up living like sheep. And to find that they had read Shakespeare and James Joyce! I'd talk to them and say "how can you live like this?" and they'd reply say "well, actually we can't understand how you live. We are shocked. You women in the west are just sex objects." In the same way that we caricature women under the Taliban a little bit, they caricature our lives – we are available to every man, and a lot of men there act assuming that. They think if you're a western woman you're available.'

Did you have experiences of that?

The Reporter

'Yes. More, oddly, with Pakistanis than Afghans. Afghan men tend to be very honourable. This is something I can't explain to myself – what happened prior to the Taliban to change that. Now everybody tells stories of how awful it was, women being raped all the time and it must be true because lots of people swear that this happened.

'Yet I travelled a lot of times with Mujahideen for weeks in the middle of nowhere and I was the only woman. Many may never have seen a western woman. I was very young and never once did I have any problems. I know their commanders used to say to them at the beginning, "anything happens to her I'll chop you up into pieces".

'What always worried me about travelling with the Mujahideen as a woman was something else, that you were a liability and they would think of you as that – somebody else would be risking their life to help you. In fact I was always chatting with Abdul Haq, the Kabul commander who lived near me and he refused to take me with them because, he said, "you're a woman". It made me more determined. As a woman doing this type of work you have to be much more determined than men – you're not as physically strong and you can't show that. You have to compensate for it. In the end he did agree.

'Being a war correspondent is addictive. I was completely addicted to the whole danger and adrenalin of it in the two years I lived in Peshawar, going in and out of Afghanistan. I was fascinated by Afghanistan and what was happening, and I never ever thought anything would happen to me. I think most war correspondents are like that and it's very dangerous. When I left Afghanistan all I wanted to do was go and cover another war.

'When I came back the first time from living there I felt really foreign *here*. It was the Thatcher years and everybody was obsessed by making money. Because I'd only graduated two years before, lots of my friends had gone into very high paying jobs – investment, banking, trading – and they were earning huge amounts of money. That's all they thought about and I found it so odd because I'd seen people being killed. I also thought that what we were doing in the west was not helpful because it brought in people like bin Laden. I was very shocked to come back – I couldn't talk to people about it because people weren't really interested.'

When she finished her time there, still addicted to war, 'I was furious because I was working for the *FT* and they said "oh, we'd like you to go to Brazil and be our South American correspondent."'

No matter that Lamb went there, soon enough she would be putting her knowledge of Afghanistan to good use. 'On 9/11 I was in Portugal. I was on sabbatical from my newspaper writing about exploration of the Amazon. I'd spent a couple of months in the Amazon and come back to London for about a month. Because my husband is Portuguese and we have a place at Estoril[6] – very quiet – we decided that it was better to live there while I wrote my book. Our son is still very small and we wanted him to speak some Portuguese. We went by boat to Bilbao and drove down through Spain, arriving on September 9.

'The flat is in a condominium, on ground floor, and there's a swimming pool. We spent a couple of days getting it ready – I needed to buy a desk and things like that, because it was a holiday place. Lourenço started at nursery on the 11th but was back by lunch time. I was getting ready to start writing the book. I switched on the TV to catch the news and saw what was happening. I couldn't believe it.

'Watching the second plane hit didn't look real, to start with. Lourenço was just at the age where he likes planes and knows the word plane. He thought it was very exciting and kept shouting "mummy, plane" because they kept showing it over and over again. It was Portuguese news. They were showing CNN but with Portuguese commentary and they were saying "there's going to be an attack on London". The *Sunday Telegraph* office is in Canary

The Reporter

Wharf'[7] – an obvious comparison with the Twin Towers, she thought: *we are in Portugal and we are safe*. At the same time, 'the news hound in me wanted to know what was going on. I phoned the Foreign Editor and said "can I go to Afghanistan?" He said, "why would you want to go there?" At that stage they didn't quite realise the bin Laden link.

'Next day he phoned and said, "can you come back to London?" and that was the end of my sabbatical. I came back and I was fixated on Afghanistan and Pakistan. Everyone was still focusing on what was happening in America, all trying to get to America and there were no flights. At the end of the week they said "how do you feel about going to Afghanistan?" I went the following week.

'I didn't go to Afghanistan, I went to Pakistan. Like everybody else at the beginning, I was *trying* to get in but that was very difficult. The Taliban made it clear that they had banned all foreigners and expelled all foreigners. They kept issuing these edicts like if you were caught with a satellite phone you'd be hung. But I was planning to go.

'I met Yvonne Ridley[8] early on, she went in and was arrested. In fact two things happened. John Simpson [of the BBC] went in wearing a burqa and then – annoyingly – broadcast to the world how he'd done it. So what did the Taliban do? They put women guards on all the checkpoints so that they could look under the burqas. That made it much harder. Then Yvonne Ridley was arrested and it was clear the Taliban were looking for people. I didn't know what to do. The problem was that you couldn't go on your own – because of the language, you needed a guide. I speak some Pashtu[9] but not enough and I am fair haired and green eyed and don't look Afghan in the least.

'I had Afghan friends that I talked to about taking me, but that created a problem. One aspect of the Yvonne Ridley episode was that she was arrested and released, *but* her guides were kept. It's all very well putting your own life in danger but now you were very

The Women's War

much putting someone's else life in danger. We can always fly away but they – drivers and interpreters – have to live with the regime. It really was a danger, because if they were caught helping you get into Afghanistan they faced a very serious regime which wasn't playing games.

'I hadn't thought it would be a problem for me getting in because I knew lots of Afghans from going in before. I am very friendly with Hamid Karzai[10] who was my closest friend when I lived there before. I went first to Quetta and saw him, probably about September 16, and asked him to get me in to Kandahar. He said "no. I could get you in easily but what will you do? You won't be able to talk to people – you'll be exposed – and it's pointless just going in and seeing without being able to talk." I was furious with him.

'I tried all sorts of ways because I had had experience before of the border being closed when they didn't want journalists to go in. For example, during the first battle after the Russians left – Jalalabad – they closed it. I was arrested at the border and taken back to Peshawar, *but* I did manage it in an Afghan ambulance which was going in. There were cushions in the back and I hid under them, then they put blankets and medicines and things over me. The drive from Peshawar to Jalalabad took about four hours and for all that time I was under these blankets – which had been soaked in Dettol disinfectant, so I was breathing Dettol fumes. I was completely high by the time we got there!

'Now – in September, 2001 – I thought *well, maybe I could do this again, go in an ambulance.* I got a black burqa, which is what lady doctors wear. I have a friend at the hospital in Quetta – and Kandahar – and he was to take me. It was all set to go, and on that day we heard that Yvonne Ridley had been arrested. My Editor phoned and said, "do not go." I said, "look, it's all arranged" and he said it again: "Do not go." We had a long chat about it because he was convinced I was going to try it and he insisted, "I just don't want you to."'

The Reporter

Why did you want this so much?

'It was the best place to be. We were all sitting in Quetta talking to refugees that were coming out. The only journalists inside were with the Northern Alliance. What we wanted to know was what was happening inside Taliban Afghanistan. After all they controlled 90 per cent of the country. It was so frustrating. We weren't very far away – you were five hours from Kandahar.'

Was that a professional thing?

'Yes, but it was more than that because I had been there before and I cared about this story, I cared about Afghanistan. I care about everything I write, and I had always tried to cover the forgotten places and people, but I cared most about this. Maybe that's because it was my first foreign assignment, but in a way I had really fallen in love with Afghanistan. It had and it has that effect on a lot of British people. I don't know if that's for historical reasons but there's a bit of an affinity and a lot of mutual respect. *And* I'd been close friends with Afghans, like Hamid Karzai, and seen what the fighting had done to them. *And* I felt guilty because that time when I got to Jalalabad I left after the end of the battle. I was very traumatised by what I'd seen and I never went back to Afghanistan.'

What traumatised you?

'It was the first time that the Mujahideen had tried to capture a town [March 1989].[11] Everyone was saying then that once the Russians went away the [Soviet-backed] regime would collapse because it had no support. The Mujahideen would go straight in. That was completely wrong, and I knew it was wrong – it was clear if you were living there and covering it a lot. The Mujahideen won the war against the Russians partly *because* they were so disorganised: there was no central command to destroy and they never took any towns. From that to suddenly trying to capture Jalalabad required a much more strategic plan and more conventional fighting. It was a disaster.

'I got there – at the beginning it was only myself and one other journalist, an American. I had never seen anything like it. I had been into Afghanistan ten times before and I had seen death, but that was something completely different. The Mujahideen were rocketing the city from outside. The civilians tried to flee with these rockets coming in and the Afghan regime was bombing the roads. These civilians were getting caught between the rockets and the bombs. Thousands of people were killed, they say 10,000, but nobody knows. I saw hundreds, and I saw the fighting between the different Mujahideen groups. It was clear that it was going to be disastrous from then on. I didn't choose to leave, I was deported by Pakistan.'

How do sights like that affect you as a woman? Do they make you want to resign and become a librarian in Islington?

'It was only when I went back to Peshawar that it hit me. I had to go back to Peshawar because in those days communications weren't the same and you didn't have satellite phones or anything. I went back to Green's Hotel, and only when I was writing it on my Tandy[12] did I realise what I had seen. It's curious. You know people have a way of distancing themselves when they are watching something so that, somehow, they are not part of it. It's a mechanism for survival.'

In the long run up to 9/11 when the Northern Alliance had power in Kabul and were beaten back by the Taliban, you must have known what the Taliban ruled entailed in a way that most western people couldn't and didn't. What did you think about them? In the documentary,[13] as someone said, women had less rights than animals.

'That's what I mean about feeling guilty about not going back when I could have gone back. I felt I had had many more opportunities – and access – and I didn't go.'

Did you feel that this was something a western woman with freedom of expression should be writing about on their behalf?

'Yes, sure. I felt guilty because I cared about the place. It wasn't just a country to me, when I think about Afghanistan I think about people I know.'

These people you knew – the women – were going to be denied all rights.

The Reporter

'But a lot of the people I knew, men and women, were in exile in Pakistan and I felt they had given up their lives. Because I'd lived there for those two years I'd met these people socially and become friends. Some of them were very young then. In the first place, they'd given up their lives to the Jihad,[14] that hadn't achieved anything and they ended up in exile in Pakistan. I knew them as figures in their twenties – those glamorous Mujahideen warriors I mentioned before – and suddenly their lives have gone by and they still haven't got their country back.

'I want to say something else, because this concerns me. It wasn't the Taliban that started the whole thing about the women, it was the Mujahideen. They began closing the schools and the Taliban took this to extremes. OK, the Taliban has gone and now it's the Northern Alliance back. They are as hated by educated women as the Taliban were and I find that quite disconcerting.'

And we have also heard disturbing things, like when the Northern Alliance had power before they hung children from lamp-posts.

'I think there is a tendency too much to see the issue in black and white and it is not. There is this feeling at the moment that the Taliban were all bad and now they've gone everything will be fine. It's not like that.'

You wrote a piece which carried the headline READING, WRITING AND COUNTING RIFLES. *How did you feel about writing that?*

'Having a school child who is at the age of starting to learn to count made it even worse for me. It is very disturbing to see that and it is one of the big effects of what's been happening in Afghanistan. For those children, war is part of their lives to the extent that they learn to count through guns.'

Was that difficult? If I was in Kabul writing about boys who had been denied any education but for girls it was fine, I'd feel rage.

'I cared about it more, I guess, because I was a woman. More than being difficult to write about, it made me angry.'

But the anger is not in the piece. It is objective.

'I see it at different levels. I have spent so much of my time listening to people's stories and that's all my foreign experience, not just Afghanistan. I have always covered the developing world, remote parts of Africa, Latin America so I have heard stories from many horrible places. I'm not saying that you get inured to it because I don't think you do – and if you do you should give up – but you can ask the questions almost unemotionally. Of course many times in Afghanistan, or afterwards, or thinking about it, you start crying. Sometimes I wanted to just shut my notebook and go away because it was too horrible. And everybody – everybody – finds it horrible. There is nobody who is immune to that sort of thing.'

It's interesting that it hasn't put you off.

'No, because I think it's important that you stay and write about it and tell people what's happening.'

I want to give you a proper feel for what Christian Lamb wrote, although of necessity it will only be chosen paragraphs.

Here is the story on the Kabul schools from the *Sunday Telegraph* of 23 December 2001, starting appropriately with the introduction:

> Five-year-old Sonita is learning to count. Instead of the colourful ducks, cakes and rabbits that British youngsters use to learn, the textbook in her Afghan primary school opens with the following illustrated lesson: one Kalashnikov, two grenades, three rifles, four armour-piercing bullets, five 9mm bullets.
>
> In her learning-to-read book, a picture of a carrot with a caption saying 'Vegetables are good for you,' is followed by a huge page inviting the learner to colour-in a Kalashnikov assault rifle. Underneath, it says: 'The bullets of the Mujahideen will fall like rain on the enemy.'

The Reporter

And . . .

'I feel like we've been let out of jail,' said Fatima Ismati, 36, a primary school teacher. 'Our homes were our jails for these last years.'

And . . .

The United Nations Children's Fund . . . estimates that 30,000 children in Kabul – two thirds of them girls – studied in secret home-based classes.

And . . .

Most young people have been traumatised by 23 years of war. A 1997 study by Unicef found that two-thirds of Kabul's children had seen someone killed by a rocket, and more than a third had been involved in tending to a wounded or dead relative or friend.

Lots of people do things to make their names but I never get the impression that's why you're writing it.

'To me there are a lot of aspects to it. For instance, interviewing the women in Herat that were very brave. That makes you feel guilty that you've had things so comparatively easy and taken so much for granted. I felt a bit powerless a lot of the time. I wanted to write about how people were but I didn't think it was enough, I wanted to do more. I'd like to have filled their libraries with books, found food for all the children. Instead I had to watch mothers bury their babies dead of cold and hunger. Nobody should be dying of that in the 21st century.'

Thus, the helplessness of the journalist, eternal witness to the actors and their parts. In the *Sunday Telegraph* of 16 December 2001 Lamb wrote a piece about the Sewing Classes of Herat, 'an underground network of writers and poets who risked death to keep alive the culture of their ancient city' by pretending to attend sewing classes which were, in fact, 'cover' for studying forbidden subjects like literature:

The Women's War

One student, 23-year-old Zena Karamzade, was in her second year as a medical student when the Taliban ended female education. With her dreams of becoming a doctor in tatters, she was on the verge of suicide when a friend introduced her to the sewing classes. 'We didn't live under the Taliban,' she explains. 'We just stayed in our rooms like cows.'

Maybe if you hadn't loved the place, it would have been just another unpleasant assignment and then you'd have moved on to the next one.

'But it's very much an unfinished story, anyway. None of the issues are at all resolved so I wouldn't want to leave it.'

Did you feel that you were covering a defining moment – thrown into sharpest relief by 9/11 – between what one might call east and west?

'Most of the time I didn't think about it but there were times – like when I was arrested or sometimes in very hostile situations – that you suddenly realised *you* were the enemy to these people. They were not used to the fact that you're just covering it and that you're not actually involved.'

Was it a moment which defined the place of women east and west?

'It's funny, I never thought about it in that way. The treatment of women has somehow become symbolic of everything that was wrong with the Taliban – and their laws and rules against women *were* terrible *but* they were also terrible against men: tortured, killed, not being able to listen to music, play chess, meet in gatherings and so on. OK, men were allowed to go out on the street and, OK, boys could go to school but the syllabuses had completely changed. They weren't studying in the same way. At Herat University, the English course suddenly became mostly Islamic studies and the lessons suddenly became mostly on Islamic culture – so that was what they were learning. In fact I was slightly annoyed that people were making it a *thing* [solely] about women, because they didn't care about that before and everyone had known for years what was being done to women.'

How can it come about that people think like the Taliban?

'They basically thought that the answer to Afghanistan was what they were implementing. You have to look at where they're coming from. Before the Taliban, the situation was bad and everybody was frightened. My friends say that women were not going to school at that time because you could be attacked or raped so they were being kept at home, anyway, by their parents. The Taliban institutionalised that.

'At the beginning this whole idea that women needed to be protected was what they were about and only later on did they seem to become convinced – like Mullah Omar – that they needed to take Islam back to the time of the Prophet, and that only then would Afghanistan be really pure Islam. A lot of them had studied at the Madrassahs[15] and they reject everything modern and everything from the west. A lot of them were also Pashtuns who had this very strong Pashtun code. What happened was a combination of both.'

I can understand why you reject everything modern, because it doesn't sit with your beliefs, but to reject your mother?

'But they didn't see themselves as rejecting them, they were protecting them. A lot of Afghan women, when they have visited Pakistan, have said to me "how can you possibly live that way? Isn't it horrific that you go out on the streets and you're not completely covered? That men can speak to you?" It's a different culture, a Pashtun culture.'

Yes, that's cultural, but to actually say 'I will deny my mother medical treatment . . .'

'They didn't deny women medical treatment, but you had to be seen by a woman doctor.'

And denied education?

'They argued that they were protecting women. They would open the schools eventually when they had worked out the way of protecting women. And a lot of the girls' schools had been destroyed, too. As I say, in the Pashtun area in Pakistan which I knew quite well that's how women live, anyway. I'd been horrified, but they'd been horrified by my life.'

Although you had the choice and they didn't.

'To them I had no choice. I was being forced to go out and work.'

In February 2002 Lamb managed to interview some Taliban leaders who were hiding in Pakistan.

It took me a few moments to come to terms with the fact that I was sitting cross-legged in front of some of the world's most wanted men.

'You see, we don't have two horns,' says one of the ministers with a smile as he poured me tea and offered me boiled sweets in place of sugar. 'Now anyone can say anything about us and the world will believe it. People have been saying we skinned their husbands alive and ate babies and you people print it.'

During the interviews, one man – Maulana Sahadi, who had been Director of Defence – said that the Talbian were 'not broken, still whole. We weren't defeated, we agreed to hand over rather than fight and spill blood. Our people went back to their tribes or left the country. Now we are just waiting. We are regrouping. We still have arms and many supporters inside, and when the time is right we will come back.' That seemed the perfect lead-in to:

If there were more women leaders would there be fewer wars?

'I'm sure that's true because women spend more time listening than men and women think more about family and what's likely to happen to their families. I think it was reflected in the newspaper coverage in this country which are very male dominated the men were very gung-ho for the war and it was all about boy's toys.'

The Reporter

What would you have done after 11 September?

'Very difficult. I think Bush had no choice. He had to react. It was an attack on the heart of America and he had to counter attack. Yet in some ways [the US-led coalition] hasn't achieved anything. They have replaced one regime with another which can only survive as long as foreign troops are there. The Taliban is still there – very few were killed – and they'll come back. I repeat that I don't think Bush had any choice, and who knows if the Americans hadn't done it whether there would have been further attacks?'

A final question. What is it that takes you back and back to this strange place – something deep down inside you?

'Because I care about the place and know it quite well, I am maybe able to get insights that other people aren't. I want to use that. It's this naïve thing of thinking you can change the world.'

SILENCES AND OTHER VOICES

I want to quote Valerie Powell, a 54-year-old British nurse, here because her work is radically different to that of Christina Lamb, and yet both share – if I may put it this way – similar motivation to make things better. While Lamb arrived in Pakistan with a large suitcase and no immediate prospects, Powell, the daughter of a Cornish businessman, went to the Canadian Artic to look after a village of Inuit indians some 400 miles from the nearest doctor. After that, she went to Siberia.

She works for a charity called Merlin[16] and these are Powell's own words, as she sent them to me from Tajikistan, with the most minimal editing.

'I had been working in Tajikistan when I first became involved with the Afghans who, after fleeing from the Taliban, became stranded on the 'islands' on the Afghan-Tajik border. When my contract for the Tajik programme ended I knew that I wanted to work full-time on the islands and I was returning home from Tajikistan to London on September 11.' That took her to Munich to change flights – and took her to a Munich Airport deathly quiet. She saw people in front of a TV screen in the restaurant and watched the coverage of the attacks from there until she had to board the London flight.

'Although I could not understand the commentary in German I watched the horrifying events on the screen, I realised the implications and I knew then with an absolute certainty that I would be returning.'

She explains that the term 'islands' is 'slightly misleading: it is actually a flood plain with a wide, meandering river that divides and changes course as the water rises by 3 to 4 metres when the snows melt in the summer. It is a flat and featureless area with muddy banks, low scrubby bushes, tall reeds and some grassland. The area is about 25 kilometres wide and 40 kilometres long. The tall cliffs of southern Tajikistan – guarded by the Russian Border Forces – are on one side of the river and, on the other, the arable land and mountains of Afghanistan.

'Without an aerial view or map it is impossible to tell how many islands there may be, although all but one site have to be reached by crossing water. This can vary from a muddy channel crossed by 4-wheel drive in winter, wading knee deep in the spring or using a raft made of inner tubes – or a wooden barge – in the summer. Sometimes two boats are tied together so we can take our vehicle across.

'Because of the security situation with shooting and shelling from the Taliban across the river, access could only be obtained from Tajikistan by passing through the Russian Border Force gates. It could be a lengthy procedure involving obtaining permissions and a drive to collect a RBF soldier to escort us through the border post area – which is mined – and onto the "islands".

'We are not allowed to stay overnight and have to return to the border post well before dark each day. It involves a lot of travelling and waiting, which limits very much the time we can spend on the islands. I work with a wonderful team of Tajik doctors who accompany me. We provide mobile clinics, vaccination campaigns, supplementary feeding programmes, training of health workers and traditional birth attendants. Basic drugs and medical supplies are given to health workers on completion of training.

'The population was approximately 10,000 and consisted of many ethnic groups including Turkman, Uzbek, Tajik, Pashtun and Arab. There were four main settlements with their own commanders, and most people lived in holes dug into the ground with a reed roof. This was partly as a bunker to protect against shelling and wind. Initially I used these shelters as a clinic but they were very small, damp and dark and we often used animal shelters.

'As the people became more settled they built clinics for us out of reeds. I was so surprised the first time I saw that they had made a clinic for us. The only problem was a slight design fault: I was too tall and couldn't stand up in it! Soon after they made a mud building with two rooms that we furnished with rush mats and mattresses.

'They began to re-establish compounds, as they would have had in Afghanistan, with tall fences made of woven reeds. When the first summer came they were able to make bricks of mud baked in the sun and gradually more substantial buildings appeared that were dry and windproof. They built their own mosques and schools for each main settlement. Water was collected from holes dug in the ground – usually dirty and contaminated – or from the river, where they risked being shot. There was no sanitation.

'Ovens were made from mud, but food was the biggest problem. There was no agriculture on the islands and no edible plants, so scurvy (vitamin C deficiency) and anaemia were noted in the population. Few people had animals and most were dependent on sharing food rations sent to the Northern Alliance combatants on the islands. They had no agricultural tools or seeds to cultivate the poor sandy soil.

'Until September 11, humanitarian aid was restricted on the islands due to the presence of combatants amongst the population who did not want to be separated from their families. After the fall of Mazar-I-Sharif the combatants all left and more aid was given, especially in building latrines, and insulated tents were provided for school programmes. Clothing, shoes, blankets and hygiene kits were also distributed. As most of the families had their homes destroyed in Afghanistan they were allowed to stay on the islands til the spring 2002 when it is possible to rebuild again.

'I return to Tajikistan each night so I have relatively comfortable conditions.

When we first held clinics on the islands, all the health workers were male, and women could not access health care from them or reach hospital facilities. We established a good relationship with the community leaders and they were supportive of our plan to train some women in safe deliveries and basic health care.

'According to their culture, these women had to be accepted by their husbands and the community [in order] to be able to travel around the settlements. They are mostly older, illiterate women, often widows. Training therefore had to be based at a very practical level using life size dolls and other visual aids.

'I dress in loose clothes and a veil respecting Muslim traditions and my team has been praised by the mullahs for the modesty of our dress!!

'The local women are unused to going to pre-natal care and initially their husbands were reluctant to let them. After attending a young girl at delivery with a dead baby and severe haemorrhage due to scurvy, I found that her husband had not allowed her to come to our clinic. Meetings were then held with the leaders and groups of men explaining the necessity of women attending and allowing the female health workers to visit them in their homes.

'The health workers are very shy when they first come and it is lovely to see them grow in confidence. Despite being busy with

The Reporter

household duties – collecting water and firewood, grinding wheat, baking bread and caring for the family – many women welcomed the opportunity to leave their compound to work in the clinic and visit other families, often for the first time. The women were very enthusiastic once they had discovered that illiteracy is not a barrier to learning and we had a lot of fun in our training sessions.

'Myram, a young widow left with four children after her husband was killed by the Taliban, was one of our female health workers. She really enjoyed the chance to learn some skills and visit around the community, whether it was advising a young mother about a child with diarrhoea or assisting at a delivery. Rano, a respected older woman, also enjoyed the interest of attending the clinic and helping her people. Najiba, a second wife with two children, became pregnant and was delivered by Zulhyar, another female health worker. Najiba hopes to find work in a clinic when she returns to Afghanistan – she would love to train as a nurse, which would never have been possible before.

'This week [14 April 2002] all the people are returning to their villages after eighteen month's refuge on the islands. It is a time of great uncertainty for them and many long to remain in the security of the islands. The country they are returning to is vastly different from the one they fled in terror. The Taliban may no longer be in power but the Taliban mentality remains. Whether these women will be able to continue to work in their villages on their return – or their husbands, if feeling threatened, will revert to the former Afghan tradition of keeping their women within their compound – remains to be seen. Will they be able to work in clinics and train as nurses?

'What will happen to fourteen-year-old Salima, whose father was killed by the Taliban and mother died in childbirth leaving her five siblings to look after? Who will help rebuild her home and will she be able to continue her school studies on her return?

'The islands are emptying and I will be returning to the UK, my work finished but I cannot forget these people who have been so much part of my life these past eighteen months. They arrived in fear and terror, many injured and with little or no possessions. Using reeds and mud they built homes and re-established their communities, started schools and small businesses making reed mats and bricks. I hope that they can take this enthusiasm and commitment back to a new Afghanistan.

'For the women of these villages a door has been opened and they have had a glimpse of a better life. Let us make sure this door does not close again.'

Would there be fewer wars if there were more women leaders?

'Of course. Having worked in Grozny, Armenia, Kosovo and Afghanistan I see that there are no winners in any war, only losers.'

What would you have done after 11 September?

'I would have tried to get funding to continue support to the island people.'

In May 2002 Save the Children produced its annual State of the World's Mothers' report. On the situation of children, the report said that

> Afghanistan finished last behind 155 other countries. One of every six children dies before his or her first birthday, 71% are not enrolled in school, 88% are without access to safe water, and 25% are suffering from moderate to severe malnutrition. The situation is equally grim for mothers: a woman in Afghanistan is 1,200 times more likely to die in childbirth than a woman in top-ranked Switzerland.'

SEVEN

The Fiancée

People were jumping from his building and as I'm watching this I'm thinking if they're jumping it must be horrible, it's got to be that bad if these people are jumping to their deaths. *Then I'm wondering if Brian is one of those jumping.*

Debbie Barrett was born at Hackensack, New Jersey. Her fiancé Brian Cummins, a partner and equity trader with the firm of Cantor Fitzgerald, was thirty-eight. Barrett had been married at twenty-three and had a son – Troy – but she was long divorced. A graphic designer, she'd had her own business 'for eleven years, marketing and advertising'. Then Cummins came into her life two years ago like an irresistible force and she'd given it up to become a home-maker.

'It is a funny story, actually. I was at the World Trade Center with a fellow that I was on a date with and a group of friends. Another brokerage were having a St Patrick's Day party and Brian was at that. The gentleman I was with was a director, he was off talking to everyone and didn't spend much time with us. I was kind of by myself and Brian was very . . . attentive. He was very set on getting my phone number, me taking his phone number and he proceeded to follow me round the entire night. He was persistent that I speak to him and go out with him and so forth.

'I was really attracted to his personality, the fact that he was so persistent and he was very funny. He had this wacky sense of humour – he was known for that years ago. He was thirty-six then. He was a partner at Cantor Fitzgerald, he was one of the top equity traders on the hundredth and fourth floor.

'He proceeded to follow our group. We left the party and went to a place across the street called *The China Grill* and he followed us. He picked up the tab. Each place we went he picked up the tab! It really insulted the other man but Brian was so persistent and so funny. I was with another couple and the girl had a boat which was for sale. He bought the boat to get near to me! He was holding my hand saying "we are going to be together".

'By the end of the night he was saying "you have to agree right now that you'll have lunch or dinner with me." I said, "look, you've got to go away – I'm on a date right now! This other guy is getting very upset." The gentleman I was with was like *I'm going to kill this guy*. I was having a great time! Finally I said to Brian "OK, I'll have lunch with you but you've got to go away now because this is causing quite a problem."

'Several days later, after about twenty phone calls, I came into the city and had lunch with him. Again it was a real funny story. He wanted me to come to Manhattan. This is our first date' – and this is how it went. Debbie Barrett knew that Cantor Fitzgerald had a car service they could use.

Barrett: 'I'm coming in to the city to meet you. Can you send a car for me?'

Cummins: 'Come up to my apartment.'

Barrett: 'I am not coming up to your apartment. I don't even know you! You can send a car for me and I'll meet you at this certain restaurant. If you can't send a car I'll take the train and meet you at Penn Station but I'm not going to meet you at your apartment.'

Cummins: 'I'd rather be in a rock fight in Beirut than come down and meet you at Penn Station at that time of day.'

Barrett: 'OK, well then goodbye.'

She put the phone down and immediately it rang again.

Cummins: 'I'm sorry I said that. I'll meet you anywhere you want.'

From that day on they spent almost every day together.

'I live in an historic little stone house, my house that I bought by myself. Brian had an apartment on the Upper East Side in New York City and he had a beach house – he called it a beach house but it was a summer house – in New Jersey. Brian would spend weekends there in the summertime. It didn't really have heat, it was pretty much a summer house.

'Shortly after we met we started spending a lot of time at that house at the weekends and a lot of time at my house during the week. After we decided to make a commitment to each other, get engaged and so on and so forth, he sold the summer house and we were purchasing another home together. That was going to be our house. He took the train or ferry to work.

'How he proposed to me is a good insight into his personality. It was a Christmas morning and he'd been planning it for over a month, designing the ring and so forth. He was very proud of it. Christmas morning he jumped up in the bed, tossed the ring at me and said, "if you want to be my wife, you'd better get up and make me breakfast!" And I said, "how would you like your eggs!?!"

'We were officially engaged. He asked my father for permission to marry me and we had a beautiful engagement party, both sides were there and my closest friends. There was no big hurry, well, he wanted to get married immediately. He would have got married the first night we met! Any time a man was speaking to him he'd say "she is going to be my wife".

'I was a little unsure at times, believe me. I had been married once before, a long time ago, but I had a business, a nice little home and, you know, you're a bit once bitten twice shy. I just wanted to make sure it was the right person. He had not been married before, I was determined never to get divorced again and if I got married again this was going to be *it*. He wanted to have children immediately. He couldn't wait, he could not wait. He was becoming very successful, a partner there and he was ready to get married. He wanted to get out of the city and live down here, a coastline with lots of water – have a big yard and a bunch of kids and live happily ever after. A lot of people here commute.

'He was extremely dedicated to his job and a very hard worker, and he would be at his desk by 6.30 in the morning. He got up at 5.0 and when he took the train he could get there earlier because the boat didn't leave until a later time. If he had to be in extra early he would take the train.

'He liked to get there and read the newspapers from around the world. I think he had a sixth sense that maybe there was trouble coming because of some of the conversations we had and some of the things that happened before 9/11. He couldn't sleep at night, he was waking up with horrible nightmares. That was unlike him. He was always a sound sleeper.'

A couple of weeks before 9/11, over dinner, Cummins said he had made her his beneficiary.

'Looking back I think he may have had a bit of a premonition. In 1993 he was stuck in the stairwell[1] for thirteen hours. Trapped in the pitch black with many, many people all squished in there together. He mentioned it a few times and I would try and talk to him a little bit about it but I don't think the thought that it could be a target again that ever crossed his mind although I don't know. I never asked him that question.

'Actually, I was thinking *well, if it happened once they would have better planned escape routes and emergency precautions in place as a result of 1993*. That seems to be the way things happen: you learn from disasters. Not that I ever considered it could happen again, I really never did. I just don't think he did, either. The subject

The Fiancée

was so upsetting to him [after his 1993 ordeal] that he didn't want to talk about it. He would expand on it a little bit then quickly change the subject.

'Brian was always at his desk so early and he would call me. He would call me eight times a day. 9/11 was a Tuesday morning. We were together over the weekend and we were together Sunday night. Monday was a regular work day, Monday night he stayed in the city – so he was not with me. He stayed in the apartment. We spoke on the phone for an hour or so before we fell asleep and said "I love you". We had good conversation. I had this rule, because he called me so often – the second he got to his desk in the morning – that I wouldn't allow him to call me until after nine o'clock. I used to get mad because he'd call me at 6.0, 6,30.

'That morning the phone rang at just about nine o'clock. I was sound asleep, I had no idea what was happening in the world. I answered the phone thinking it was Brian but it was a very good friend of ours, Joe Reagan, who works for – I think – JP Morgan a few blocks away.[2] He and Brian were on the phone constantly for work and they did business together. Joe had been on the phone with Brian when the plane hit.

'Joe Reagan was screaming hysterically, "Brian's building's been hit, Brian's building's been hit. I don't know what's happened. Turn on your television. We're under attack." He thought [the area] was bombed. That's what he told me: it was a bomb. *Wall Street's being bombed.* As he was speaking to me I could hear explosions and he said, "Oh my God I don't know what's happening." He said his building was shaking and he thought he was being hit next.

'He asked, "does Brian have his cell phone with him?" I knew Brian wasn't allowed to use the cell phone during the trading day inside the building – strict rules and regulations – and he rarely brought it to work with him. It was possible he did have it with him but in the days just prior to this his cell phone wasn't working properly. I was really on top of him about that. "Please get that fixed, please get that fixed." There's a phone store right next to his office and I'd say, "leave it there and tell them to fix it." So – I knew the phone wasn't working very well in the first place, and I thought he probably didn't have it with him, anyway.

'During this phone call Joe Reagan said "Debbie, I've got to go, we're under attack, we've being evacuated." He hung up very quickly. Within seconds my phone rang again and Brian's brother was screaming hysterically. "Turn on your television, turn on your television. Does Brian have his cell phone with him? What's his number, what's his number?" I gave him the number but I said, "I don't know if he has it with him."

'My phone is portable and I was switching the television on while I was talking. They showed the building, they showed a plane coming around and hitting the building, so now I'm seeing exactly what is happening and I knew exactly where Brian's office was. I knew it was Tower One and I knew exactly which floor he was on. I'm looking at the television trying to count the floors and trying to calculate which *part* of the building Brian would be in: above or below or right where the plane hit.

'I started to panic because I realised he would be just above where the plane hit – or very close to where the plane hit, if not where the plane hit. I wasn't quite sure but my guesstimation was right around that area.

'I actually crashed on to the floor. I couldn't believe it. I thought it was a freak accident. How bizarre is that, that a plane hit the building? I thought it was a complete freak accident – somehow engine problems or something and it veered off course and it hit this building. Now my phone is ringing off the hook. The calls are coming through right on top of each other, Call Waiting, Call Waiting, Call Waiting. "Is Brian at work? "Yes, he's at work."

'From that point forward, I didn't remember a lot of what happened to me that day and for days later I didn't remember who I had spoken to. Someone would say "Debbie, I talked to you," and I'd say, "oh, you did?" Then I'd remember the conversation.

'Watching the television then I see the second plane coming in. I mean, this is live. I'm watching it hit the second tower and immediately I told myself *two planes hitting the two buildings – this cannot be a freak accident.* So it's not a freak accident and it's like the world's gone crazy. What's going to happen next? I didn't know what to do. My immediate instinct was to go into New York, to go there.

'I guess it's just the way it works with your mind, but I really believed he was still alive and had gotten out and was at a triage centre or a hospital somewhere. I had a lot of hope for many, many days but every minute of every hour that went past it was *I should have heard from him by now.*

'I have a couple of different phone lines in my home. They heard what was happening at high school and Troy was sent home immediately, so he came in. I had him on one phone and I was on the other. We have several friends in the area that I was calling. I was trying just to find out if they had heard from their husbands who Brian commuted with, if they knew anything, what they had heard. One of my girlfriends was friends with a top management guy at Cantor Fitzgerald – he was in another office. She was getting a lot of information because her husband wasn't killed but his brother, also at Cantor Fitzgerald, was. I was on the phone to her because she was getting as much information as she could possibly get just as I was. My son has a friend, Brad, who lost his father – at Cantor Fitzgerald also – so I had this network of women who were all comparing notes at any little bit of information.

'There were tremendous rumours flying – we heard that this guy got out and that guy got out. Every time we got a tiny bit of information we'd call each other. It never occurred to me that the buildings would collapse, it never occurred to *anyone* that the buildings would collapse. I thought of people getting up onto the roof and being rescued from there. Helicopters were sent in to evacuate the roof and they were circling. In fact I found out later, in conversations with wives and girlfriends, that some of the phone lines belonging to several of the men on the same floor as Brian were still working. They were saying "we're OK, we're being evacuated" so I still had great hope. The alternative didn't even occur to me – that wasn't going through my mind. I believed he was OK.

'The second tower collapsed first and we were in total shock. I thought *oh my God, if that one can go his can go, too. They've got to get him out of there.* People were jumping from his building and as I'm watching this I'm thinking *if they're jumping it must be horrible, it's got to be that bad if these people are jumping to their deaths.* My logic is saying *Debbie, this is a very bad situation.* Then I'm wondering if Brian is one of those jumping and that's all I could think about. The bodies were falling and on TV you were seeing them fall. Some of the firemen said later it was raining bodies.

'I called my parents. My step-father is a very rational, wise man and I have great respect for him. I told my parents what had just happened and at that point they had seen what had happened also, they were watching it. I said Brian had to be at or near where it hit and "I'm going into New York." He said, "oh, no. You're not going to New York. Just calm down, calm down, sit by the phones, stay by the phones, stay by the phones." While I was speaking to him I saw the building come down. I knew Brian was in it and I just completely . . . that's when I just completely went down on the floor. I just completely collapsed. I went to my knees. I freaked out completely.

'There was a very strong possibility that he didn't get out although I still believed he did, but I can tell you, when that building went down it was just like somebody shot me in the heart.

'The phone network was going on for the first hours of the day, but every point in the day went by without a call. I knew he would call me first out of everyone, that if there was any way he could get to a phone a call would come to me. And it was six hours and I hadn't heard, it was twelve hours. I was completely convinced that he was unconscious and that was why he hadn't rung. I was trying to figure it all out. I knew the phone system was wiped out in the entire area so possibly he couldn't get to a phone or he was injured, or a combination of both. I was still very hopeful. I believed that there were still thousands of people trapped in the area and they were alive. You heard that a large group was taken to Jersey City, and a large group was taken across the river to New Jersey so I was still convinced that he was somewhere in one of these other locations. For days I was convinced.

'Immediately they'd set up emergency triage centres all around the area and brought in personnel from the entire New York metropolitan area. I had a list of every hospital and triage unit. You couldn't even get a phone call to them. By now there was no physical way for me to get into the city. They closed down all the trains, they wouldn't let you drive in and the boats were cancelled. I was determined that I was going to go in and start searching for him even though everybody wanted me to stay by the phones.'

'My sister lives in Manhattan. She and a male friend would drive, take a train or whatever as close as they could and then walk to all the areas where they heard bodies were being taken. They'd go and search for Brian's name or see if he was there.

'They walked throughout the night talking on the cell phone with me from one location to the next looking for him. And he wasn't there.'

Barrett did get to New York on the Thursday. 'Understand I hadn't slept since Tuesday or eaten at this point. My sister's with me and now I'm extremely distraught and thinking *OK, I'm going to go to the apartment and just rest for a little while.* We were posting pictures and missing persons information all over the city. I was making photocopies, writing up large posters with his description and photograph. IF YOU HAVE SEEN HIM PLEASE CALL. People were doing this all around. They'd break your heart. It was overwhelming, the amount of people. They were everywhere. Everybody had hope, everyone thought someone had taken them in.

'I got to the apartment door but my keys didn't work. I was told that the locks had been changed and that I was not allowed in. Every move I made I was calling his family and telling them, giving everybody whatever information I could find. I was hoping Brian might have called them. We were in communication every step of the way quite normally, trying to help each other as much as we could, and then something went wrong.'

That Thursday, Barrett had travelled by train and 'my sister met me at Penn Station. Cantor Fitzgerald had set up emergency quarters at the Pierre Hotel [overlooking Central Park] dedicated to Cantor Fitzgerald families. We got to the hotel and they had lists of people who'd made it out. Nobody else was being qualified as dead, only missing, because they didn't know. It was very well organised, very well done by Cantor Fitzgerald.'

A senior executive, Peter Depuzzo, had been a close friend of Cummins and now sought Barrett out. She had never met him face to face before. 'Oh my God, Debbie, I've been looking for you. Brian's told me so much about you. He was so happy and so excited about the wedding.'

That gave Barrett a good feeling because 'it was the first acknowledgement that I had had from anyone. It was huge thing for me.'

Sensibly, Cantor Fitzgerald made those who had come into groups of four. These groups were arranged at a big table for those who'd worked on the 104th floor, another for the 101st, the 102nd and so on. 'It was amazing how many were lost.' Originally Barrett had thought Cummins worked on the 106th floor but 'that had never been important.'[3]

Peter Depuzzo came up and said 'I have to tell you that I have not heard of one single person getting out above the 90th floor.'

'He was telling us in his way *no chance*,' Barrett says. 'That was the turning point in my mind, the overwhelming moment. He was

The Fiancée

telling us *there are no miracles here*. I still had hope but that was the moment when I began to accept the possibility that he wasn't alive any more. In my mind I had to start considering *if this is true what do you do now?*

'They found his body in October. Was he on the roof or on his way up to the roof? Did he jump? That's part of my nightmare, the thing that haunts me every night. He was found in a relatively short period of time in regard to where some of the other bodies finished up. You know, being someone that you loved, you just want to know every bit about what happened to him. Was he in pain? Did he bump his head and was he unconscious? Did he go for the fire and smoke. Did he burn? Where was he – on the stairwell, on the roof? Did he go through a lot of suffering?

'From what I understand, the fuel created a fire of such intensity that the heat disintegrated *so* much evidence and *so* many people, and there is no way of ever knowing. A lot of the questions for a lot of the women are *where was their husband or fiancé? Were they trapped and wondering if they were going to get out? Were they trying to make phone calls? Were they burning alive?* You are haunted by all of this. *Were they just at the base of the stairs, ten feet from the door? Were they on the roof waiting for the helicopters?* It's a very haunting thing to wonder exactly all this.'

Barrett became 'so depressed I couldn't get out of bed, very horribly depressed and suicidal at times. Just what is the purpose of life? What I believed was the course of my life had completely changed. All of a sudden there was no hope and no expectation. It makes you examine every little tiny detail. What is this if it can *all* change tomorrow? I don't know how to explain it exactly, but I didn't care about anything.

'My son was one thing that kept me going. I knew that I had to be there for him and take care of the house and continue to do all these things for myself. Brian and I had had plans for the big house we'd bought. I was very good an interior design and I was focusing on that.

Now I didn't have that any longer. I didn't have the man, which women tend to hang a lot of their purpose in life on. I don't have the home that I thought I was going to have, which was going to be my career as well: making it beautiful.'

The situation was very distressing in another way, because the girlfriends and fiancées suddenly discovered that, whatever commitments they had made, unless they were married they were entitled to nothing under law. Some were a week away from their weddings, everything organised, but that made no difference. Nor did engagement parties and engagement rings.

Debbie Barrett decided to try and do something about this, and she did.

'What happened was that the lawyer I was talking to said, "we have another fiancée we're working with." I said, "could you please give me her phone number?" I contacted her and after finding a few other women through word of mouth I'd find a fiancée, get their number, and we'd start contacting one another. That's how the group began.[4] I didn't know any of these people. We'd meet a girl who knew of two other fiancées and there was another fiancée group we found, and so on.

'There were support groups and there was counselling but as fiancées we faced separate issues and separate struggles. We had our own set of problems because we weren't wives. We had no rights, we weren't being considered as anything. In a lot of cases I couldn't even get information. They said, "who are you?" We weren't able to find out when they found the body.

'It's given me a new purpose, it's helped me so much that you can share experiences and share information – like about whether we can get help for different things and we weren't aware of them. Sometimes it's just to cry on each other's shoulders in the middle of the night. It's been tremendously helpful.

'What we are trying to get is basic rights and recognition in some way. We have forty-five people in the group – no, almost fifty now

The Fiancée

[March 2002]. We have four men. The first man in the group was having a horrible time, because being a fiancé is a difficult position and being a male fiancé he had no one he could talk or relate to. He was one of the group's founders and when a newspaper article came out he was thrilled that all of a sudden we were contacted by a few men who said, "thank goodness another man that I can talk to." Men don't particularly relate their feelings very well, anyway. Now we have a policeman in the group and a computer designer.

'At this point we have been getting recognised as the forgotten ones – some of our group had their marriage licenses, they were going to be married in a week. They had it all done, everything booked, ready, bridal gown sitting there, gifts and now they have zero standing. They have been cut off completely. It's a very strange situation. They've lost houses, properties, their cars – because they cannot afford them. All or nothing. A week later they would have had everything, even if they'd only been married for one minute. We're trying very hard to change the state laws and a lot of what keeps us going is that we have hope. They're hopeful. If this turns out that things don't change and they are still held to zero and they lose their homes, how do you deal with that?'

If there were more women leaders would there be fewer wars?

'You have to say yes to that, of course. The way men solve problems or issues is with force. They go into fight mode. My observation has been that, when something like this happens to them, they react by going into that mode. They get very angry and aggressive and frustrated – maybe if they lose a loved one or a brother – and they want to do something about it. Women handle it a little bit differently. Men have to figure out why it happened and how it happened and some way they can fight who did it. *Get the bombers out and let's go get them.* Women's nature is not to make an immediate response. There would be a lot of other steps taken before war.'

What would you have done after 11 September?

'Let me tell you something. A certain sort of comment has been made to me several times and the people making it assume I feel like they think I must feel, and that if anybody felt like that it would be me. I've had strangers sitting next to me and when they hear my situation they make statements such as "you should kill every single one of them" or "we should be going in there dropping bombs and annihilating the whole area". It infuriates me – I *don't* want revenge. What I say to them is "that only spawns more hate and I don't think it's the solution to this problem in the world. This happens because of hate, and for us to react that way continues the cycle."'

And what is the answer?

'I don't know what the answer is, otherwise I might be President.'

SILENCES AND OTHER VOICES

My interview with Debbie Barrett took place in a hotel on the New Jersey shoreline. Through a broad window you could see a bay with boats moored along it. Large, wooded gardens flowed down to the water, and each had a house of some stature set among the trees. It looked an idyllic place to begin married life.

Ms Barrett sensed that the people who ate at the next table were talking too loudly for the comfort of my tape recorder and we moved to the other – inland! – side of the lounge. Here the sun shimmered through equally broad windows and she thought we ought to move again, because it was too hot. I explained that though this was March in New Jersey it was the equivalent of August in Britain and I didn't want to miss a moment. We laughed about that, and so did Lucy Aita, a member of the group she'd brought along.

It was all a compromise between grief and living on in some kind of normality, and who can say at any given moment whether you've got the compromise right or wrong?

Aita says, 'I called the DNA hotline[5] every two weeks to see if they'd found my fiancé.' He was Paul Innella, thirty-three, and

The Fiancée

another who worked for Cantor Fitzgerald. 'He was on the 103rd floor and I didn't hear anything from him that morning. He was confirmed at his desk at eight o'clock by his immediate boss – his supervisor – who did not go into work that day. He was the last one that talked to him. And then that was it. Nothing. We never got the chance to say "til death do us part." Death parted us first.'

Ms Aita recounts a disturbing tale. The week before we met, she and Ms Barrett had been on the *Good Morning America* television programme talking 'about different issues. Charlie Gibson, who's the host, had asked Debbie a question [about the $100,000 life insurance she would not be getting] and he asked me if I was in the same situation. All I did was mention a little story about Paul "saying I took care of everything" – something I'd only remembered after 9/11 because I was so grief stricken.'

To appreciate the point, you must understand that a great deal of money was now in play through a Federal fund [see below] and the money called everything into question: relationships between fiancée and families, motives, integrity, the depth of the relationship between fiancée and deceased. More than that, it was extremely difficult for honest people to *prove* they were honest. In this particular case she had no way of proving that her fiancé had said what he'd said.

Aita 'got hate mail – an anymous e-mail – that I was pretty much lying and misrepresenting myself. They wrote through the *Fiancées of 9/11* site and I got it forwarded. It upset me. I did write back. Everybody said, "don't write back," but I felt compelled to. I said I was "sorry about whatever insulted you and I hope that you find peace within yourself". I told him not to write back with a faceless e-mail. If someone has something to say you write your name and you are welcome to talk to me. I will not reply to and I will not read faceless e-mails. I have not heard anything since.'

The situation with the fiancé is amplified by Jennifer Middleton who works for Lambda Legal, which 'does gay and lesbian rights work.

The people we've been representing after 9/11 lost same sex partners, many of whom were in relationships of ten, fifteen, twenty years. We've had about a couple of dozen come forward, which seems lower that I would have expected. I bet there are more out there who are either not asserting their rights or not accessing the organisations which are available. The longest relationship among my clients is twenty-six years, but even after that long they have very little legal protection.'

Middleton has also been working with 'people in New York, New Jersey and Connecticut who are interested in changing state law to cover same sex partners, domestic partners and fiancées so that the people making the decisions in the Federal fund can look to the local state law and say "these folks are covered".'

The male/female split among same-sex couples suffering bereavement is 'just about fifty-fifty, which is interesting because the split among the people who died is about 75–25 men to women.[6] The fiancées you've talked to in New Jersey [where so many businessmen commuted from] feel like widows, but if they weren't married they have almost nothing in the way of legal protection. That is exactly the position with same sex partners. However in many cases – this is my impression from the fiancées I have talked to – they were in relationships of one, two or three years rather than the kind of lengthy, financially intertwined relationships of some of the same-sex couples, but their legal situation is exactly the same.'

What is your feeling? Do you think the same-sex people, who have made a commitment for years, and the fiancées – who have engagement rings and have set wedding dates or fully intend marrying – will get anything at all?

'Well, here's what I'm advising my clients. There are no explicit protections in the regulations under the Federal fund. To read those regulations, many lawyers would think they won't get a dime. I think there are a couple of places where we can make arguments that these partners ought to get some portion of the award. I am in the

The Fiancée

process now of making claims for a couple of people and we will see what Feinberg[7] does. He had said publicly a variety of different things. In some venues he says, "I am going to follow state law and if you're not protected by state law you won't get anything," and at other venues he says, "well, I'm very sympathetic to these problems, we will do everything we can and I want to sit down and work with the legal next of kin and see what we can do to come up with a mutually agreeable result."

'Who knows? But it seems to me it's possible to make a couple of arguments. You look at the charts the Department of Justice has published. The charts show a "typical" award. They go by how much money the person made, how old they were, whether they were married or single, how many kids they had. Depending on those three factors they crunched the numbers and came up with a potential award for the family that ranges from $300,000 – £400,000 to over $3 million.

'People who were married get a lot more money than people who were single under this system. The reason is that when you calculate out how much a person would earn over their lifetime and then subtract the amount they would have spent on themselves, which is how wrongful damages are calculated. Economists say people who are married spend a lot less on themselves because they share their housing expenses, contribute to the family and so on. You combine finances, life is a lot cheaper! And so those awards are higher.

'The argument I want to make for our clients is "look, that economic analysis about the shared households applies exactly the same to our clients as it does to a married person." Feinberg has the discretion to say who gets what and he can increase the amount of the award to take into account the household situation of the person who died. He sits down with the legal next of kin and says, "look, if I treated this person as single they would have gotten (let's say) $1 million, if I'm treating them as married they're getting $1.4 million. Let's *at least* give the $400,000 to the partner" – and there are other arguments, depending on what state they're in, that the partner ought to get more. That's all within his discretion but we don't know how he will exercise it. There is no clear right.'

Up until now there's always the risk that you lived with your boyfriend or girlfriend and they were killed in a car crash and you accepted that risk, however remote – but suddenly now you've whole masses of people who are horribly exposed.

'Absolutely.'

It is a tragedy upon a tragedy, particularly for those people who were preparing their weddings. One couple apparently were only a week away.

'Yes, absolutely. With a few opposite sex couples, the people involved made a conscious decision not to get married. It's hard to be in a relationship with somebody for many, many years and not have your whole family and society saying "so when are you going to get married" and "why don't you?" For those people – whatever reasons they had, maybe political or whatever – there is a part of me that thinks "you made that choice not to get married and it's too bad that that gamble didn't work out for you, but it was a consciously considered gamble." But then I step back and think, "no, what's really wrong here is that this whole system rests on the construct of marriage – where two people are dependent on each other and committed to one another. They should receive support."

'And then there are the fiancés who wanted to get married and the same sex couples who don't have the right to get married. Just about every lesbian or gay person I'm working with would have got married if they could have. The events of 9/11 show very clearly the limbo that people are in: the government says, "we are not going to let you get married," and yet it turns around and says, "since you're not married we are going to deny you these benefits."'

The Taliban, who were so insistent that women should have absolutely no rights at all, may just have bestowed rights on lots of women all over the United States, including lesbians.

The Fiancée

'I hope so. It's fuelled a movement for people – maybe a movement is too strong and a push is a better word – for couples to get married. I've actually heard of more than one different sex couple since September 11 that has decided "well, let's finally tie the knot" after eight or ten years of living together. "Why not?"'

At the moment we know the answer to that question.

'Whatever you feel you're entitled to as a committed partner, you risk having if you don't.'

So what happened to you on 9/11?

'I was at the top of Wall Street right across from the Stock Exchange at my gym on the *Stairmaster* – the treadmill except it's actually stairs, which you go up and down – when the first plane hit. We could smell the smoke and immediately it came on the TVs at the gym that this plane has crashed in to the World Trade Center. Then shortly thereafter the second one, which we all watched live, and they evacuated the gym, I believe because they were worried that the Stock Exchange was a potential target.

'I left there and I walked out into the street and there were ashes. The smoke was thick and things were falling from the sky, mainly office papers snowing down from the sky. And shoes: that was the other really creepy thing, random women's shoes, mostly, scattered around the street.

'I walked down to my office which is about two blocks further away from the World Trade Center and it was all so . . . surreal. I can't describe how odd it was to have had this major disaster occur a couple of blocks away and then, in classic New York intrepid fashion, it was *gee, that's horrible but there's not much I can do about it. Might as well go to work.* So I went to my office, we were all standing around and we couldn't get news because the TV and radio transmitters were at the top of the World Trade Center. It never crossed our minds that the towers would fall.

'We were booting up our computers thinking *this is all very scary but what can we do at this point?* Our executive director got a phone call from someone outside of the Wall Street area saying "there's another plane in the air, the Pentagon's just been hit and you guys should get out of there" – which hadn't really occurred to any of us before. We evacuated and by the time I got down the first tower had fallen but I didn't know that. I think it must have fallen while I was in the elevator. There was white ash everywhere outside and we were standing around in the lobby thinking *should we even go outside?* I didn't think it was that the tower had fallen but maybe debris from around where the plane had hit. I ventured out and there were people just running and shouting "get to the water" – we're right near the East River. Police officers were directing people who were running. It was so – again – surreal to walk out into that: from what felt like my safe office, into this.

'Maybe five minutes after I headed north to go towards my home, the other tower fell. I heard an enormous roar that for all the world sounded like another plane coming in very low overhead. Even though I knew that there was another plane in the air, and even though they hadn't figured out where it was – it was the Pennsylvania plane, in fact – my mind didn't go to that, but instead I thought *it must be our military overhead zooming in to do who knows what.* My mind didn't compute the thought that another plane was headed my way with evil intent. As it turned out, it was the second tower and the sky turned completely black. You couldn't see very far in front of you and everybody was covered in ash and soot. I walked and when I was a mile or so from my office there were crowds. People at hardware stores and places like that had TVs out on the street and people were gathering. It wasn't until I saw it on TV that I realised both the towers had fallen. I had heard, but I thought it was just the top halves.'

If there were more women leaders would there be fewer wars?

'I think we can't know the answer to that question. I like to believe so. I'll tell you something that I have found fascinating. One of the things I do in addition to serving lesbian and gay clients is work with trans-sexual people – people who identify as another

The Fiancée

gender, male to female, and female to male – and many of them undergo sex re-assignment. What I have been told by a couple of my clients – ones who went from being male to female and took the hormones, the whole thing – is that they say that their thinking patterns changed. They take into account love and relationship and personal happiness more than aggression and competition. That's only my anecdotal experience, but I think it's telling.'

What would you have done after 11 September?

'I was very proud that our country did not immediately go rushing to Afghanistan to drop bombs willy-nilly and I was disappointed when we did start to do that. My whole life I've been quite an anti-war person. I see very few reasons for people to go to war in general and certainly, in particular, for this country to flex its muscles around the world. I demonstrated against what we did in Central America and various other places. I did have a different feeling about this, because I'd had the experience of being so close to the buildings which fell and then went through several months in New York City where I felt my personal safety was threatened on a daily basis.

'You didn't know what might come out of the sky at you or through the subways or whatever. It felt like we needed to do something and I had quite a bit of a struggle about what the appropriate something would be – because it seemed to me that bombing in Afghanistan was probably not going to solve the problem. So a part of me reserves judgement on that question. I do have to say that I have fears about what the war we have waged in Afghanistan will do to Middle Eastern politics in general. We could have started a conflagration that's going to be way out of our hands. But what we should have done I can't say.'

EIGHT

The Naval Chief

An Army colonel is coming at us. The skin is hanging off of his hands and his arms. It's like somebody took a vegetable peeler. His face was all chalky and I noticed he had blood spots on his blouse.

If you'll forgive me, certain aspects of Sheryl A. Alleger's life had been cryptic. You will see. She was born in Sandusky, Ohio, which is likely the first time you've heard of it and, equally likely, the last. She joined the US Navy and has served in Alaska, Hawaii and Spain. Now thirty-seven, she is married and has three children: Nichole (seventeen on 11 September), John IV (sixteen) and Michelle (seven).

'I graduated in 1982. I went to nursing school for about four months and I could not get a grasp of Freudian theory. Psychology and sociology are both parts of being a nurse, they are one of the curriculum requirements and I was not doing very well. I reached the point of *what am I going to do?* Sandusky is a very small town. I came home one day and said to my dad, "take me to the recruiter's." My dad said, "OK," and we hopped in the car. My dad was Army long before I was born. If that was what I thought was going to be good for me, then he was behind it, so he took me to the recruiter's and about three weeks later I was in!

The Naval Chief

'I really wanted to be a corpsman, which is the equivalent of a nurse. The recruiter said that recruiting is done on a quota basis and they didn't have any quotas for incoming female corpsmen – we're talking in the early 1980s here. There was a waiting list for something like a year and a half. I asked him what else he had and he said "I've got this one and I don't know anything about it. It's cryptology, whatever that is"[1] – this is a Navy guy that I'm talking to.'

You didn't know what cryptology was.

'No, I didn't. He explained by reading the stuff out of the book and that tells you basically what a cryptologist is. He said, "go home and think about it. Talk to your folks." I went home and talked to my dad and he said, "your cousin was a cryptologist in Vietnam, call him." I called him and he gave me the run down on it. I said, "sounds like a good job" and he said, "oh, yes, definitely." I signed on the bottom line and that was twenty years ago this year. I've done this job ever since.'

Chief Alleger was working in the Pentagon – 'attached to the Under Secretary of the Navy staff and it just so happens that day I was in her office when the building got hit. It was about 200 yards from the point of impact.'

Alleger's own office was 'relatively small – in fact, two offices, mine and my boss's. We are on the Fifth Floor and look into the area between the E wing and the D wing.' We're on the Mall side.'

Subsequently she wrote a personal account of 9/11 which was sent to the Naval Archives Historical Division, and I am grateful for permission to reproduce extracts. Like the NYPD's Terri Tobin, the power of the document comes from its slightly stiff understatement.

> On Tuesday September 11th, I started the day like any other day. I arrived at my office about 0830 and did turn-over[2] with my immediate supervisor, Georgia Osterman. Shortly after arriving, Georgia left to deliver documents to one of our supported offices. I then received a phone call from a friend who told me I needed to be downstairs watching CNN.

'I have a girlfriend in the air force, Julie, that I had been stationed with and she called me that morning. She said, "I know you don't have a TV. You need to go downstairs." – 'cos I work on the fifth deck. "Just go." So I did.'

I went down to the Under Secretary's outer office. There was Col Ferguson, Ms. Totman, and YNC[3] Davis watching the CNN broadcast of the first plane hitting the tower. All of us stood there watching as the second plane hit and then the President's opening comments from the school in Florida. About that time the phone rang and the Col. answered it. He really didn't say much, hung up the phone and turned toward all of us. He said, 'that was the Command Center and they are reporting an unconfirmed aircraft headed this direction.' It couldn't have been thirty seconds after he said this that the entire building felt like it was lifted up and set back down. Chief Davis and myself were standing next to the windows overlooking the Mall Parking Area, we both looked out and down and saw a man standing next to his car looking off to our left (toward the corner by the helicopter pad). We just knew what had happened.

Chief Alleger remembers the colonel saying 'we need to move' when he hung up and how short the thirty second to impact seemed. They knew 'instantly – and that it was a plane. The building shook, oh yes. It was incredible, a huge boom.' After all, as she points out, 'if you're going to hit anything, the Pentagon's the building to hit. It is not a hidden target. The guy standing by his car was half in and half out – like in the process of getting in or out – and he's looking to what would be our left from the office window. It was *OK, now we know where it hit.*

All of us ran out of the office and into the E ring, going into offices and telling people they needed to get out, and get out immediately. I headed for the Sixth Corridor from the Seventh Corridor.

'The E wing is all the executive offices. Chief Davis, the other chief, went to the left and I went to the right. We started ducking our heads in office doors telling people "you need to get out, you need to get out now." We started doing the evacuation. I headed towards the Sixth Corridor because we were between Sixth and Seventh. Some people were coming out of the offices, some didn't have TVs on, didn't know what was going on. My initial thought was *oh God, my boss Georgia*. If you look at the pictures taken right after the collapse, the fifth floor was one of our offices and she was supposed to be over there. I was thinking *was Georgia in there, was she on the way back to her office?*' (In fact Alleger didn't find out that she was all right until that evening.)

All I could think about was that Georgia had headed that direction and was she still there or somewhere in between. When I reached the Sixth Corridor, Defense Protective Service (DPS) was directing everyone down the corridor to the A ring and Courtyard. Smoke was already starting to fill the corridor and people were making their way out.

'I didn't actually see smoke. There was some coming into the passageways but it was being funnelled away towards the courtyard, although I did see the plume of smoke [from the plane and the impact] when I got to the courtyard. We were all looking at it and nobody was moving – well, hardly. It was like OK, *the building's been hit* and everybody stopped. The courtyard was still: shock – shock and disbelief. It *was* unbelievable. You could see smoke and pieces of things were falling into the courtyard but, from the inside, hardly any damage. I saw an army guy – I can't remember any more what rank he was – coming out of the building. The stairwell is on the second floor and he yelled out that there were people that needed help so they called 911.[4] Then it kind of got chaotic: there were people coming out that had ceiling tile debris on them.

Once I made it out into the Courtyard, I started heading toward the A ring entrance of the 3–4 Corridors. People were streaming from every doorway. Most were coming out and gazing about looking to see what happened. I noticed a few folks sitting on the benches right across from the 5–6 Corridor entrance. Some were covered in dust and debris. One lady was holding her head and just rocking back and forth. There were other people around her, but they were all looking up and around at everyone else. I went over and was talking to her, checking out the top of her head, where she said she'd been hit by something falling from the ceiling. She wasn't bleeding, she just kept saying her head hurt. I talked with her for a few more seconds, when someone came out on the second deck landing yelling for someone to call 911 or get some medical help in there. I looked up at the guy who was standing by me and asked him to take the lady out towards north parking where they should be setting up a triage area, then ran up the steps and back into the A ring.

What made you do that?

'Second sense. [Pause] I don't know. Before coming here – when we were stationed in Florida – my husband got involved in a group called Escambia Search and Rescue, an all-volunteer group.[5] They provide you with your training. We did it to meet people but we also did it because it's a good organisation. We were trained how to go out and find missing people. Most of our cases were Alzheimer's patients who had wandered off from care facilities or from their homes, or lost children, or lost hunters – you'd be surprised. They can't find their base camp.

'We were taught how to man track – follow a person's trail through the woods. We took it very seriously and acquired two dogs, one a bloodhound, that we trained for finding people. In the three years down there I probably did 5,000 hours – getting called out at two o'clock in the morning to go into some not very safe area to go find grandma who's walked away from the house and nobody's seen her since eight o'clock that night.

'We did mass casualty drills, train wrecks, plane wrecks. We did triaging and assessing injuries, moving people and all that. As a matter of fact, the commander of our unit use to drive me to the training facility and I'd think *what am I going here for? I don't want to learn how to do this.* He made me qualify as a basic EMT – Emergency Medical Technician – and ride on the ambulances, learn what to do in an emergency. So in a sense I had been prepared for this moment although I'd never thought I was going to use the training – but it was that training, plus the naval training I've had coming up through the ranks, that made me go back in.'

Are you a pretty level-headed sort of person?

'I like to think I am.'

You have to be detached in circumstances like these.

'You get detached very quickly and pretty much learn how to cope without emotions because you *can't* freak out, and the 11th was not a day to freak out – because there were plenty of people doing that. That's one of the things that surprises me about the 11th, how calm I was. I never pictured myself going back in and I went back in several times.'

So now you go back in the first time, you've got the smoke. What do you see?

'An Army colonel coming at us. There was three or four of us standing in the middle of an alcove off the stairwell and the skin is hanging off of his hands and his arms. It's like somebody took a vegetable peeler. It was just hanging off of him. His face was all chalky and I noticed he had blood spots on his blouse. I didn't know if it was internal, because he had his hands against his body, or external. He came walking out towards us and collapsed right there in the alcove. We started working on him. There is not a whole lot you can do for burns: wrap him and keep him wet.

'He was so calm. He wasn't screaming. He just lay down on the floor and about that time one of the folks from the flight surgeon's office, which is on the fourth floor, they came running up with equipment bags and emergency kit that they had grabbed. So we started assessing him, wrapping his hands in gauze and pouring water over them. One of the ladies, I guess she'd be a secretary but obviously not medical, was sitting at his head and holding his head in her lap and reciting the Lord's Prayer. He was conscious, talking to us.'

When I got inside, there was an Army Maj/Lt Col (couldn't distinguish his shoulder boards), laying on the floor right at the bottom of the stairs. His arms were burned from his shirt sleeves down . . . [his] face was ashen, but I couldn't tell if it was ash, ceiling dust or what. I knelt down and started talking to him, another guy was standing there saying we needed to get help, there were more people in the hall that couldn't find their way out. I stayed with the obvious victim, started doing the initial assessment, asking if he hurt anywhere else.

'We were asking him questions, because part of the medical assessment is to find out a patient's background, like any allergies – you are going to give him medication and obviously you need to know that, or if they're on any medication, their medical history: anything to keep him talking, keep him lucid, keep him with you.

'That was my training, definitely. The hard thing with him was that we needed to get an IV[6] into him to give him some fluids immediately. We couldn't do it through his arms. I don't know if the army blouses are polyester like ours are, but his looked like it was melted. He had obviously taken part of the heat blast. We slit his trousers and pulled off his socks and put it in through his ankle.'

About this time a group of Air Force people showed up (from Flight Medicine Clinic) and started opening aid packs. As a couple of AF

The Naval Chief

[Air Force] Colonels started working on him, I told them I was a First Responder [equivalent to basic emergency medical treatment] and to tell me what they needed. They told me to find the IV pack and prep[7] him. I couldn't IV him through the arms so we started cutting away his trousers legs looking for a good vein and any wounds on his legs. I used one of his socks as a tourniquet to do an IV. The med. kit didn't have much in it, but we used what we had. About this time one of the hospital carts showed up.

'We have motorised carts that run around the building and the hospital has a couple of them. One of those came up and we slid a backboard on him, put him on the cart and off he went. It was like *OK, next* but we hadn't seen anybody else come out. The smoke was so thick in that alcove area that we couldn't see down the hallway – it was as if you were looking into a curtain. I thought *if anybody's in there they are not going to be able to see to get out. We need to do a floor sweep* – that's floor by floor.'

As the cart rushed off, we picked up what was left of the kits, and one of the Colonels said we should check the rest of the area for more people that might need help. The entire area was filling with smoke: I couldn't see the snack bar, which was about 10 feet away. The Colonel, an Airman, myself and one other gentleman went up the stairs to the Fifth Floor and started into the 5 & 6 Corridors yelling to see if anyone answered.

'We ran up to the Fifth and a couple of us went this way, a couple that way yelling down the hallway and listening to see if you could hear anybody yelling back. We had to listen – it was dark because of the smoke and the lights were out. There was nobody there.'

We waited a few seconds to see if we could hear anybody and then headed down to the next floor to do the same thing.

'We went down to the Fourth Floor and went back down the hallways again and we did that until we got all the way to the first floor again and we heard people coming towards us. We kept yelling "come this way, come this way".'

The smoke was thick and everything was dark. No lights were showing anywhere, no sounds at all. Three people were coming out, and we walked out with them into the courtyard. One lady looked to have burns on her hand and arms. One guy laid down, he was having a hard time breathing and his nose, mouth and teeth were covered in black. Another lady came out and sat down behind us with an obvious head injury. We split up to take care of them best we could until more help got there.

'The guy was the biggest I ever saw in my life. I can't even tell how tall he was – I'm kind of short but even so he was big and he was *solid*. He came out into the courtyard area and collapsed. My thinking was *OK, so he's the next one*. We jumped right to it and started working on him. He and another lady came out so we were talking to them and he was having a hard time breathing. We put a nasal airline on him. He was on his side, I was behind him and I leaned over to help them put the nasal in and his nose and mouth were just black. His teeth had black on them and it looked like he had tar in his nose. I'd never seen so much smoke in somebody before.'

What was wrong with him?

'It was the smoke. His office pretty much took a direct hit. The *Washington Post* ran an article and I read it. I think his name was Gonzalez or something and I thought *who's that?* and then *that's him, I worked on him*. I remember the one Air Force man I was with had a walkie talkie and they were trying to get a feel of where the victims were coming out of, what room numbers. We kept asking "where did you come from? What room number were you in? Was there anybody else in your office?"'

Christina Lamb. (*Courtesy of Andrew Crowley/the* Sunday Telegraph, *London*)

The merciless terrain facing charities in Afghanistan. (*Courtesy of Médecins Sans Frontières*)

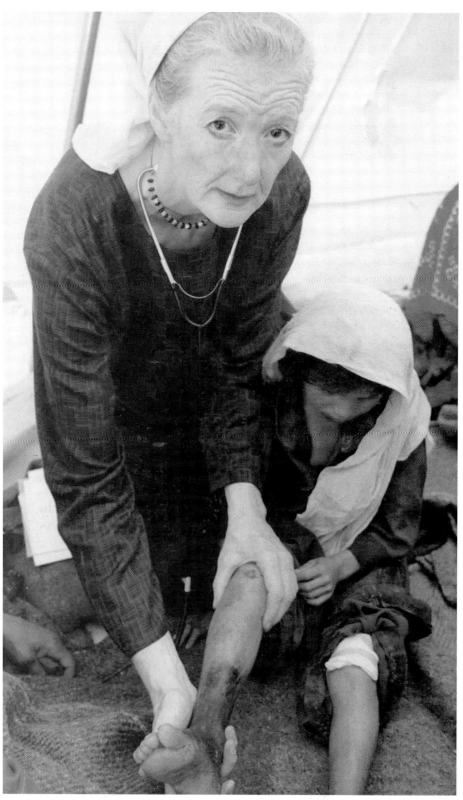
Valerie Powell treats a patient in a temporary clinic. (*Courtesy of Merlin*)

River transport – from the Tajik border to the island where Powell worked. (*Courtesy of Merlin*)

The huts the islanders built for themselves and Powell. (*Courtesy of Merlin*)

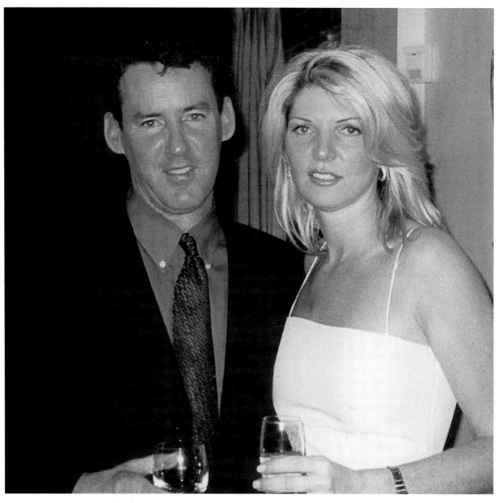

Debbie Barrett and fiancé Brian Cummins.
(*Courtesy of Debbie Barrett*)

Lucy Aita. (*Courtesy of Lucy Aita*)

Naval Chief Sheryl A. Alleger in the Pentagon. (*Christopher Hilton*)

Jacqui Tong's field surgery in operation. (*Courtesy of Médecins Sans Frontières*)

Jacqui Tong back in London. (*Christopher Hilton*)

Women spinning thread from goat's hair in the Atora Khartuk refugee camp, Pakistan. (*Courtesy of Margaret Owen*)

The brutal brickfield. (*Courtesy of Margaret Owen*)

The Jalozar refugee camp on the Afghan-Pakistan border. (*Courtesy of Margaret Owen*)

Seema Ghani and her 'children'. (*Courtesy of Seema Ghani*)

Renée Mangalo and fiancé Frank Carino. (*Courtesy of Renée Mangalo*)

The Naval Chief

What was the atmosphere around you like?

'The courtyard was pretty much empty, but then we had a rumour of another plane inbound. They did come round and told us "you need to evacuate, you need to evacuate." It was the Pennsylvania plane[8] – but in the courtyard you don't know. There really is only two ways to get out, you go down the eighth corridor out into North Parking or you go out second corridor into South Parking, but in a panic people forget that. The DPS[9] was good about coordinating everybody and they came by and told us that we needed to leave. We told them "we're working on somebody here, we'll move just as soon as we can move him." There was no way we could carry this guy out and I wasn't leaving him. We finished working on him and a trickle of folks started coming back in, a lot of the medical folks.'

> Folks were coming by asking what we needed; mostly it was . . . water. They'd run off to try and find some close by. Hospital carts were flying back and forth trying to load up folks as quick as possible and return with needed supplies. The folks we were working on kept talking about people still in their office area. One of the Colonels had a hand radio and was passing information on to someone as fast as we could get it: information like location of their office, number of people, condition of spaces,[10] anything we could get to help get rescuers in there.

'I moved over to Fourth Corridor and they were working on people. You jumped in and helped wherever you could. Then they came by again and said, "there's definitely another plane that's inbound. You need to move." By then the fighters were flying over the building and I thought *if the fighters are up we need to go. This is serious. This is not just a suspected plane. Obviously there is one.* We loaded a guy onto a flatbed[11] motorised cart and loaded a lady, too, jumped on the cart and went flying through the courtyard towards North Parking.'

People were scrambling from all over the courtyard. [On the cart] I [was] holding the IV bag up to keep the flow going, since we didn't have anything to hook it to.

'There were people walking almost leisurely: the shock, very much so. They were going out but kind of *strolling*. The driver of the cart was honking the horn and telling them to clear the way. It was amazing.'

Near the exit doors there was a bottleneck of people trying to get out.

Do you think you went straight onto autopilot – 'this is what I've been trained to do and now I'm doing it' – and it helped you that you were doing something which helped?
'In afterthought, yes. In the courtyard you are isolated. You don't know what is going on outside the building. All you see is this plume of smoke and it's blowing over the courtyard. I still hadn't seen the outside of the building, hadn't a clue how badly damaged it was. The plane could have been hanging outside the building and I wouldn't have known. I only saw the outside of the building much later, in the afternoon.'

One of the people on the cart relieved me of the IV bag, and I saw some other people carrying a lady out on a sheet of ripped plywood. I jumped off the cart and ran over to help them as they were trying to get a better grip on the board to make it out the doors. She was pretty lucid and kept saying that she just wanted to get out of the building. Four or five other people jumped in to help relieve those that were carrying her and getting tired.

I started talking to her just to keep her calm by asking her name and where she worked, things like that. We finally got her out of the building and found an empty cart sitting inside of the pylons waiting to go through. We loaded her on the cart, but with the board it was too wide.

'Around the building going towards the parking lots are concrete pylons that [for security reasons] keep cars from being able to drive up. We have this cart loaded with victims and it won't fit through the pylons.'

All of a sudden five or six guys – Army, Marines, Navy and a couple of civilians – grabbed one of the pylons around the base and started pulling it up out of the ground. It seemed like those things were in there probably a good three feet and made of solid concrete, but they finally got it up and out.

'They manhandled that thing up out of the hole so that we could get through. When they got it out, a big cheer went up – like a stress reliever, almost. *Hey, we accomplished something.* We got the carts through and got the people out.'

We moved the cart on out into the grass area next to the water.[12] Somebody brought over a litter[13] and we had to roll this lady off the board where she lay and onto it to make moving her easier. She appeared to have a possible broken leg but no other obvious injuries. When we got her off the cart and into the grass area, we assumed a more typical triage state. We obtained her info and passed it to someone who was walking around writing down victims' names and other pertinent information. Somebody came by and handed us gloves. A pharmacist came by and handed me a Field Injector[14] to give her. I started asking for a doc since I am not qualified to give injections. We got her stabilized and lined up for evacuation out of the area.

'We set up a triage and, by then, some of the medical people from the Annexe[15] came out and they had supplies, like oxygen tanks and gloves, that you need and we didn't have. An ambulance finally came along and we loaded up the most serious. Then people started going into the parking lot and getting their vehicles – mini vans, station wagons, whatever – and we started loading people into them. We were saying, "OK, do you know where this hospital is?" The medical folks took over in terms of "OK, take these to this hospital or this hospital". We were just loading people up and getting them out.'

After that it is a blur of people who needed help and assistance being loaded to be taken out to hospitals. Some were minor injuries, some weren't. We just tried to do what we could for everyone. I saw a couple of other people I knew working there and we tended to try and stick together with folks we recognized. Everyone was asking about people that were known to each other, people from other offices. Once most of the victims were evacuated somebody started forming up teams to go back in. Teams were a mixture of military, civilian, medical, and anybody that could go.

You still didn't know the overall picture.
'I didn't have a clue. We just knew it was a plane. Somebody decided, "OK, let's form up teams – we need so many people with medical experience on each team. We're going back in." I jumped on to one.'

We gathered up triage equipment, anything we could lay our hands on and went back through the North Parking Entrance into the Courtyard and the Three, Four, Five & Six Corridor areas. As the teams would get to the Courtyard, Fire Department personnel were directing them into areas to be searched for victims.

The Naval Chief

'We started going into the building on the first floor and trying to go back as far as we could go. That was hideous. The smoke was so thick it was like putting your head in the fireplace. We had no masks so we used T-shirts. The guys that had T-shirts took their outer blouses off, took their T-shirts off and put their blouses back on. We tied the T-shirts around our faces. You go until you can't go any further. It was very kind of eerie. There's no lights, it's very dark and you're crawling over debris, crawling over ceiling tiles. There's pipes and wires and all kinds of stuff hanging from the ceiling. It was like crawling through a spider's web – you know how that clings to you. You couldn't see but you knew there had to be people in there. And you keep going.'

Corridors 4 & 5 were thick with smoke. It made your eyes water and your nose and throat burn. The smoke was heavy with the odour of jet fuel, burnt carpet and burnt paper. In some of the areas . . . debris filled the hallways and water from the fire fighters flooded the floors. Most of the teams didn't stay in more than maybe 10–15 minutes at best. You just couldn't see anything when you did get in and breathing was getting harder. We were only allowed to go in about four or five times.

Did you think anyone could have survived the smoke for this long?
'Initially, yes. [Pause] Initially. We figured that there had to be pockets of air – and this was probably well after the [front of the] building had already collapsed. People could have been in a conference room, under the table for protection, and had air for a time. There was a possibility.'
And was there?
'[softly] No.'
Was there a moment when you thought nobody's made it?
'Yes, when we were told to leave the building by the FBI and the Marshals service.'[16]

In the courtyard, triage areas were being set up in teams to treat a vast array of casualties. Several of us were running from the courtyard back out to North Parking ferrying additional equipment as it arrived. By this time though, it was pretty obvious we wouldn't be seeing many more walking victims. Those of us in the Courtyard were evacuated several times when word filtered in that another plane was inbound. Also by this time the FBI and Federal Marshals had arrived in the courtyard. They essentially sealed off the building, nobody in or out. The teams were told to stand down and wait. We were also told it would be another three to four hours before we would be allowed back into the building for any recovery attempts.

'As a matter of fact, the last time we went in I had to come back out. I couldn't breathe any more. It reached the point of *OK, it's either going to be the victims or me and it can't be me. If I go down here's one more casualty and one less helping* – and I've got my kids to think about.'

Had they been on your mind during it all?

'Not initially. [chuckle] Bad mother! [Pause] My husband was in Florida – I'd put him on the plane on 9 September. The kids were in school. When I think about it now, I wasn't so worried about my real little one who's seven. The teachers are going to shield him and others of that age. The two I worried about were my high schoolers, one eighteen and one sixteen.

'My eighteen-year-old was in school and they watched it on TV. They were watching the Trade Center and an announcement was made that the Pentagon had been hit. She got up and left, went and got her brother then went and got her sister. She grabbed the portable phone from the house and went to the next door neighbour's – a non-working mum who's home all day – and they fielded phone calls.

'We were working on the people out in North Parking, and if anybody had a cell phone you were up to them asking "is your phone working? Are you getting out?" – because you couldn't get calls out. I tried a couple of times on a guy's. I tried to call my husband's cell phone, which is a Virginia number even though he's down in Florida, but the Virginia network was down. I just wanted to tell him "I'm fine" but I never got through.

'Once things had settled down in the afternoon, the guy who's phone I'd used – I don't remember his name – went through all the calls that had been made: his phone recorded the numbers when you used it. He rang every single one of those numbers and explained "hey, I'm at the Pentagon. Somebody was trying to get a hold of you. Can you describe them?" He got word out that I was fine – although I'd just gone back in with oxygen tanks . . .'

When did you discover the full extent of the collapse?

'I happened to be standing where an ambulance came by [during one of the evacuations]. "Jump in, you've got to get out of here." They took us around and out and we went past the impact site, which was the first time I'd seen it. I thought *oh my God*. There was the smoke and the flames but you couldn't see any bits of the aeroplane, that was the thing that got me. I was thinking *this had to be a big plane judged by how big the boom was*. I expected to see the tail sticking out, although there were so many emergency vehicles around that if anything was on the ground you wouldn't have been able to see it, anyway. But – nothing. It was just like the building swallowed the plane.

'Later, they took us back in and we were in the courtyard. We had just raided every soda machine around, broke them open. We had had no food, no water, nothing to drink. I remember someone taking a fire extinguisher, smashing the lock and popped it open. At one point we took all the soda bottles and dumped the soda out, went into the cafeteria [in the middle of the courtyard] and filled the bottles with water. Number one, you don't want to be drinking soda because it's got too much sugar in it and will dehydrate you faster but, number two, we didn't even have any water to pour on anybody.

First thing I ate was a *sugar* doughnut! [laughter]. We brought out a whole tray of doughnuts from one of the cafeteria areas.

'They formed us up into a group and said, "OK, the FBI and the Marshals are here and the whole area is considered a crime scene. We are not going to be allowed back in until they give us the OK." I said, "Wait a minute, there's still people in there. This is wrong. OK, I understand this is a crime scene. However, in this time that they're not allowing us in there somebody could be pulled out alive" – even though we knew pretty much it wasn't going to be the case. We were told we might be allowed in with the Fire Department under escort as long as we don't touch anything that's considered evidence but basically we were stuck in the courtyard for about three and a half hours.

'They did open up a fire control access panel – that had fire alarms and stuff in it – and there was a phone in there. They said, "OK, anybody that has not gotten in touch with family or somebody, you can use this phone. Just dial 99." I was thinking *my cell phone is up in my office and it has every number I could ever need and I can't think of a one. Who am I going to call?* By the time I finally got to the phone I remembered my girlfriend Julie in Florida and her number at work. I called it. She's at the same base as my husband. After about fifteen minutes of trying to convince her that I'm really OK, I told her to phone John and calm him down. "Tell him I'm fine, tell him you've talked to me and I will call him whenever I get home." I asked her to "call my ma. She can take care of the family side" – it was around 3.0 and I was thinking my kids were still in school. I didn't call the house because there'd be nobody home and for the life of me I couldn't remember my next door neighbour's number. So she called everybody for me. I didn't actually talk to my kids until about 5.0, 5.30.

We were told to get something to eat and drink or try and rest if we could. There was nothing more we could do at the time to get through. The Marshals service escorted half the personnel from the Courtyard out to South Parking where a large triage area had been set up. During this reprieve of activity, the decision was made to make ready for recovering remains. Commander Way went into the building and recovered any sheets and blankets he could find so we could cover the remains. There were not any body bags available yet.

'Whenever people were not working on victims they were trying to make calls on cell phones. Everyone was doing it. I did get through at one point because I figured I could circumvent the system. I dialled information and explained to the lady "I'm at the Pentagon, I've been trying to get word to my kids that I'm fine, can you please connect me to the school?" – and I gave her the school's name. I talked to the lady at the office and they were all very nice about it. Little did I know that my daughter had already left. She never got the message that "mum's OK. Take care of your brother and sister. I'll be home when I get home."'

Discussions about where to set up the morgue were radioed between South Parking and the Courtyard. The morgue was initially set up in South Parking and then moved into the Courtyard. Those of us still in the Courtyard started laying out the plan for setting up the morgue and how best to handle the remains and identification if possible.

'When I finally spoke to my daughter she wasn't hysterical, she was very calm. She's a lot like me, I guess.'
And this is the way it went with Nichole, then all of seventeen.
Nichole: where are you?
Alleger: still at the building.
Nichole: what are you doing?
Alleger: well, we've just set up the morgue and I'm taking a break.

Nichole: oh yes. [Pause] What is the number one rule in this house?

Alleger: what are you talking about?

Nichole: what is the rule in this house? IF YOU ARE GOING TO GO SOMEWHERE YOU TAKE THE CELL PHONE. And where is your cell phone?

Alleger ('I'm thinking *attitude* here'): it's in my office.

Nichole: well, that's a stupid place for it. DO YOU REALISE YOU ARE GROUNDED?

Chief Alleger thought *these are my words coming back to me.*

'We were sitting on our thumbs waiting and we said "let's go back with the fire fighters." We had an armed escort from the Marshals service. We didn't touch anything. We started recovering remains and lined them up in the hallway in the 5th Corridor. I think we had thirty, thirty-five bodies but we didn't have any bodybags, we didn't have anything. One of the commanders and I went down into the Medical Annexe and started ravaging the clinics: sheets, towels, anything.

'There's a little stage area where they do a lot of ceremonies. We decided that that was going to be the morgue. Finally we'd got some bodybags and as the bodies came out we did an initial identification if we could. In some ways it was easier because at the Pentagon we have badges with our names on and many of the badges were fine. Wipe it off and you could see. Others had name tags. The civilians were a little harder because most of them were pretty burnt.'

Did that distress you at all?

'I was still pretty much on adrenalin, and I'd seen a few dead bodies before, although drowned not burned.'

Shortly after the morgue area was established and everyone was briefed on their role when recovery efforts started again, individuals in camouflage uniforms arrived and took over the operations in the Courtyard. Everyone was interviewed (so to speak) as to his or her qualifications and training. Shortly after that, most of us,

The Naval Chief

who had initially remained after the attack, were told to leave. I had tried explaining that I was qualified as a First Responder and had also been a member of Escambia Search and Rescue in Florida for three years prior to coming here. I was told "thank you but go home." So I headed home to Springfield and my children.

'Getting home was the first trick. I don't drive all the way to work, I ride the Metro – and the Metro station for the building was closed. *How am I going to get home?* In the backpack that I carry there's all my IDs, my car keys, everything but that's in my office. I'd tried and I couldn't get up to it – full of smoke, wasn't able to see. The only two things I had on me were my badge and my Metro card. I thought *what I've got to do is get to a Metro station and then I can get home.*

'I walked from North Parking and crossed over the highway – no cars, it had been cut off – and then over towards a Metro station twenty-five, thirty minutes walk away. There's cars everywhere. I walked a couple of blocks and saw guys in full battle gear with guns and I had taken my badge off. I put it back on – *let's put it in plain view, I don't want to get shot.* I caught the Metro and there was nobody on it – well, three people. I got off at my station but I had no keys for my car. Luckily where I park my car is five minutes from the house. I explained to the Metro workers "look, here's the story. I work at the Pentagon, I don't have any keys and please don't tow my car. I'll come get it as soon as I can get my keys." They were really good about it. Then I got on the phone, called the house and said "OK, this is mom. I'm at the Metro station. Come get me." My daughter jumped in her car (they can get licences at sixteen) and I'm standing at the Metro waiting.

'During the day I had changed from my uniform into surgical dress. I'd been wearing a skirt that day and I didn't need to be in that or nylons. Someone found me sneakers and the surgical stuff. I had my uniform in a trash bag and I felt like a vagrant standing out there with my clothes in my bag. Nichole pulled up and I still say she was out of the car before it stopped moving. She ran over and hugged me. Told me I stunk! It felt good to hug her . . .

'When Nichole picked me up, one of the neighbour's girls rode with her because the neighbours didn't want Nichole driving by herself. Another neighbour had sent half a pack of cigarettes, a book of matches and a couple of bottles of beer with Nichole – "your mom is going to need the cigarettes" – they knew I smoked – "and drink both of those beers. That's an order." I did on the way home and they were *so* good. Never tasted a beer *so* good in all my life.

'Bear in mind I had not seen any television. I didn't know that the Twin Towers had collapsed. There was so much I didn't know – I didn't know a plane had come down in Pennsylvania. We'd heard rumours, though, while we were in the courtyard that Camp David had been hit and that we had taken a plane down somewhere. The rumours were running rampant.

'Of course when I got home I had to call everybody. Mom and dad weren't satisfied that I was fine until they heard from me. I spent the evening pretty much talking to everybody and convincing them I was OK. The neighbours fixed me dinner. A neighbour works at the State Department – luckily she wasn't at the building when the car bomb went off there[17] but another building. She filled me in on the mass exodus from the DC area, everybody trying to get out, and the towers collapsing. I guess I was pretty much a vegetable. They hadn't see the Pentagon attack so they wanted to know "where did it hit? Did everybody make it out?"'

We all have visions of the Twin Towers but the Pentagon . . .

'. . . was quiet. There's a reason for that. The Pentagon is always quiet.'

'I didn't sleep that night, I didn't sleep for a while. The adrenalin goes away. I didn't know until next morning that I had blood on the uniform. I had left my uniform on the dining room table in the bag, didn't even open it or anything. When I came downstairs I wondered if I'd be able to salvage it because I hadn't really paid any attention to what shape it was in. It was smoky and I understood why, of course, but there was blood splattered across my skirt. I held up my blouse and somehow I'd got blood across the back of it, I think when I was helping someone and they were leaning on me but I'm not sure. I was going to throw it in the trash. My daughter said "don't do that, we can wash it. I'll wash it right now" – but when she took it out of the trash she saw the blood . . .

'My son forbade me from going back to work but I had to explain to him I had a job to do, and because the building got hit doesn't mean mummy can't go to work anymore. That Wednesday I brought the kids to the Navy Annexe up the hill [adjacent to Arlington National Cemetery] and showed them the impact site. I said, "OK, now you see it." I wasn't so much worried about the little one as my older two. Nichole brought her camera – she's into photography – and we went down to where the press corps was. She said, "explain to us where your office is." All my kids had been to it but hadn't a clue where it was in relation to the view from the outside. I said, "you see the hole, see all the smoke on the left hand side and see the corner. It's around that corner. That's all you need to know."

How long did it take you to get back to some sort of normal life?

'I came back to work the Thursday, came in early. The service quarter [on the Seventh Corridor] was still closed off. It was very strange because I got up to the Fourth Floor of the E wing and it was pristine. I don't know how else to explain it. I didn't realise the cleaners had already been in. I thought *this can't be so bad, you know*. I went up the stairwell, got up onto the fifth floor and it was . . . black, the desk, the walls, everything. There weren't even lights yet but there was police tape where the structural engineers hadn't been through to say OK it's safe and sound. I thought *well . . . under the tape and down the hallway*. I did that and I left little footprints. All my stuff was in my office.

'I had read things about the Taliban but even after the 11th, when I came back to work, it was just so hard to believe the Twin Towers and the Pentagon had been hit: the timing of it, the amount of destruction caused. The Pentagon is military, there's a lot of military here and when one country attacks another they attack the military – but the Twin Towers weren't. The Twin Towers were different nationalities, different religions and some of their own people. How stupid is that?'

If there were more women leaders would there be fewer wars?

'If bin Laden had been a woman – wearing a veil, a second-class citizen – it would never have happened.'

Supposing it was men and women as leaders, fifty-fifty?

'Every election cycle, they say, "the United States isn't ready for a woman president." Who's to say? What's the difference? Men and women are essentially equal or supposed to be. I was raised with the belief anything they can do I can do and I have raised my daughters to be that way. You had The Queen and Margaret Thatcher and they did well but it didn't matter: there was still conflict, there was still wars.'

What would you have done after 11 September?

'I'd have done exactly what Bush did.'

SILENCES AND OTHER VOICES

Since this is a military chapter, and since by definition most of the book is cast in dark shadows, I can't resist including a quote from a report about women serving in the US forces in Afghanistan. An eighteen-year-old private, Eileen Schnetzka, responded to a question of having to change in front of men with: 'They know what we've got, we know what they've got. End of story.'

There was, too, a 26-year-old US Navy pilot – known only as Ashley for security reasons – flying combat missions in an F14 Tomcat over Afghanistan. Ashley, an American citizen, grew up in England and was evidently known as Mumbles by her service

The Naval Chief

colleagues because she retained an English accent. Speaking as an Englishman, I won't comment on that.

Anyway, she was pretty and inevitably there was talk of a major book deal and a Hollywood film. I mention this because, of course, if she'd been a man there'd have been no interest whatsoever. Just occasionally, discrimination cuts both ways.

I must be discreet now. When Chief Alleger was walking me out of the Pentagon we fell entirely by chance into conversation with a uniformed soldier (I won't be any more specific) who, unprompted, recounted a tale of how he'd been part of a detachment in a Central American country with 500 men sleeping in a large hangar. Two French nurses arrived and they, too, did not have any inhibitions about changing – or indeed one evening doing personal things with two of the 500 – in full view.

'It's true,' he said.

I think we ought to leave the rest of this particular story in – silence.

Postscripts, one happy and the other sad. Chief Alleger was given a Navy Commendation Medal and I don't think you need me to tell you that she'd earned it. As you might expect, she doesn't dwell on that. She did, however dwell on the sad postscript, and this is what she said.

'There was a man in the Pentagon, probably about sixty-five – around the mid-sixties, anyway. He was a civilian employee and didn't matter where you were. If you passed him in the hallway he'd walk up to you and hand you a piece of candy. This would make you smile.'

It made everyone smile and everyone called him The Candy Man.

He was a victim of 9/11.

The corridors of the Pentagon are busy and bustling and full of talk, all as it was before – and silence wherever The Candy Man might have been, any minute of any day.

NINE

The Coordinator

I was joking that I come from a small town in New Zealand, there's nowhere in my social conditioning that has prepared me for this: nature nor nurture. Can I blame my parents that I am not married to a doctor, with two children, and living in the suburbs? Instead, I'm in the middle of the biggest political emergency since World War Two.

Jacqui Tong is gently amused because, like everybody else, I assumed from her surname that she would be of Chinese descent. 'It is,' she says, 'a Cornish name.' There's a light coincidence here because Valerie Powell, who we've already met (in Chapter Six, and also a medical person) is from Cornwall. In fact, Tong is from a small town in New Zealand. She turned forty when she was working in Afghanistan in 2002 for the charity *Médecins Sans Frontières*.

'I have a nursing background. I also have a degree in political science, a year of law school and a Masters in humanitarian studies. My background is pretty much middle class, what would be termed working class here in the UK, but of course there is quite a different class system – not that in New Zealand we like to think we've got a class system! I'm . . . more lower-middle class.

The Coordinator

'I got into charity work more by accident than design. It was through the Rwanda crisis.[1] It was *MSF* that I went to Rwanda with. I had contacted them to see about going to Cambodia – I'd been back-packing through south-east Asia. They said, "do you speak any French?"[2] and I said, "a bit of rusty schoolgirl". So instead I volunteered to go to Rwanda and suddenly I was on the way there.

'I discovered that I was quite good at being put into chaos and being creative. It was pretty heavy, it was sink or swim and I swam. I can organise things well: from a cultural perspective I have the idea of fixing chaos and adversity with a bit of number 8 wire – the old colonial mentality! Somehow or other this must have gone down through the generations: you are in a bad situation, you've got to find solutions and you're not going to find the normal solutions so you are creative. I found it suited my way of working.'

Volunteering for Rwanda is a big thing for a normal person to do.

'Some people wouldn't call me normal. It's a bold assumption to make.'

How would you describe yourself?

'I lived on the wild side.'

Rwanda is on the wild side after cosy New Zealand.

'Hmmmm.'

All those sheep and beating our cricketers.

'I'd rather beat the Australian cricketers but we don't want to get into that.'

Rwanda didn't put you off at all?

'Well, I'd seen a lot of things but some of it is the capacity to work through these things, put up the appropriate psychological barriers and keep on working. You deal with the after-effects afterwards. Of course there is an impact. It actually felt more stressful for me going to work in the [British] National Health Service here because of the rigidity and the hierarchy than to work in these situations. It demands a lot of creativity, a *lot* of energy and responsibility.

'Afghanistan was my seventh mission with *MSF*. The joke was that I was going out there for my summer holidays. Half way through August 2001 I had been asked by the emergency pool in Switzerland – it was over a couple of glasses of wine one night – if I'd consider going and I said, "yeah, but only for a short term because I don't want to be long-term in the field anymore." That's when it began as a joke about my summer holidays.

'I'd never been to Afghanistan and it was somewhere I was never going to go. With my personality I didn't think I would work too well there, because I'm very pushy and outspoken with anyone who doesn't see things my way [soft laughter]. Yes, I went out that August.

'We flew to Pakistan and then to Faizabad, northern Afghanistan, where I was based. It was in the Northern Alliance zone and we had projects across that part of province. The real joke became that something had gone horribly wrong with my summer holidays because [as the crisis deepened] I stayed on. Everyone was evacuated – except *MSF*, and we were the only ex-patriots in Afghanistan, apart from the ones in jail in Kabul.[3] We downsized from seventeen people to five. Then we were trapped. For me, it was actually the first time I felt a special notion of solidarity: I'd been in situations before where you had to evacuate and the national staff [local workers] knew you had to evacuate, but this time it seemed terribly important to stay.

'I was in Badakhshan. That's the name of the province, it's north eastern Afghanistan. It's very mountainous, not much arable land, a very desolate area. Before all these years of war it was the most under-developed part of Afghanistan and it still remains the most under-developed part.

'I was medical coordinator which means that I was responsible for all the medical aspects of the project. I certainly have played emergency nurse but what medical coordinator means is that I am responsible for medical aspects of programme orientation, technical and ethical working with the Head of Mission to help define things, set up procedures. You have to make sure the strategy is correct to meet the objectives, and it's a pretty tough job.

'We were in charge of the only referral hospital in the area and there are about 400,000 people in Badakhshan. We were also in charge of several clinics, some community work and traditional birthing attendance. Because a lot of women need permission from their husbands to be able to leave the home, we tried to do as much in the home as we could.

'I used to seethe in silence over this male permission, but interestingly enough some of the Afghan men I met didn't like it very much either. One area we were working in was basically Taliban in everything but name, it's just that they never just actually joined the Taliban movement. The Taliban were very, very restrictive on the women and this was just as restrictive but not as institutionalised.

'The burqa, incidentally, is not a Taliban invention, it goes back a long time. That quite surprised me when I arrived. I didn't realise I'd be seeing people in the burqa [in that province controlled by the Northern Alliance]. I'd gone there with the misconception that it was a Taliban idea.'

What sort of problems did you have personally? They're not supposed to look at women.

'Because I had a position of quite a lot of responsibility, I was dealing with local counterparts and I found a couple of them quite difficult. I felt that I wasn't actually taken seriously because I was female, but that didn't happen so often. I can't pinpoint any specific difficulties. I learnt very quickly what strategy I needed to get the job done: to be quite manipulative as opposed to being very open and pushy, which had been my normal style. You just have to play things along a little bit more.'

Again as a woman, how did you feel about having to be like that?

'It created stress sometimes but it wasn't overly stressful. It's just a different sort of stress. I mean, having to be pushy all of the time to get things done is stressful. It was just another way to get the job done.

The Women's War

I can't say it didn't bother me, but I can't say it bothered me enough that I was lying awake at night about it.

'Our accommodation was purely basic. We had our own compound, spot latrines, no running water, just the bucket showers – comfortable. It was a bit more than your average Afghan would have, but actually quite spartan: kerosene lamps and things like that.'

In fact, on 9/11 Tong was in Faizabad, the centre of *MSF*'s operations in northern Afghanistan.

'I can run it through my head like a movie. I was inside my bedroom. I walked out into the common room and there were three of my team who lived outside. They were ex-patriots from Germany, France and Switzerland – we were a very large team. One of them grabbed my arm and explained to me quickly what was happening. We felt shock. Then we turned on our high frequency radio to the BBC. I can still remember the eyes of the person I was looking into the whole time across the time – completely stunned. Then we were saying "it's bin Laden" – just a calculation that he would be capable of something like that. Then some people came from the office and said someone from *MSF* UK had called to speak to me.

'We had a double whammy. On 9 September we'd had the assassination attempt on Massoud,[4] which was subsequently successful. After that it was: *Ok, we're evacuating, who's out? who's in?* It was decided that five of us would stay. Everyone else would leave, and I was one of the five staying. I was the only female ex-patriot in Afghanistan at the time apart from two ICRC members and the prisoners in Kabul. We were very worried for them, we kept thinking *this is just awful*. At some stages I felt like leaving, but professionally it would have made it very difficult for the rest of the people to stay – the ex-patriots – because I was the medical coordinator, which means I am in charge of all the medical aspects of the programme. What would have been their purpose in staying apart from solidarity with the national staff?

The Coordinator

'For us it was a very surreal experience to be in the centre of attention. I remained in Faizabad for a bit of the time, then it was suggested by a couple of key national staff that I move because it just wasn't a good idea to be the only female ex-patriot – it being inherently more difficult to travel quickly as a female if we needed to get out quickly because of the anti-Western feeling. So I moved to Eshkashem on the border with Tajikistan and from there, apart from other things, I monitored one of our projects by radio. In Faizabad we were starting to have a few little clashes inside the team, and understandably so. Everyone was flipping out and we're in a war. Anyway, just for my own perceptions I wanted to work nice and quietly. What I was doing was on the computer and I could jump in the vehicle to visit the projects each day but I still thought I would prefer to live away from Faizabad.

'I came under tremendous emotional pressures to get out from family and friends and so on, and it was terrifying for everybody. I confess I was whipped out of sleep some times thinking *OK, it's really happened, I'm really in Afghanistan, I am the last Kiwi in Afghanistan and there's a bit of a media circus about me in New Zealand. In a country of 4 million people and 60 million sheep one of them is lost in Afghanistan!* Everything had a very surreal quality about it, like living in a bubble and you know the world is looking into it.

'I was joking that I come from a small town in New Zealand, there's nowhere in my social conditioning that has prepared me for this: nature or nurture. Can I blame my parents that I am not married to a doctor, with two children, and living in the suburbs? Instead, I'm in the middle of the biggest political emergency since World War Two.

'I couldn't work on analytical or abstract things, just figures and numbers. I kept myself very busy setting up computer programmes for inventory tracking and things like that: numbers and formulae were no problem because they are very concrete things, but the abstract or the analytical, no. I did this newsletter [see page 161]. It was like emotionally vomiting on to the computer screen but, even after that, there are still some things I need to deal with for myself.

'In some respects we had good information about what was happening and in other respects we were completely dependent on the BBC to get updates on the world situation. We heard the American hostages had escaped through the BBC. We were following the news every night. We got TV about ten days after September 11th and finally we were able to watch the images on TV – very, very poor reception but *OK, now we can all understand why we're getting hysterical e-mails.* I was still in Faizabad and we managed to borrow a satellite dish – this was a rudimentary satellite system. The reception was bad reception but even so the pictures were just extraordinary. We also had what we called "radio bazaar", which was the gossip in the bazaar. "What's the gossip? Is there anti-Western feeling?" It was an extremely strange time, but I think it was important in concrete terms for the local staff that *MSF* stayed. In Taliban areas they did evacuate but they really had no choice.

'When we were getting a bit paranoid – I think justifiably paranoid – about these anti-Western feelings, I had an incident which might have been awkward but turned out to be funny. I was walking outside the office in Faizabad and this little boy came running up to me. He said in English, "why aren't you in your own country?" I said to myself *oops*. This kid's about nine years old, hands on hips looking very aggressively at me. I said I was in *MSF* and we were at the hospital looking after people blah blah blah. He was still looking very cross and aggressive and I'm thinking he's going to throw stones. Then he goes, "well, thank you very much, mister!"'

We heard one of the reasons they wouldn't get rid of bin Laden was because their code of honour demanded that they protected strangers who came into their midst. Did you feel they'd do that to you?

'Yes and no. The people who we were associated with, yes. Then again these were very crazy times and who could predict outcomes in

The Coordinator

that respect? To be quite honest, everyone was on alert for our benefit to pick up any anti-Westerner feel. As much as what happened on September 11th impacted on the western psyche, it impacted very, very gravely on the Afghans as well. Everyone was confused and scared and asking *what is going on here? What is happening?* The ordinary Afghan hadn't gone looking for it in the first place.

'Some people were happy with these outsiders [the Taliban] and some weren't. You can't generalise on that point. In Kandahar they were very well accepted because it had been gang land beforehand. In other areas like Mazar[5] they were not well accepted at all and the Taliban conducted a more violent offensive than they had in Kandahar.

'I met hard-liners, yes, but they were not Taliban, just very, very ultra-conservative. We actually had a couple working with us. They were doctors, educated in Pakistan and very hard-line. Did they not want me there because I was a woman? I wouldn't go that far, I just didn't feel I could get any respect or that my opinion was probably not respected. That was the impression I had. Of course that would never be said.'

I'm surprised you weren't moved to comment.

'You know, you work in different cultures and there's a game that must be played in order to balance what needs to be done versus what your constraints are. The country was fragmented, this is clear.'

What did you make of the plight of Afghan women?

'Pretty deplorable, but it was true of Afghans in general. I mean, the average lifespan for an Afghan man is only 43. Regardless of gender they have a very, very hard existence. When you look at their figures for life expectancy regionally, Afghanistan is a catastrophe and it's not being made any better by the drought. So specifically, yes, they have it very hard. They do need their husband's permission to leave the house and that makes it harder, but I don't think anyone has it very good there.'

You didn't have the police of vice and virtue in the streets?

'No, no. Certainly there was the Sharia law[6] in some parts and there were some public executions on the basis of Sharia law. We were invited to the bazaar one day for a public hanging but we declined. It was a man, and he was duly hung for murder. He had apparently murdered someone, although there were a lot of rumours as well. I didn't go because I've got a thing about the death penalty. I don't think anyone's got the right to take another life, certainly not the state and certainly not governmental institutions. I am very, very clear on that. If someone has committed a heinous crime, I think the French have got it right: set up a Devil's Island, make life a living hell but don't take another life. So no, I wouldn't go.'

Eventually, 'I said I needed to come back to London for a couple of weeks. I'd left for Afghanistan thinking I was going for two months [in August] and my friend in London was having to forge my signature on cheques and things like that in my personal life. Then I said OK, I'd go back for three months more. I came out about November 7 and went back about November 20 and stayed until the end of February. We'd got our full team back, the front lines had gone down, the media circus had moved from where we were – we had a big media circus – to follow the fall of the front lines and the fall of the Taliban. We were starting to get to the stage where the projects needed rebuilding and re-orientation, we needed to do team building and stabilisation: take steps towards normality. It wasn't something I could articulate at the time but there was unfinished business for me there, so I went back and now it feels more or less like finished business in terms of that part of what I went to Afghanistan for.'

If there were more women leaders would there be fewer wars?

'I don't think it's a matter of gender, it's a matter of the system. The system that we live in, the dominant western system, rewards the people who compete rather than the people who cooperate. It rewards success on the basis of monetary terms as opposed to human terms, and by human I mean how you look after your environment as well as other people. While we are dominated by that system I

The Coordinator

don't think it matters if it is women or men. If we changed the system it might make a difference.'

What would you have done after 11 September?

'I really haven't thought about it because I've only just come out of Afghanistan [March 2002]. I haven't really allowed myself to think about it too much yet and I need time to do that because it was a very big psychological impact staying there. In answer to the question, that acronym that the military is famous for comes to mind: *all options stink*. Do nothing: what's going to happen? Do something: what's going to happen?'

I am indebted to Ms Tong for allowing me to reproduce, in full, the newsletter she mentioned during our interview. Like so many documents of its kind, it gets its power from the strength of its content rather than the artistry of its writing – and if it revisits some of the ground covered in the interview, never mind.

Dear ——,

My name is Jacqui Tong and I am writing to you from Badakhshan, in northern Afghanistan where I work as medical coordinator for *MSF*. This is my seventh mission with *MSF*: at home I have been working in the Acute Medical Department at the Royal Sussex County Hospital in Brighton. When I came here on a six-week mission in August, my friends joked about it being my summer holiday. Well, I'm still here and now the joke is that something went wrong with my holiday plans.

MSF's work here includes full support to 4 clinics, community health networks, the only functioning hospital in Badakhshan and an emergency project with displaced people in Tahkar province near the front line. We place a strong emphasis in our work here on improving mother and child health.

The infant mortality rate is staggering – one in four children die before the age of five. Their mothers are also at risk. We don't have exact figures, but it's common for women to die during and after childbirth. Many never make it to the clinics or the hospital. Most of these deaths are preventable, and our biggest challenge is to make health care truly available to all those who need it.

So one of my biggest priorities has been to set up a functioning network of health workers who can make sure that people suffering from disease, illness or accident are promptly referred to the nearest health post. In most cases this is one of our health centres, but serious medical cases have to be sent to the hospital in Faizabad[7]. We have brought the hospital up to a decent standard, it's basic but clean and has all essential facilities, including X-ray, and ultrasound. *MSF* provides all the drugs and medical materials for the hospital, trains and supports the medical staff, and has even donated generators to ensure that frequent power cuts don't stop work.

Even so, delays in reaching medical care are often fatal. I remember this one little girl, 8 years of age, whose family brought her into the hospital. The poor child was already suffering from end-stage cerebral malaria – fitting and foaming at the mouth by the time she arrived. She and her family lived in a very remote area and it had taken her parents two days to bring her by donkey. Despite their efforts, and ours, it was too late to save her. This girl should not have died. If only she had been given simple drugs a few days earlier she would still be alive. Cases like this make me realise how much we still have to do.

There are also success stories. When our staff hear of people sick and unable to travel to see our doctors, *MSF* arranges for them to be collected by one of our vehicles. This was the case with one poor shepherd we heard of who had been shot in the leg. He was in one of the most remote areas in the whole world, Wakhan, in the 'Panhandle', a long thin strip of mountainous territory sandwiched between Pakistan, Tajikistan and China. The shepherd was probably shot by accident, as all the men there carry guns to ward off the wolves.

The Coordinator

News of the shepherd reached us in the nick of time. When our team eventually arrived to pick him up, gas gangrene had already developed in his leg. The bullet was still lodged in his hip. Our doctor stabilised him as best he could on the spot, then we brought him back to the hospital to have the bullet removed and the infection treated. He is now improving daily and feeling anxious to get back to his sheep.

September started badly here in the Northern Alliance area. The assassination of the leader of the NA, Massoud, on September 9 left us in shock, with real concerns that the front line would move rapidly towards us. Two days later we were hit with news on the radio of the World Trade Center attack. All other aid agencies, apart from our colleagues in the ICRC,[8] quickly evacuated. It was a surreal time for us all as we felt in the centre of events, according to the media, but yet outwardly life went on the same.

I do remember feelings of raw vulnerability and the eye contact with our national staff; they were as confused and as worried as we were. We use the word 'solidarity' when we are in proximity to the people in need. After 7 missions with *MSF* this has been the strongest experience I have had of this need being expressed by our staff and our patients. The need just for us to be there with them, and not leave.

Some days it was hard to stay and work as the airwaves buzzed with furious political rhetoric and threats. We were often pulled by emotional e-mails from family and friends asking us to get out. My colleagues in the Taliban-administered areas were forced to leave the country, relying on our Afghan staff to continue the work. I really have to remark here on the fantastic efforts of *MSF*'s Afghan staff; keeping medical facilities continuously open and functioning in many locations, despite great personal risk.

At the same time though, it has been difficult to accept the way that solving the humanitarian crisis is presented as a war aim, knowing only too well how little the outside governments seemed to care about the people of Afghanistan before 11 September. We have watched with dismay, and spoken out, about the motivation and profound lack of efficacy of the military food and medicine airdrops. Humanitarian aid has to be delivered by people who are seen to be impartial and neutral in war, otherwise it is not trusted and unlikely to be effective. *MSF* always struggles to protect that independence, so that we can never be seen as part of any enemy.

MSF's international staff, travelling through the remote and rugged Panshir valley, returned to work in Kabul on the 13 November, the day the front line crossed the city. We went without any military escort and completely independently of any armed group. In the same way, *MSF* was the first international aid organisation to return with ex-pats to Mazar-I-Sharif and Herat, to emotional reunions with our Afghan staff, and rapidly resuming full-scale operations.

It is your support, and that of people like you, that makes this possible. *MSF* has stood alone in not taking funds from governments involved in the fighting. And *MSF* has only been able to work in Afghanistan, since 1979, regardless of media coverage, thanks to the commitment of private individuals. On behalf of *MSF* volunteers working throughout Afghanistan today, our Afghan colleagues, and the people we assist –
Thank you.

Jacqui Tong,
Medical Coordinator,
MSF Badakhshan.

SILENCES AND OTHER VOICES

Margaret Owen is a formidable lady. The night before I spoke to her, she'd been to a meeting at the House of Commons where Dr Abdullah Abdullah, the foreign minister in the Kabul interim administration, was speaking. He is, she says, 'the spokesman they put forward, a dentist. He's the polite, cosmetic front of all that. Jack Straw[9] sort of grovels at him and licks his toes.'

One questioner, an Afghan woman, was 'quite aggressive about what the Northern Alliance have done and also there being only 160 women in the Loya Jirga[10] out of 1,500 people. Abdullah is going on and on about how "it's our culture to go very slowly" and she was absolutely screaming at him "what do you mean, we're not ready?"

'If we are going to talk about representation, the widows have to be represented – and we don't even know how many there are. They say that on the Loya Jirga there will be representation for refugees: well, 80 per cent of the refugees are women and probably 70 per cent of those are widows.'

Margaret Owen describes herself as 'terribly, terribly old. I tell people I'm 90 and then they look at me and say "gosh, you look really young." That's good. In fact I'm 70 [in May 2002]. I am an international human rights lawyer based in London. I founded Empowering Women in Development,[11] which is the only international non-governmental organisation representing widows of the third world. I've been in Kosovo and Rwanda and Sierra Leone and East Timor. I'm a consultant for the UN on widowhood.

'After 11 September I founded a spin-off of EWD. It's actually a network called Widows for Peace and Reconstruction. I am a conduit pipe, I hate being called a moving force. I am the channel for voices that are never heard, faces that are never seen and people that are forgotten after conflicts.

'The reason I got into it is this: I'd worked particularly on women's issues and I never thought about widows until my husband died eleven years ago. I was teaching Commonwealth judges, the wife of somebody from Malawi walked into my house in London and said "you mean your husband's brothers let you stay here and keep all these things?"

'Apart from conflict, widows in patriarchal societies – that's Africa, south Asia, lots of other places – are kicked out when their

The Women's War

husband die. They have no rights to land, house, and they are often subjected to the most terrible violence and rape by brothers-in-law. They live in utter poverty and they have no voice. And, yes, that's how I got into it.

'On 11 September I was here in London worrying where my son, who works in the World Bank, was. He had gone back to America with his wife and baby the day before and the World Bank is right next to the Pentagon. It was 24 hours before I could get hold of him.'

She walked from her terraced house ('I suppose in the 1900s it was a workman's cottage but it's all gentrified, a pretty little terraced house in a pretty street') to her local supermarket, a 'mini-market in Shepherd's Bush, and I heard it on the radio. There were about seven of us in this place and I kept thinking *this isn't a very funny spoof that a plane's gone into the World Trade Center*. Nobody bothered and I kept thinking *that's not very funny*. I was thinking *is this a drama? Is this a play? It's a bit early for the afternoon play*. The shop was run by Asians and they weren't paying any attention to it either. I came home and the phone rang. A great friend of my son said, "put on your television."

'You couldn't get phone calls through [to Washington] and then I got the e-mail which I have always kept. It said *Being Evacuated* and then there was a description of what had happened.

'We'd had a Conference in London – to which two Afghan women came, one a wonderful woman called Latifa – so we were already talking about the plight of widows under the Taliban and in the refugee camps. And when the attack happened we knew there were uncounted numbers of widows in Afghanistan who would not be able to even flee. Then we had the American bombardment – which I marched against. They were all patting themselves at the House of Commons last night but some of us didn't feel too good about that.

'The first time I went to a camp was with RAWA. The camp was on the Peshawar-Pakistan border, a camp made of mud housing.

The Coordinator

As I walked in there somebody ran out and said, "Margaret!" It was Latifa. RAWA was running everything in the camp, the clinic, the orphanage, the literacy classes for women – it was mostly widows and children, I saw hardly any men.

'I felt it was more at peace – and people were working together and being kinder and caring to each – than in the Dorset village where I have a cottage and where everybody's at loggerheads about something or other.

'I was at the camp in February [2002]. Remember, in developing countries you are deemed an orphan if you're father's dead. It is also reflected in the fact that if you've a widowed mother she's got no money to look after you or educate you. What was impressive about the orphanages and the schools was that they had Pashtuns, Uzbeks, Tajiks, Hasaras all together, all working with each other. This does not reflect the situation in Afghanistan or, I'm afraid, the future.

'There were girls at the schools – the women kicked out of their jobs in Afghanistan were the teachers. They were also refugees. One girl had only arrived three days before: her parents had been killed in the American bombing. There were girls who had never been to school. Maybe they had come the year before and they were fourteen, fifteen. *They had never been to school before.* They were amazing. They were speaking English – in just a year their English was brilliant – and they were doing sciences.

'They all came from villages and when you asked them what they wanted to be they wanted to be doctors, engineers, lawyers, journalists. One little boy wanted to be a king! Another wanted to be an actor and I said, "can you do something for us?" He hammed up running around pretending to be a Taliban, pulling people by their hair, throwing and kicking them around.

'I spoke to lots of widows and some were still completely traumatised because in their flight in the mountains they had lost babies who had died from exposure. They also told me stories – I don't want to go into too much detail – of how their husbands died, shot by the Taliban, how the frozen corpses were left in front of their houses, how they used to have to boil water to try and get the corpses off the ground because the blood was frozen. They told me they had to carry them because the Taliban wouldn't let them put them on a cart.'

Why?

'Just the terrible brutality of it: they wouldn't even let them do that. There was one brother-in-law who'd not been in the village when they killed all his brothers and he'd had to lie to his sisters-in-law [to spare their feelings] about how he'd found these corpses. I remember one woman: she doesn't speak any more. She's got maybe a four-year-old son but her baby died when it was six months old in the mountains – exposure and hunger – and she just makes a hysterical giggling sound. She is completely traumatised and has lost her mind.

'This is an extraordinarily well run camp in terms of people looking after the orphans, everybody knowing each other, people being really kind, but the only heating we had was an electric lamp. You put it under a stool, covered the stool with quilts and put your feet under that when you ate and when you slept.

'The women say, "how can we ever go back? Who will rebuild our houses? We don't know what's happened to our houses. Who will educate our children? How can we go back? Who's going to give us money? Who's going to train us for jobs? How can we have jobs?" They were absolutely terrified that they would be forcibly repatriated.

'I went to another camp, a terrible camp outside Peshawar, where I had to be smuggled in wearing a burqa. I had to disappear suddenly because it was very dangerous. They said, "go, quick, quick – the commander knows you're here." This was run by a Pakistani ex-policeman who actually doesn't allow RAWA or any NGO's to have direct access to the refugees. There are allegations against him and I wrote a report to the UNHCR.

The Coordinator

'He screams at them when he sees them: "if you're widows, why haven't you got married again?" The Prophet married lots of widows – Mohammad was always for the remarriage of widows and his first wife was a widow. This is what they say to the widows: "Get another man. Why aren't you married?" These women have absolutely nothing, and nothing for their children. They walk about three hours to the nearest town begging and looking for washing to do. The children collect garbage and paper. Some of the women try to spin thread out of goat's hair – 30p for a kilo of thread, and it takes three of them with their children about three days – or they work as slaves in the brick fields. They go out at night to try and make bricks, and again it's a pittance for three days work making 1,000 bricks.

'All of them, illiterate but articulate, were saying "this interim government, it's the Northern Alliance, they committed all these atrocities before". They are very nasty people, there is no security and the whole thing about "isn't it wonderful that 20,000 refugees have returned, some in gaily painted lorries" is rubbish. There are uncounted thousands of women in the camps [in Pakistan] and there are ad hoc camps in remote rural areas, heavily mined, no roads, no nothing. It is *rubbish* to talk about everybody going back to school and isn't it wonderful?

'The whole pat on the back for Bush and Blair is about Kabul, and even Kabul isn't safe. And of course as soon as the [American] bombardment finished – we knew this would happen – the traffickers were there very quickly. It's the particular sort of blonde blue-eyed Hazarahs – women and children – who were immediately targeted. The traffickers have had a field day in Afghanistan and nobody's looking at that. I mean child prostitution, I mean the trafficking of women and girls through Pakistan and into the brothels of Bombay, and then maybe to the Gulf, and then all over the place.

'Also, there is a lot of rape – as there always is – in these situations. The Taliban raped women and they refused to allow widows to work at all or go outside without a blood relative. At the same time, they were raped if they went outside and there was a lot of prostitution and begging. It was a peculiar paradox: they said a woman has to have the blood relative to go out and the widows didn't have anybody.

'If you are raped – and a lot of these widows have been raped – [it's] also a crime of honour. It means they could be killed by their relatives because they have brought dishonour on the family. It's impossible to prove under Sharia law that you have been raped – you need four witnesses – so women who've been raped mustn't even speak about it. There are a lot of Kosovo Albanians who have never spoken about what happened. That's dishonour. It's the same everywhere, and all of it is horrendously chilling and terrifying. Even if there were laws, women wouldn't access them because the local authorities are warlords.

'I did immediately protest on September 11. Within a few hours Blair – without going to the cabinet, without going to the House of Commons, without going to the country – stood shoulder-to-shoulder with Bush. My heart sank into my knees at that because I knew this was the beginning of real problems, which would go downhill. One, in terms of our democracy what was he doing? Two, I had huge concerns about what Bush would do to placate the Americans. Three, we know from 200 years of history that you can't wage a war in Afghanistan and win. Four the actual objective – to find Osama bin Laden and get rid of the *al-Qa'eda* Taliban – was going to be impossible. It was a war which could never be short term, a few weeks.'

If there were more women leaders would there be fewer wars?

'Oh, yes, I am convinced. I think that the sort of women leaders we have had haven't been always the sort of women we would liked to have had as leaders – for example Margaret Thatcher. Take Golda Meir.[12] I remember what Henry Kissinger said: "When you've had an afternoon with Indira Gandhi[13] you don't look forward to an evening with Golda Meir." OK, there are women who kill – Tutsi women

The Coordinator

who kill Hutus, there are women who are for war. Mrs Thatcher sent us to the Falklands. But also I think there are huge numbers of very wise women who are not in decision-making caucuses at any level but do have a much longer term view of the importance of peace and dialogue. They understand that violence breeds violence. Also, women – and particularly widows – are often the most equipped to cross ethnic and national divides because they all have in common the fact that they are bearers of children.'

What would you have done after the 11 September?

'I wouldn't have done anything so quickly. I would have certainly had much more careful dialogue. I felt it was un-thought out, the immediate getting into bed with Pakistan because, after all, it was Pakistan and Saudi Arabia – to whom we all sold arms – who actually funded the Taliban. I would have studied the connections much more deeply – and particularly the connections with what was going on in the Middle East with Israel and the Palestinians, because that's the very heart of it.

'I'd have taken very, very careful thought about how one could win back some sort of confidence in that area and I'd have tried to find out why there was so much resentment against the United States. I'd have worked from that.'

An Afghan Red Crescent[14] report says the regions surrounding Herat are some of the poorest in Afghanistan and the plight of women there reveals that. The twenty-three years of war has claimed the lives of many, many men leaving widows and children without fathers everywhere. The subsequent drought has cut into whatever resources remain.

The Red Crescent in Herat is running several programmes to help the needy, 'including the widows. They, the handicapped and the elderly represent the majority.' The Red Crescent runs a relief centre feeding 15,000.

'I have two sons, but they have both gone to Iran as there was no work for them here. I have nobody to help me. I work a little bit, helping another family, but the salary is almost nothing,' says Zalikh, a 63-year-old widow. 'During the Taliban rule, life was even harder because women were not allowed to work. Now at least we have the freedom to walk on the streets and try to earn an income. I have nothing now except the clothes I am wearing, I do not even have a blanket to keep me warm at night.'

'The Red Crescent gives food to my family every week,' says Malin, a seven-year-old girl who comes to the relief centre with her neighbour Mirian. 'I have nobody else to support me and my family. My father died in the war, and my mother is sick and cannot leave the house.'

TEN

The Exile

Women have a softer heart. They always think of the consequences of what they do: if I kill this man, who's going to look after his child and his wife? In our religion, Islam, women are not allowed to be judges and that's because they are very kind.

We're sitting in a café opposite Victoria station in London. The soft-spoken Afghan lady is perfectly assimilated, slightly feline and slightly formidable, and preparing to go back. The vivacious Afghan lady opposite her talks in short explosions of sounds laced with laughter. Cumulatively, these two ladies are so expressive – so evocative – that we might be watching the sunset over the parched ruins of Kabul rather than all the red buses backed up in regiments as they come and go at the station.

Seema Ghani, the soft-spoken one, left Afghanistan in 1990, a family decision 'because my father thought it might be dangerous to stay. He was a retired army officer and the communist regime wanted such people – experienced retired officers – to work with them in an advisory role – or if they were not willing to work they just hassled them, asking questions, imprisoning and in extreme cases killing them. I had never been out of Afghanistan before. We went to India and then Britain where my brother was already living. That was what brought us to Britain: our family thought they should at least try to get together.'

She was ten and 'I wasn't looking forward to coming. In the first place I didn't want to leave Afghanistan and my idea was that other Afghans are being killed so let me die with them rather than leave. We had already suffered how many years – twelve? – of the communist regime and I thought I could put up with a little bit more. *My people are in pain, let me be in the same pain.* However I had no choice. I couldn't live in Afghanistan by myself – there was no way that women of the age I was then could live alone.

'So I hadn't been looking forward to leaving Afghanistan. I was coming to Britain on the plane – from Delhi to Heathrow – and I wasn't looking forward to anything. In fact I was really worried. I kept thinking on the way *well, what am I looking forward to when I get to London?* There was only one positive thing I could think of: a friend of a friend I hadn't met was there and I thought *good, I can see that friend.*

'Then you know what hit me. The plane was landing and you could see the ground really well because it was a clear day in June, you could see houses. One of things which made me smile was their style, with attic windows in their roofs. It's a pretty little style for me. What I'd been afraid of was finding a city of high rises and I don't like them, I like lots of green. When I saw the houses I thought *thank God, at least the houses aren't high rises everywhere.* That was a second positive.

'I had the fear of the language because although I knew the basics – table, chair, "my name is" – that was about all, so I had to learn the language. However, being in London rather than anywhere else was another positive. You were communicating with different people and the city is so cosmopolitan. Although I had heard a lot about the racism of the western world – towards the non-whites – to be honest I have never experienced that in the twelve years of my life here. The community is used to seeing lots of foreigners and I was impressed.

The Exile

Later on, I travelled around quite a bit – Europe, America, Singapore and other places – but I came to the decision a few years back that if I was to live anywhere outside Afghanistan it would have to be London. I like the society.

'Culturally, it was not a big adjustment because there wasn't a lot of difference in terms of life style – my life was good here. It didn't bring any specific changes. I dressed the way I used to dress in Afghanistan, trousers, skirts – I still do that – and I lived with my family.

'As women we had had freedom when the king was in Afghanistan[1] and afterwards. During the communist regime that is one thing they didn't really touch: whatever women were doing they continued doing it. That's why I say that coming here was not a major adjustment culturally.

'There was, however a lot of oppression under the communists. People of my age went through their school and then university years thinking that we needed our political freedom, and we didn't have this freedom we wanted with that government. You'd hear of people being killed and tortured. A member of my family was imprisoned for three years and tortured. It started from when the communists took over – it was a coup, you know – and as soon as they took over they started bringing in rules and killing people.

'In terms of citizenship, I have both Afghan and British now but I think I am more Afghan and that is why I am going back. I look at London as my second home although I'm not foreseeing living here again. I am thinking of visiting for maybe short periods. Therefore, I think I am more Afghan.'

Very often when you are away from a place you feel it more keenly than if you were living there.

'But I had these feelings when I was in Afghanistan! That's why I never wanted to leave. My patriotism never died down. People kept telling me from the beginning – before I even left India – "oh, you are going to get used to the life style in London, you are going to feel at home there, you are never going to go back, you wouldn't *want* to go back." People have been repeating that for twelve years and I keep telling them "sorry, after the twelve years of you people saying it to me, I still say no".

'In London I worked as a project manager with an accountancy firm – one of the big ones – but I have left now [May 2002] to go to Afghanistan permanently. I've been offered a job with a charity organisation.'

She was, of course, in her London office – an open plan office – on 9/11 'sitting doing the usual work and all of a sudden one of my colleagues shouted from the other end that a plane just hit the Twin Towers in New York and every one got up.' They gathered round and watched, 'trying to come to terms with what was going [on] and listening to the news. Some people had to go back to their desks because the phones were ringing.

'I felt real shock. At the same time, I knew my phone was ringing but I just couldn't bring myself to go and pick it up. By then it was probably twenty minutes afterwards and you could hear from the radio it seemed to be a terrorist attack. You just don't want to do anything and actually I think my day stopped then. My manager was sitting behind me and all the other staff were there but I couldn't work.

'By then, too, assumptions were being made. Journalists were making announcements and we were looking at websites trying to get some reality out of this. Was it the journalists making it sound like a terrorist attack? The more we listened and looked we found an assumption that bin Laden was in it – he was mentioned.'

Ms Ghani had already 'been back to Afghanistan, and to Peshawar a number of times because I run a charity there. We have projects in Peshawar which I visit.

'I went to Afghanistan in April 2001 during the Taliban regime. My dad's best friend is a religious teacher and I call him uncle because he is very close to the family. He was in Pakistan and I'd

The Exile

said I was planning to go to Kabul. Could he help? It was organised in a way that he, two of his friends and myself took one of the coaches which was going from Peshawar to Kabul. I didn't use my passport or anything – women were simply not recognised.

'I wore the burqa for the first time. I had to buy one and I went to the shop with a friend. We were trying to joke about it although I was thinking of the comfort, because I would be wearing it for a few days. The first time I put it on in the shop I thought *I can't see anything*, but my friend said, "you're doing it wrong, you have to pull the front a bit further" – because in front of the eyes [there is] a netted part – "you have to look through this." I said, "it is not good enough! I can't see very well at all!"'

If it is loose you can only see more or less straight ahead, but if you 'pull it down onto your face' and hold it closer to your eyes you have more vision to either side. Overall, 'it changes the vision completely. I think emotionally it didn't affect me at that point because I was so excited about going to Afghanistan for the first time in eleven years. The day we went I didn't wear it from Peshawar – actually, from Peshawar I did wear it for a short period of time. I wore it at the border. My 'uncle' was sitting next to me and he said whenever we got to the Taliban area he'd tell me and "you'll have to pull it down over your face."

'I think it was there that it affected me because the road journey to Kabul is a beautiful route, fantastic views, and for me going to my home country after so many years I wanted to see that view, I wanted to see from the window but I couldn't all the time. My 'uncle' was saying, as we passed each of the Taliban checkpoints, "pull it down now because somebody is stopping the bus", and I'd do that and we did it almost all the way.

'Again emotionally it affected me *because I couldn't see how other women felt until I got to Kabul*. When I got off the bus I saw more women wearing it and that was the point I felt "OK, traditionally a lot of women wear it" – although it is not our culture, it comes from Pakistan. Our culture was not to your face, just to the shoulder. Anyway in Kabul I wondered how many women were wearing it by culture and how many because the government told them to. *That* was when it affected me emotionally, because I wanted to know how these people feel. Or maybe I didn't want to know. All sorts of things were going through my mind. I think I started weeping then and I wept for three days on and off.

'It was also the fact that I was seeing Kabul for the first time for so long, and how much was destroyed. Most of the destruction happened during the Mujahideen time back in 1992 because they were fighting with each other, different groups hitting each, trying to destroy the other group's buildings.

'At the same time it was the expression on men's faces – I naturally couldn't see women's faces, I could only talk to these people at home or when they came to see me. I talked about their emotions. They'd walk in the street with their heads down being afraid that any minute they could be stopped by a Talib or the religious police. We were stopped once in the car. My friend was driving, his wife was sitting in the back and the religious police stopped us. It made me think of probabilities: I was there four days and was stopped, and if you were being stopped every four days all the time . . .

'The religious policeman asked my friend to play the tape – he had a cassette in his stereo, not playing, just protruding. He said, "switch it on," my friend did and it was religious recital, a holy Koran recital. He said, "OK, you can switch it off now," and he just stood there – I thought he was trying to think what else he should ask: he'd assumed it would be music on the cassette. He said, "who are the women in the back?" and my friend said, "my wife and my sister." All legal. Again he stood there thinking and at this point my friend got really annoyed. They spoke the same language.[2] My friend said, "if you don't have any further questions I am going, I have things to do." The policeman said, "well, off you go then" – he was very happy to see us go.

The Exile

'I was born and brought up in Kabul, although the family was originally from the north of the country. I recognised it despite the destruction, all the roads and streets – and finding my way around wasn't a problem because we went by car or taxi. And I had been living with it, although I had been outside the country I had been living with it.

'I think I was prepared, coming from London to a society where you couldn't see women at all. I knew what I was facing because I had heard of it so much and by the time I went in 2001 we had had many years of publicity. We met women at the refugee camps through our own projects in Pakistan, we did a lot of research and interviewing. It meant I was already familiar with what was happening.

'What I wasn't prepared for was the emotional side, the emotional meaning, my own emotions. I wasn't sure how I would feel. I knew that I would be sad but I didn't know how sad and I didn't know what I would see on people's faces. My brother had been there a few months before and he'd told me not to expect too much. "People have changed, people are really sad. You see them on the streets and they're not jolly, they're not smart, they're not talking." The city was dead. That is how I felt: the city was dead.

'One of my decisions before 11th September was that I was going to stay in Britain for maybe a year or two – maximum – and then, if the Taliban were still in Afghanistan, I would go and live in Pakistan, and work with one of the charities. I'd go in and out of Afghanistan but I couldn't live there because the patience that other women have – I don't have that. At some point I would have snapped with the Taliban.

'Once every few months as a student I used to send some money to my friends in Pakistan to give to the people in need. These were small amounts but when it got there it made a difference. In 1999 I decided on a project and I'd try and get other people to help. The one thing I had been thinking about for many years was an orphanage because I knew there were too many of them and no one to care for them. During the communist regime the majority of them were sent to Russia and almost brainwashed. But I never managed to find the right people to work with me. Someone volunteered to set up a health clinic and I said, "fine, if I can't set up an orphanage I'll do that." So we started the clinic for women and children. It was free of charge and open two days a week – it's still running. It is called the Khorasan Clinic – Khorasan is the old name for Afghanistan and it also means the land of the sun. The clinic is in Peshawar and I am the managing director. We are all volunteers.

'Then in 2001 we set up an orphanage, fairly small, fourteen children – boys and girls in the same house. I am the mother, they are my children and they call me mother. We are planning to move the house to Kabul, hopefully very soon.

'For some reason I am a very optimistic person, very positive. Everybody gave up on Afghanistan but I didn't. When the Mujahideen destroyed Kabul I didn't give up. When the Mujahideen started fighting each other and the whole Afghan community gave up I didn't. I thought, *no, it's going to get better*. Then when the Taliban took over, people said, "Afghanistan is finished," but I still didn't give up. I believed something would change, something would happen. I used to say to my friends, "I'm going to live in Pakistan until the Taliban are out and then I am going to Afghanistan." I thought the Taliban would be out if we could get the international community to pay attention for once in their lifetimes.

'Of course I had no idea they were going to attack America. There are things that you can never predict – what they are going to do and where they are going to move to next. It's amazing how things change.

'I had mixed feelings about the US bombing at the beginning. The first time I heard Bush saying revenge and war I hated him. I hated him for mentioning the word revenge about Afghanistan – because it's not *al-Qa'eda*'s country, civilians live there. How can you mention the words revenge and war in a country like that? There have been people dying for the past I don't know how many years. How can you mention it now? And to think how low that could be: ignoring the country for all that period of time and – now that it's in his interests and those of his people – he's suddenly talking revenge: he wants to go and bombard the country.

'When they started the bombing I think that was the worst moment in my entire life. I don't think I will ever forget the feeling. I was sitting at home working on my lap-top and watching the television. A news flash came on but before they said anything my heart sank. I knew they had attacked. The news was that they had attacked. I shut down the lap-top because I couldn't work any more.

'I was very much for diplomatic talks – everyone knew they were in contact with the Taliban, they were communicating about *al-Qa'eda* for I don't know how many years and there were rumours through Saudi Arabia that – somewhere around October – Mullah Omar was prepared to hand over Osama bin Laden. I was really annoyed . . . instead of them bombing the country the least they could do was move diplomatically, a bit quietly, talk instead of just guns.

'Bush had to show the American people he was doing something and that's the only way they could think of, but for me that was too much, for me as an Afghan I knew they were bombing my country. How could I understand that? There was no way because there was no justification. If somebody lets a next door neighbour in as a guest, are you going to attack the whole of their house for doing it? You don't do that, you find that guest.

'They started bombing Kabul. I have come across a family friend from there and they have grandchildren. The grand-daughter is three years old – she was two and a half at the time – and now it's very peaceful but if she sees a plane she runs inside the house, goes to a corner and shivers. I know because it happened in front of me. No matter how many times she is told "this is a civilian plane", she says, "no, no, they are going to drop bombs." She is afraid of the sound of aeroplanes – and she's three years old, for God's sake. What is the future? This is only one child. How are other children in Afghanistan? How many more years can the country put up with this sort of thing?

'The good thing was that [Taliban resistance] ended very quickly and I really did say I was very grateful to the Taliban for walking out of Kabul without fighting. For once in their lives they made the right decision. Otherwise Kabul would have been destroyed completely.

'Looking ahead, the country has enough resources for its own population. Afghanistan is very rich in terms of resources and we have never used them. The rest of the world has been trashed but Afghanistan hasn't. Now we are starting almost from basics and if we do it the right way – and we're not exploited by the multinationals – we will get to the stage where we have a government that is providing and supporting the economy. Then we'll have education and that will bring educated people who can think of things like equality. When I was there in February [2002] one of the biggest changes was in people's morale compared to just one year before. We know that the [interim] government is not perfect but at least it's broad based and recognised by the United Nations. We got an agreement in nine days[3] – something we haven't been able to do for twenty-three years, for God's sake.

'Some people say to get to western standards will take hundreds of years, and a lot of our generation and – maybe even older – say "we have to die, all of us. The children being brought up today will be the educated population of the future and they will build their lives. It won't happen in our lifetime." That's not what I believe. I believe in the ten-year plan that the United Nations is giving, the $15 billion that they are talking about.

The Exile

'I couldn't be moving back to the country if I wasn't committed and I think the country needs people like me – the mad ones that are prepared to take that extra risk! I have experience. I have lived in the east and the west, I have seen both, I can compare and pick up the good things from both and practice them. The people of my age who stayed in Afghanistan are all war-torn and they haven't had an education. They are the ones with the guns. The 6 million exiles should show their interest by going back. People like myself have to return to show them: "hey guys, you've done well, you deserve medals, you've fought for freedom for many years, thank you very much. Now sit down and rest and we will find you jobs."'

If there were more women leaders would there be fewer wars?

'Yes. Definitely. Women have a softer heart. They always think of the consequences of what they do: what will happen to the men, the children. If I kill this man, who's going to look after his child and his wife? We just wouldn't allow that sort of thing. In our religion, Islam, women are not allowed to be judges and that's because they are very kind. A combination of men and women would work.'

You have seen both sides. Can you ever see women getting equality in Afghanistan in the way that we understand it here?

'Hmmm. Interesting. I don't see equality here in Britain. How many women are in Parliament? How many women are chief executives? You don't have equality – yes, if you look at the standards in the west this *can* be achieved but, saying that, we also have to consider religion and in my religion there are some restrictions on women. That is accepted within our society[4] by women, by people like me.

'To expand on the example of judges, I'm too soft hearted, I know the criminal has ten children and his wife is not allowed to work. I don't know any organisation that's going to look after those kids. So I'm going to forgive him and it's not safe for society, this forgiving of criminals. What I'd like to do is keep him under control – but I can't. How many days can you watch a man? The paedophiles in

Britain, you can't watch them every single minute. The majority have been in prison, they've been watched and they do exactly the same thing again.'

What would you have done after 11 September?

'Diplomatic talks. Put pressure on the neighbouring countries – Pakistan, naturally, is playing the key role. I would have promised money, talks, whatever.'

SILENCES AND OTHER VOICES

So we're sitting in the café opposite Victoria Station and the vivacious one is debating what she should call herself. She has family still in Kabul and elsewhere, and you can't be too careful. She ponders Miss X, Miss K of Kabul and decides Miss Afghan would be better.

I venture that she might like something more mysterious.

'No, I think Miss Afghan would be fine – or you could call me Miss XX!' She makes a joke of that, something about XX being a woman's designation, and when she laughs she seems gloriously alive. The incongruity of this – and what she will be doing in a moment, conjuring glimpses of Kabul – seems sharper in the plainness of the café. The area around Victoria Station is many things, but not exotic or mysterious.

Miss Afghan is just into her thirties and 'was born in the south of Afghanistan. On 11 September I was in England – I've been living in London for four years. On that day I was working in the Social Services in the Home Counties, looking after mentally ill patients. In the early afternoon my colleagues told me that the attack had happened. Of course I didn't associate it with *al-Qa'eda* – terrorist activities are going on everywhere. I didn't actually know anything about that side of it until it came on the news. It might be very naïve of me but I didn't know anything about *al-Qa'eda* until it was on the news and everybody was talking about bin Laden, who claimed

The Exile

asylum in Afghanistan and was staying in Afghanistan. He was kind of a famous person so I knew about him but I didn't know anything about *al-Qa'eda*.

'I was already a doctor when the Taliban took over. I'd graduated from medical school in 1991, which was the last year of the communist regime and the Mujahideen took over. In meant that when the Taliban took over I had already been working in [the] medical area for five years. Of course there was a lot of difference when the Taliban took over Kabul. We had an announcement on the radio next morning that woman were not allowed to go to work. I already had information about what the Taliban were doing when they had taken over many other provinces and they wouldn't allow women to work, so on Thursday before, I gave out a caution to my staff because all of them were female and I was responsible for their safety.

'I said to them they should take their belongings home from the mother and child care clinics where they were based and if the Taliban did take over – which was likely – they shouldn't return for work unless they heard from us. The Taliban came on the Friday and the first thing was a few announcements on the radio: women were *not* allowed out of their homes unless accompanied by a male relative, they should be covered head to toe, the keeping of birds at home was forbidden, men should grow beards and if they cut their beards they would be punished according to Islamic law, they could not listen to music or watch television – and they should destroy television sets. These were the main announcements.

'This was early in the morning, six or seven o'clock, and I was listening with my father to find out what was going on. One of the hopes we had had was that although the Taliban took most of the provinces, as soon as they came to Kabul the situation would be different. In the provinces, yes, most of the women are illiterate but in Kabul more than 50 per cent of the staff all of the ministries – teachers, all the workers – were female. If they banned them, all the government places would be shut.

'So we thought they only wanted to take the side of the illiterate people in the provinces and make them think they were doing the right thing but as soon as they came to Kabul they would change their minds. Unfortunately I was wrong and when we heard the announcements it was a shock. I didn't go to work that day and no one went after what we had heard. To be honest we didn't know what to expect.

'What should we wear? In the beginning they said women should cover themselves from head to toe – and can cover yourself with a piece of cloth which we call chadour.[5] You put it around your head and you can have a piece of it in front of your face. You cover your face but not your eyes. Then they changed their minds.

'I was there in Kabul with my father and I felt I had no choice – I had to leave. My family were in Pakistan. We decided we'd go there until we would know exactly what was going to happen. I gave a notice to one of my male staff who is in admin. I wrote that the project was postponed until further notice. The reason was because all of our staff – apart from two admin people and six or seven drivers – were female: the midwives and doctors were all female. In the office we had a female secretary.

'We actually left on the Friday and drove to Pakistan. There were lots of horrid things going on but I didn't see because first of all I was scared – and my father was scared. I was travelling only in a chadour, my face covered but the eyes showing. I didn't have the special thing [the burqa] they might have been requesting – we still didn't know what they wanted.

'I stayed in Pakistan with my family for about twenty days, during which time I heard from one of my colleagues – he was working with a foreign organisation, one of the main donors to our project. He came to Pakistan and he said the Ministry of Public Health had given permission to restart our project and given permission to all the women to return. I decided to go back.

The Exile

'By now, of course, one of the rules were that women should be covered if they were going to work.' She returned in the black veil, and 'although the car was stopped in several places nobody said anything because they knew we were coming from Pakistan.' Next day she went to market and bought chadaris[6] for 'all my female staff. I sent the drivers to deliver a notice to the staff because we didn't have any postal service or anything like that. I gave a message that the project is re-starting but one of the conditions was that only medical staff could return. Of our admin staff in the beginning, we only had two cleaners and one cook.'

Tell me about your normality.

'First of all I wasn't used to this chadari – in my whole life I had never worn such a thing. My eyes are weak and I have to wear glasses. It is extremely difficult to use glasses under those chadaris and I couldn't see anything. I would get headaches. However, I was lucky enough because I had a driver who came and picked me up from home so the only time I wore it was from my door to the car – and my car had curtains. I sat in the back and I had black curtains between me and the driver. That was one of the government's conditions allowing us to go to work. Also I had curtains on both sides and behind me and nobody could see me. As I got into the car I took the chadari off. When we reached the office I'd just pull it briefly over myself. It took about one minute from the car to the office and then I would take it off completely.

'At that time the offices were divided between men and women so we had to hire another office [for women]. We only had two men in the office and it was easy to get rid of them. Our main difficulty was that we didn't have admin staff, no secretaries at all. That was one of the things I wrote a letter to the Ministry of Public Health about and also the religious police.

'I explained my problem: "I am doing this project, I have permission and you say I can work as a doctor but I can't operate without women – my secretary, my pharmacist, my cleaner and my cook.

187

I know some of these women are not medical but if you don't allow them to return I cannot function. The other choice would be to hire men, but if I do that I wouldn't be able to sit in the same room with them – not allowed, because that's against your law. If I don't sit with them – and I am the coordinator of this project – how can I coordinate my staff without seeing or talking to them? Give me the solution. Either you should ban the project completely or let the female staff return."

'It was a bit of a dangerous thing to do but they accepted my argument, the women came back and it was a great joy. I could only treat women but that was my job anyway – I was a paediatrician. A general doctor was restricted to women.

'It was not, however, so simple. One problem, for example: I was working in the children's section and usually they were accompanied by their mothers, but occasionally by their fathers if they'd travelled a long distance from the provinces. The hospital was the main teaching hospital in Kabul and if there were any complications the children would come. The men couldn't bring their wives because they'd have another five or six children and the wife would stay to look after them while the man brought the child.

'That was one of the difficulties, talking to the men, but we would get round that. No-one was supervising us inside. The religious police would be walking around and that was the time when we'd be careful but other than that it was normal hospital function.'

What about when you stepped outside, though?

'It was really difficult. Life was really, really difficult.'

Who did the shopping?

'The shopping was done by my brother. I had a busy life and it couldn't be a normal, typical Afghan woman's life – because I know the situation of women. They came to me and they were crying because they wanted to commit suicide: to die is better than this life. Most of them were widows but they were looking after their children. They were asking for jobs but no one can hire them.

The Exile

They didn't have a family around them and they didn't have men. Depression was one of the biggest problems. I actually had a commander advising them to go and remarry. You could marry a commander because he's allowed four wives and she could be one of them. Yes, all the commanders wanted to marry four or five times – but they wouldn't be interested in widows. They weren't that good Muslims! They were interested in young girls, they would like to marry a young girl not a widow – who may have two children already. All these things were rumours, however, because they weren't happening in Kabul.'

You went to these women's houses to treat them.

'Yes. Most of them were very poor and hadn't had anything to eat for maybe days. Most were suffering from anaemia caused by iron deficiency and there was also malnutrition among the children. I couldn't help the whole community, of course. Some people were able to survive and others were in really bad condition. About those, I went and talked to people at the World Food Programme.[7]

'I said, "look, this is what is happening. You are not allowed to go and see women in their houses but we are. We can evaluate the conditions better than you. Anyone and everyone can come to your office and say they need food but most of the needy people are at home – and they don't even have the courage to come and ask for food. If we gave you the addresses of those people, would you be willing to help them with some of the basic foods like wheat and oil and sugar?" They said, "fine," and these people survived.'

What did women do all day?

'Sat at home and shouted at their children – because of the anxiety, depression and trauma of not being able to do what they wanted to do. A lot of them never had a good life, anyway. Most were illiterate and the only jobs they could have done were either cleaning in offices or factory work. But the factories were closed, and even the more professionally qualified women were not allowed to go to the offices. That made for an extremely difficult life and in those circumstances it was obvious everyone would go through depression. And they didn't know what was going to happen, when – or if – it would ever end.

'You don't have control over your own fate and that leads to the depression. You feel guilty, you have all these symptoms and there is nothing you can do about it.'

How difficult was it for a woman to ask the man 'can I go out?' because he had to go with her.

'The normal man in the community was more sympathetic towards women. Although it was more difficult for women, to be honest it wasn't that easy for men either. They had to grow beards and so on. If, for example, they were accompanying their sister or wife or mother and the woman had bright clothes under the chadari or wore nail varnish – well, at the beginning it was the women who were beaten, but latterly the vice police were beating the men. They wouldn't touch the woman, they'd say, "this is your woman, she lives in your house, it is your responsibility to make sure she doesn't dress like this." Most husbands were sympathetic towards their wives but they were suffering the same.'

What is it that could conceivably make human beings behave like this?

'Being brought up in that environment and under strict rules. The original Taliban were from religious schools in Pakistan, where there is a very extreme version of Islam, anyway. Very fundamental. In Afghanistan we have a very small number of religious schools. There is another thing: Afghanistan is suffering from twenty-three years of war. Anyone twenty-three or younger knows nothing apart from killing. All these young men, the Taliban and some of the Mujahideen – grew up fighting, *severe* fighting. Every day the thing was either to kill someone or be killed. I repeat: they have learnt nothing apart from killing. They don't have any skills, they've never been to school, never been to a factory or anything like that. They don't know what a normal life is and if someone is like that – they don't have a perception of peace – you change psychologically. There are lots of personality changes in society directly because of the trauma of the war. This needs a lot of counselling and psychological help, replacing their normality.

'If a child sees that he was the one asked at the age of ten or twelve to come and get a gun and fight, and his sister wasn't, he would say, "I am better than my sister." They have seen this from a very early age. Now consider: men now in their twenties or even early thirties were five or six or seven years when this started. And the twenty-three years killing has put a huge amount of sort of stress on their minds.

'The fundamentalism of the Taliban wasn't good Islam but what I'm saying is, apart from that, it is very easy for foreigners – like bin Laden – and foreign countries to use the illiterate Afghans who have known only the killing. They would say, "well, these people can't read and write. They don't have any education about Islam apart from what they've been taught," – they can't even read the Koran so they don't know its meaning. If a mullah or a religious person tells them that killing a person is a holy war and if they die they go to heaven, they believe it. This is a simple thing very easy to inject, but it is almost like using young children.'

If you have illiterate people so familiar with cruelty and killing, they are not going to feel much sympathy for women.

'Exactly. And if I say, "look, this is wrong," and a mullah says, "no, it is right," they won't believe me. They'd say, "you are an educated person, you haven't used the burqa, you haven't covered your face – you are doing all these things against Islam, you aren't even a Muslim." There is no way round, this would have to be extreme counselling and behaviour therapy: complete reconstruction of the personality. I am not just talking about the Taliban, I am talking about some of the Mujahideen still in power.

'I lived under the Mujahideen as well [as the Taliban]. They are not better. What about the rapes? Girls threw themselves from the third floor of buildings because the commander wanted to marry them. In that one sense, I think the Taliban were safer. [Ms Ghani, interrupting: 'I have met women who were raped by the Taliban. They were living in the north of the country. It was soldiers lower down doing this, at least it was not sanctioned from above.']

'I hate the Taliban as much as anybody, but if there are good aspects you have to say so. I reasoned with them and I got my female staff back. I know I was watched all the time and it was a horrible life.'

How many children would an Afghan woman have?

'She didn't have any rights over contraception, which was not permitted for a long, long time – from when the Mujahideen were in power: contraception was against Islamic law. We were trying to help women who wanted space between children. It was extremely difficult to cope with children born year after year, seven or eight or nine or ten children. The midwives were going to their houses but on the fortieth day after the baby was born we discharged the women and that was the day they were asking "can you give us some contraception?"

'I had a man who was crying for contraception. He was a working husband. I don't know if they were lucky or unfortunate but he and his wife had triplets . . . and a second lot of triplets . . . and a third. She was only twenty-three, maybe twenty-four and he said "for God's sake do something!"'

Was it the man's right to make love to the woman whenever he wanted, regardless of her feelings?

'I think this was the usual thing although I wasn't married [chuckle] . . .'

Did you provide contraceptives through the back door?

'No, we couldn't because we didn't have them. Actually we were saying that we could provide condoms, but first of all the husbands were not cooperative and second the woman, having got it from us, would have had to give it to him. Most of them were asking for the pill or IUDs or something like this, but we couldn't. To be honest, some of the private surgeons would insert them in Kabul but this was expensive, I think costing 10,000 – 15,000 afghanis[8] which most people couldn't afford. What the women wanted was something that they didn't have to ask their husbands about so they would have the power, not their husbands. Many wouldn't have wanted their husbands to know – but, as I say, there were some men who did want contraception. They probably loved their wives quite a lot and couldn't take endless children.'

If the woman can't leave the house without the man's permission, and when she comes out she must be completely covered, there is no way of knowing what he is doing to her. He may be beating her. You'd never see the bruising.

'In Afghanistan, beating in some families is a normal part of life. Women are beaten by their husbands. Yes, I think in Afghanistan it happens quite a lot. Some of the educated men would beat their wives.'

[Ms Ghani, interjecting: 'They do in this country as well.']

'I have a friend – our mutual friend – who was married to one of our lecturers . . .'

['Oh my God'.]

'. . . a lecturer and he was an Afghan and he was beating her. So that's what I'm saying. It's kind of like normal. A man thinks you are his personal property and he can do whatever he wants with you.'

Meanwhile, America's senior female fighter pilot – Lt-Col Martha McSally – was stationed in Riyadh, Saudi Arabia, in 2000. She had to wear the *abaya*, the Saudi equivalent of the burqa, outside the base. She didn't like that. She had to be accompanied by a male at all times. She didn't like that. She had to sit in the back of a car and be driven. She didn't like that. As she said, how come I can fly a single-seater combat plane over enemy territory but not drive a car?

The Women's War

As I write this, she is suing Defence Secretary Donald Rumsfeld on the grounds that she was being deprived of her constitutional rights and being forced to wear the clothing of a religion other than her own. She has already shaken up the military establishment in the sense that they are relaxing the demands of these dress codes.

I wonder what a provincial Afghan woman in a distant, dusty village would make of all that.

Following the medical theme, this from the UN Integrated Regional Information Networks in Kabul, in April 2002:

> Rahema's tale is a sobering one. Three months pregnant, the 35-year-old mother of six is Afghanistan's latest female victim of opium addiction. Brought from remote north-eastern Badakshan province to the Afghan capital's only drug rehabilitation centre, she knows this is her last chance for help.
>
> 'We don't have the resources,' Dr Nagibullah Bigzad, an Afghan clinical psychiatrist at the poorly-equipped unit, told IRIN. Most women use it for remedial purposes given the lack of doctors or health services in Badakshan, but many still use it as an escape from the horrors of war or poverty.
>
> For David Macdonald, drug demand reduction specialist for the United Nations Drug Control Programme in the Pakistani capital Islamabad, the problem of female opium addiction extends far beyond Badakshan. 'There are thousands of women suffering from opium addiction throughout Afghanistan, as well as amongst the large refugee population in Pakistan and Iran. All indicators suggest this problem is increasing.'

ELEVEN

The Insurance Attorney

People started getting up and I yelled 'I'm alive, don't step on me, don't step on me please.' It took maybe a minute, maybe 30 seconds for the people to get off me. My big fear was that I'd try to lean up and somebody would stand on my neck and break it. My mind was thinking survival.

Renée Mangalo was born in Rhode Island, graduated law school in 1996 and has been admitted to the New York Massachusetts Bar. 'The legal market there wasn't so great so I also took the New York bar. I passed both of them, moved to Florida for a little while and then came to New York. I've been in New York for a little over four years.' She worked for Pattison and Flannery, representing insurance companies and dealing with large financial institutions. Her office was on the thirteenth floor of 115 Broadway. It had a magnificent view of the Twin Towers. As we have seen, the north tower was 1,368 feet tall and the south tower 1,362 feet. The normal skyscrapers arranged around them looked like pygmies.

Mangalo had a serious hobby. She was a marathon runner.

On 11 September she went to vote in the New York mayoral primary, carrying with her 'my bag with my lunch. Because I was a runner and I was training for the marathon, I do tend to eat a lot.

I knew I was going to do a ten-mile run at the end of the day – pasta was in there, tons of Gatorade,[1] carbohydrates and everything else, lots of little snacks. I'm not talking a little brown bag lunch, I'm talking a bag full of containers.' She also carried a bag 'with my gym stuff in it, which is kind of heavy: sneakers and everything'.

As she arrived at the polling station she saw the crowd gazing towards the north tower and saw the hole in it. 'You could see the hole. It was so easy to see, like it was just right there.' She rang her boyfriend Frank but couldn't get through.

He'd gone cycling that morning although originally he was supposed to work – in fact he was needed to help out with the election so he had somebody else work for him that day at the Fire Dept New York (FDNY). They'd called him at 7.30 that morning and asked, 'would you like to do overtime?' He replied, 'I'd love to but I've already declined because I have to do something else.'

It meant that, at 8.46, he was not with his battalion of the FDNY.

Mangalo 'came out after voting, just minutes,' and tried to ring Frank on her cell phone 'but nothing was working because the plane had knocked out something in the communications on the tower. You couldn't get any calls out. I realised I had better not take my subway because it was the [lines] 1 and 9 or the 2 and 3 – they went directly under the Trade Center. It wasn't flaming that much but I thought *wait a minute, the subway is bound to be backed up. Is there going to be chaos?* I was definitely shaken by the whole thing – I knew people who worked in the building – but I wasn't thinking about the danger. I just assumed I would go to work and have a normal workday. I think many people did that. Nobody could imagine this was going on.

'I did know a plane had hit because somebody had told me it had. I thought it was a one-person piloted plane or commuter plane or something like that, and that's what everybody was saying: "a commuter plane has hit."

'I proceeded to walk east to another subway line because I figured it would be the better route. As I was walking I cross from Sixth to

The Insurance Attorney

Fifth Avenue and when I looked at the towers again I see flames coming out of the second building. I think *oh my God there must have been a secondary explosion or something like that and it has set this other tower on fire.*'

That was 9.03.

'Everybody's standing around and people were in the streets everywhere, amazingly just standing there staring. I stopped and stared for a minute. I think I heard someone say "another plane's hit". The feeling was "oh, the smoke from this fire blinded this other plane and that's why it hit the other tower". I kept trying to call anybody I knew in my office to ask "what's going on? Does anyone know what's going on?" and tell them I was trying to get to work: *I'll be there as soon as I can.* No calls out, nothing. Finally for some reason I was able to dial my parents number in Rhode Island. I was very, very shook up but I said, "I'm OK, I'm fine, I'm going to go to the office." They weren't realising how close I was.'

Her father: 'I think it might be a terrorist attack.'

Mangalo: 'What do you mean?'

Father: 'Well, I don't know. They're saying two different things. Nobody knows. It all just happened a minute ago.'

Mangalo: 'All right, I'll call you as soon as I get to the office.'

That was the last thing she was able to say to them for what seemed an eternity.

'I proceeded towards my office. I get on the subway and I was crying the whole way down there because I was upset. Here's this building and something major has happened and people are dying but nobody was talking about it, everybody was very, very calm. Then one of these people did start talking to me. "You know, a plane hit the World Trade Center, that's probably why this train is moving so slowly." The train was just crawling. By now I was tearful, I don't think I was balling. I thought I needed to get off that train and get down there and see what's going on. I don't know why I would go to something that's dangerous but nothing was registering in my head. I would just go to work, I'd look out my window and watch everything. I still had no reason to think I wouldn't be going to work that day.

'I finally got out of the subway – the Wall Street station on the 4 and 5 train line right underneath my building – about 9.40 and walked over towards the building. But you know what? When I stepped out of that subway it was very clear to me that this was more serious than I thought it was because there was paper everywhere, paper just floating down, debris already everywhere, pieces of everything – and burnt things, pieces that were burned laying on the ground. I went *oh my God*.

'A policeman came to me and he said, "sorry you're building's been evacuated." I started panicking. "What do you mean? What do I do? Where is everybody?" You just want to see someone you know at this point and hear them say *you're going to be OK, you're going to be fine*. Then one of our security guards came over and said, "don't worry, I checked the whole building door-to-door, everybody's out, it's been evacuated."

'The police weren't even aware of how dangerous the situation was because there were tons of people standing around watching and looking up at the towers and they just said, 'OK, go across the street if you're going to stand." I said, "I want to find people from my office" and that's what they told me: "Well, go stand across the street."

'A co-worker of mine usually arrived around 9.40, 9.45, 9.50 so I thought I'd go and wait for her by the subway because I didn't want her to be alone if possible. What I was doing was looking just to find someone I knew – so I stood there trying to find her right on the corner of Wall, and I waited a few minutes Then I bumped into my boss, one of the partners in my law firm. He was walking up the street and as soon as I saw him I started to cry – *I know this is so bad, I know this is terrible*. My boss said, "let's see what time they're going to let us into the office, maybe they'll have an idea of what time we're going to get in. If not we'll just see."

The Insurance Attorney

'It was almost *maybe we'll go and get a cup of coffee and then come back*. So we walked over and the security guard was saying "well, I don't know, we'll wait until the police and the Fire Department give us the OK. It could be all day." My boss said, "well, maybe we can go up into the building and leave a message on our answer machine warning any of our clients and warning everyone else *don't bother coming in, the office is closed. We'll re-open tomorrow morning.* That was our thinking. The security guard was insistent, however, that "the building's been evacuated and no one can get in".

'We went across the street for a minute and looked around. I realised that I wasn't going to find my friend and my boss said, "let's go home, let's just go home." I said, "you know, I want to take one more look at the towers, I want to see them." I stepped around and took a good look. As I was looking there was a loud rumble – it was clear to me that either the building was exploding from the inside out or imploding. It sounded the way I imagine an avalanche sounds. I started to scream and my boss grabbed my arm. I saw the tower come down, it was like a flash that lasted a second and I thought *here comes the building*. It was clear that if this thing was exploding we were going to get hit with something.

'We turned to run and thank God we were behind the crowd, not in the centre of it. When I first started to run I thought *there's no doubt, I'll outrun this thing*. I figured I'd run and duck into the subway or whatever. Then I knew I was not going to outrun this thing. It was a dirty brown, dusty black cloud. We didn't run ten yards. I tried to look over my shoulder and I saw this big, huge cloud of debris coming at me and I thought *oh . . . I'm not going to . . .*

'I've always had a very optimistic thing about life. You're untouchable and now I thought *this stuff doesn't happen to me, danger doesn't happen to me*. Certainly not death. My first reaction, too, was *this is just like a movie, this isn't even happening*. I remember thinking that and then I realised I was screaming at the

199

top of my lungs – I think when I turned to see those towers I started to scream. I remember thinking *who's screaming?* and then I realised it was myself.

'When I understood I wasn't going to outrun the cloud I saw a revolving door into a building. I broke away from my boss, not even thinking I should stay with him. I felt fear and I tried to get into this building and he continued to go forward. There was a revolving door – but it got stuck. Five or six people came up behind me and started to push. Some people were trying to go one way, some people the other and I think something was stuck in the door. The cloud went right by us and started covering everything inside because the door hadn't even closed yet. I remember everything overcoming me, the smoke, the debris, you could feel there was glass. My face was pressed against the door and people were just pushing and pushing as hard as they could. I was a crazy person carrying all my bags and not even thinking to drop my bags . . .

'The door broke or it gave way and I fell forward and all these people started falling on top of me. I was not even half way round, I don't know exactly how far I was around but I do know that right away it started to fill up with smoke. I fractured my tailbone – your tailbone is almost like your butt, the tip of your spine. I fell face down, people fell on top of me and then other people were trying to get in and they started running over me. Not that many got in: once the big cloud had overcome people nobody else ever came into the building. What happened to the people behind me I don't know. I'd say that maybe six got through that door, maybe eight. I was in such a daze and everything happened so quickly. I didn't know if that was a ball of fire. You think it's an explosion and you felt glass but I'd leapt into the doorway.

'When I was in the doorway – because of the way everything was going up my nose and ears and into my eyes – I thought anyone who was out there would probably choke to death. My boss was out there and I thought immediately *he must be dead*. I couldn't breathe and I remember thinking *this isn't supposed to happen like this, this isn't the way I am supposed to die*. I was completely calm. It was as if I was going through the motions, as if everything was in slow motion.

'People started getting up and I yelled "I'm alive, don't step on me, don't step on me please". It took maybe a minute, maybe thirty seconds for the people to get off me and I realised *OK, no one else is coming through this door and I can stand up*. My big fear was that I'd try to lean up and somebody would stand on my neck and break it. My mind was thinking survival.

'I got up and there was a little area. Eventually I discovered there weren't that many people in this lobby – a bank building. It was completely pitch black and you couldn't see in front of you. I don't know whether it was the smoke or whatever that came into the building but you couldn't see anything. Also, outside was completely black. If you tried to look out the door you would see nothing, just night. I went over to where the light was and only four or five people were there. Nobody said a word – everybody was in complete shock, absolute, complete shock. My whole face was covered with dust and somebody handed me a tissue, then somebody started yelling "if you're alive and in the building, come to the back of the building, come down the stairs to the back". Somebody in that little group yelled, "we can't see anything". Somehow a flashlight appeared and it guided us. It's funny how people were thinking: you were just a couple of minutes from everything happening and people were ready to help you.

'We went down to the basement of the building and there were probably twenty people there. My first reaction was *they're taking us down to a subway system and I'm not getting on a subway* so I asked a gentleman, "what's happening?" and he said, "I don't know." He was very calm, he said, "just relax. You've made it through one stage, you've survived, now take it minute by minute."

That was very calming, and later I saw him on the TV news helping others.

'The first thing I need to be is in control and to know what's going on, so I didn't want to accept it would have to be done as he said. I wanted to know that I was going to be OK and everything was going to be OK.

'Then I started really shaking and crying – I'd realised everything. He was so good: "just take deep breaths and, yes, let's take this minute by minute. We're all here – you made it, you got in the door, you made it, you're here, you're alive." Unbelievable! And I saw in newspaper clippings this gentleman later on – probably an hour or so later – helping another woman up the street.

'In the meantime, while we were down there, a woman was there with glasses and she was completely covered with soot and I was covered with soot all over my face. We were having a conversation like nothing unusual had happened. I remember thinking *her glasses are so covered with soot but she's continuing talking* – and neither one of us wiped our faces off or did anything. We continued to talk to each other through this whole process like it was not a big deal to have your face covered with concrete dust. It was . . . comic. I was saying, "you know, my boyfriend is probably in that building, he's a fireman". I knew he would have gone to his fire station and by now he'd been down at the scene. She said, "oh, don't you worry, I'm sure he's fine, he'll be OK."

'I had time to think *let me unload some things*. I'm always on about food and feeding people and eating. I thought *you know what, if we're stuck down here for a few hours I've got food here, I could offer people some food. At least we'll have something to eat* – but I never looked down at the bag to see what shape it was in. People stepped all over it but I kept it in my hand the whole time. Apart from thinking that I had food to feed people in this basement I didn't think about it again until I'd walked for some miles.

The Insurance Attorney

'I had people's footmarks and bruises on my arms the next day – people stepped on my arms and everything else – but I was still holding on to the bag! I started to look in the bag and I was thinking *what can I save out of this?* Tupperware containers! I thought *well, maybe I'll dump the food out and keep the containers.* This is all at the same time as *I've got to get out of here, I'm in trouble.*

'We stayed there and then the smoke was coming down to that basement area and we couldn't stay forever. So many things were going through my head, but the biggest was *I've got to get out of here, I've got to get out of this building. Maybe this building's going to come down.* You don't know. You do know that to be underground and smoke coming is not good news. The other thing I was thinking was *if I could just be out in the open at least I'd know what's going on.* At least you'd see light, or whatever.

'People needed to start proceeding out. I don't know how long we'd been down there, ten or fifteen minutes. I don't know if the second tower had collapsed or what had happened during that time period. There was a security guard standing there and you feel *they will know.* People had started leaving.'

Mangalo: 'What's going on? What are we doing?'

Security guard: 'I don't know, but I suggest you follow everybody out.'

Mangalo: 'I don't want to go into the subway if that's where you're taking us. I'm not going into the subway.'

Security guard: 'just follow those people. I don't know where they're going but stay with them.'

Mangalo followed and they were taken to the back of the building, a 'kind of construction area although still inside the building. The next thing I know I see a window and it was light, there's the sun. For some reason I just felt better. Once I saw the sun I thought *OK.* I saw people walking by and everybody was covered with debris, people bleeding. The interesting part is by the time we got upstairs there was ice and water: somebody, maybe a person

The Women's War

who saw everything happening from the outside, gathered this stuff and brought it. People were yelling "where are the doctors? We need doctors".

'I was in a terrible amount of pain but just totally blocked the whole thing out. I was feeling *I've hurt myself* – I knew I had right away – but I didn't want to sit down, I didn't want to stop. I saw somebody break open a door, somebody yelled, "this way, this way, get out this way," and I followed them. You stepped out and it was like it snowed in Manhattan, a couple of inches of snow.

'You'd see people walking by just covered. I guess that's what I looked like, too. I walked past the Chase Manhattan Bank plaza and a man was laying on the ground. I turned and a guy had stopped to help him. I don't know if he was dead or whatever but the guy said, "keep going, keep going". Another guy yelled, too. It's funny. Everybody was very calmly moving down the street even though a crazy thing had just happened and it was apocalypse all around you. A guy behind me turned to his friend and said, "still get your kids and get the hell out of here".

'Sometimes people's calming calms you, then you'd see something like that man laying down on the street, probably dead, and I would get upset again.

'I walked slowly and another interesting part is how quickly people came out of their houses with water. People were stopping me – "here, let me give you some water." I remember walking by this little church on the corner and thought *should I go in there? Is this where I should go?* I didn't know. I am a Catholic, a practising Catholic. I kept thinking *I want to go home, I want to go home*.

'Now I'm walking down the street. I was sure my boyfriend would be seriously injured – something bad had happened to him. My other thing was *what the heck is going on?* One thing I was struck by in the September 11th video that was just released on Sunday, one of the French brothers who was narrating said, "the interesting part was that here we were standing in the building and we didn't know half of what was going on – unlike the people outside watching TV.[2] You knew more on TV than when you were standing there."

'It was so chaotic. We go east because at least I could be near the river and if it got really bad I'll jump into it. I'm not sure I was the only one thinking that, either. I walked as far as I could east and then headed north. Even going four blocks over, the debris got less and less and you reached a point where people were looking out of their windows at us covered in debris. They didn't even know what was going on. I stopped several times and put my bags down because my back was hurting. At one point I realised *oh my God, I am still carrying my lunch*.

'When I'd gone far enough to be out of trouble, my back was killing me the whole time. I thought I was walking around in high-heel shoes and maybe I should put my sneakers on. Finally I stopped and changed the shoes, put the high-heels in the bag, I kept them – I didn't leave a thing! I kept stopping every time I saw someone I knew. I said, "my boyfriend's a fireman, he's in that building." One woman said, "you shouldn't worry because firemen know everything about this stuff, they knew that building was going to come down and I'm sure they evacuated everyone." I said, "yeah, I guess you're right."

'I kept going. People saw that I was visibly upset and I was hurt. I was limping along. The bags? It's crazy that you wouldn't put that stuff down but instead carry it the whole way. The craziness of everything! At one point, because of all the concrete dust, I realised I was losing my vision – I couldn't see. I never thought rationally: somebody would give me a bottle of water but I'd drink it rather than wash my face with it. I guess I didn't really know what I looked like and how bad I was. I stopped again and a gentleman came over. I said, "I'm losing my eyesight," and he poured water in my eyes and helped me clean up. People were stopping to help you along the way.

'I was still in lower Manhattan and I was walking very slowly because of my back. The strange thing was that when he helped me rinse my eyes out I felt a lot better and that's when I put my sneakers on. That was when I started thinking OK, *better take care of yourself.*

'I couldn't run – well, if I *had* had to run I would have run. I think I was walking out a lot of the pain, because here I was carrying a pretty heavy bag on my shoulder the whole time and somehow I didn't want to get rid of it even though it was hurting me. I reached the Brooklyn Bridge and I saw policemen running, other people running. I said to a policeman, "what am I supposed to be doing?" and he said, "I don't know, just get out of here." He didn't even stop for a second to talk.

'At that point I put my bag down and started to cry because I didn't know what to do. This gentleman had his bar door open and he said, "come in and sit down." People were on the streets everywhere trying to help people. I didn't go in and wash everything off my face, I didn't want to stop. I said, "I hurt my back," and he said, "let me get you an ambulance." I said, "oh, no, there's other people who need them. I can make it, I can go to the doctor later." He said, "well, maybe you should take some water," he gave me water and I proceeded to walk again.

'What was strange was when I got to Chinatown it seemed like business as usual. They were bustling around and that made me upset because I wanted to say "something bad just happened" but then you start to think "well, I'm over-reacting."

'Nobody else looked like me! I don't know where the other people went! It was like I had wandered into a weird zone. Here I was covered with soot, nobody was crying – just me, the only one walking down the street balling – and they were just going about their daily thing, so I did think "well, maybe *I am* over-reacting here."

The Insurance Attorney

'People had their windows open with their TVs facing out and I started to hear news reports. Every time I sort of heard something I couldn't stop because I guess I didn't want to hear it.'

At this point, two young women from Belgium came up.

Belgians: 'Are you OK?'

Mangalo: 'Yes, but I think I hurt myself.'

Belgians: 'We'll get you an ambulance.'

Mangalo: 'Oh, no, no, no.'

Belgians: 'Well, let us take your bag for you.'

Mangalo: 'No, I can't give you my bag. What happened? Is this a terrorist attack?'

Belgians: 'No, it's not, just a plane, there was smoke, one plane hit in, another plane hit the other tower.'

Mangalo: 'I think one tower exploded and fell down.'

Belgians: 'No, it's not bad, don't worry.'

Mangalo: 'What are you doing?'

Belgians: 'We were originally on our way down there to go up into the towers but we heard what happened and we are watching from here.'

Mangalo: 'Good thing you didn't go today . . .'

The reality that one tower was gone had still not registered in Mangalo's head . . . 'even though I heard people saying "the building's down". I thought to myself *hopefully I'll be able to go by the end of the week to see the towers.* I may even have said to the Belgian women "maybe before the end of your vacation you could get a chance to go in there". It was almost as if they were still going to be there although I was a witness to one of them falling down.

'They walked with me all the way back to Twelfth Street and they kept saying "do you want to stop? Do you want to go in here and get a drink?" and I'd say "No, no, no." I was on a mission, I wanted to get home. I felt if I got home I could call somebody. I just wanted to call somebody – warn my family and my boyfriend that I was

OK, and then I would figure out if I need to go to the hospital or what.

'I got back to my apartment, which is right across the street from St Vincent's Hospital, and I thought "do I go there now? No, I just really want to make a phone call." I went into my apartment and called my mom – I was able to get the call out but my parents couldn't call in – and the tears were falling. I was hysterical. "A tower collapsed on me." I thought it was one or two in the afternoon but when I got my phone bill I checked and it was 11.30.

'My mom said what saved her was that she thought I was almost a mile away but the sad part was my cousin and my brother had visited me [some time before] and walked from the World Trade Center to my office. They knew it was only a half a block away. They were really panicking but none of them said anything to my mom or my dad – that I was right there. As I was speaking I just lost it.'

During this, Mangalo's Call Waiting beeps and when she answered it she heard one of her bosses.

Boss: 'Are you all right?'

Mangalo: 'Yes. Where's Tom, the other boss?'

Boss: 'He never went to the office. He found out early in the morning and he went home.'

Mangalo: 'No, he didn't, he came with me.'

Boss: 'What?'

Mangalo: 'I think he might have died.'

Boss: 'Stop it, don't say that. I can't talk to you, I'll call you back.'

Mangalo remembers 'screaming and yelling into the phone "I think he died," and then my mom comes back on and I said, "I've got to find out where my boyfriend is, I've got to find where Frank is." She said, "OK, call me back." I started listening to my messages and I hear a message from him at around 9.00 saying "are you OK? Where are you? Please call me."

'I think: *OK, 9.00, he might not have got down there*. I started to get reassurance from that. Then there's another frantic message from

The Insurance Attorney

him saying "listen, get out of there, get out of downtown whatever you do. Start walking, stay as close to the river as you can and walk north as far as you can. Don't walk near any buildings. Go to my apartment or go to the firehouse and stay there." He had known it was a terrorist attack and he had called my office – I found this out later and I only found out a few weeks ago [winter 2002] that every time they were evacuated he was calling my number from a pay phone or from anybody whose phone was working.

'For him 9/11 began right before he was about to leave [for the voting] – the first plane hit. He thought *this is going to be the biggest job, I've got to go to work*. His father and brother are both firemen – his father, a retired captain from FDNY, called him from Florida and said "get your stuff and go. This is bad. They're going to need all the help they can get." Frank was saying, "I'm going, I'm going". He'd rung and there had been no recall [when everyone off-duty is phoned in a major emergency] but most of the guys didn't need that. Like Frank they just headed up there. He and a couple of other guys got in a truck and went down there and he didn't arrive there until the second tower came down. It was complete darkness all around because it had just happened and he started working.'

Now, back in her apartment, Mangalo called his firehouse and back-up people had come in as cover. They were answering the telephones.

Mangalo (crying): 'I am looking for Frank and I assume he went down there. I know he's looking for me and I'm OK.'

Cover: 'Don't worry. He went down with a group and he couldn't possibly have gotten there before the second tower came down. As far as we know everybody is in one piece.'

Mangalo: 'If he calls, or there is anyone who calls to the firehouse to check in, just tell him that his girlfriend got out.'

Cover: 'No problem, we'll get him a message.'

Mangalo found it 'so comforting to hear him be very calm on the phone and say "it's OK." Then I phoned my doctor and his wife answered the phone and said he had gone to the hospital. I told her what had happened and she was very calming. She asked, "what are you doing now" and I said, "I am covered with this concrete stuff." She said, "well, go wash your face" – it was all in my ears and my nose. "Take a shower as soon as you can." Then I told her about my back but I was afraid to go to the hospital because of all the craziness and the number of casualties they'd have to be treating. She said, "I think you should go. You were trampled. You might feel OK now but you don't know what could have happened." I said I felt like I could wait until four o'clock in the morning if I had to. "I don't need to get in, I don't want to be bugging people." She said, "hospitals know how bad people are and they will treat you in order of what they can do." Across the street all the doctors and nurses and beds are lined up waiting for people to come – and nobody came.

'About an hour after I got home, when I'd already talked to my mom and everything, I didn't know there were attacks all over the country. A friend called and said she was just evacuated from the courthouse in Boston. She said, "didn't you know? They hit the Pentagon." I said I didn't know. She said they had evacuated the Sears Tower[3] and then I turned the TV on and *what the hell is going on?* This country being attacked – not something I would ever think of.

'Then my skin started to get all irritated from the fibreglass so I went over to one of the doctors standing outside and explained my situation but, I said, 'I don't want to take the place of anyone, I don't want to be in the way.' They said, "don't you worry, we can take care of you."

'I went back into my apartment and continued to call people and I didn't go to the hospital until about three o'clock in the afternoon. I waited until I talked to my boyfriend, who called finally. He was in complete shock too, I think. I started crying and saying I'd been trampled and he said, "stop – you're alive".

The Insurance Attorney

'I went to the hospital, I took medicine and the phone just kept ringing. It did not stop. Minute by minute, people calling. "Are you OK, are you OK?" Then I started to think: *when is the next attack coming? Is it coming tonight?* My parents kept saying to me "get out of the city whatever way you can," but I said, "I am not leaving until I have seen my boyfriend. I need to see him and I need his reassurance. Maybe in a couple of days." Even in the back of my head I was thinking *maybe I'll go to work tomorrow.* My mother was saying "you broke your tailbone, you can't walk. How do you think you are going to go to work?" Nothing was sinking in, nothing at all, the amount of damage, what had just happened. I just couldn't register it, I just wanted some normalcy, I was just looking for normalcy.

'My boss called me late, late in the afternoon to say he was OK. He got away, he got glass and everything but he didn't get hurt. Somebody dragged him down in a bomb shelter below a building, and he was so sure that that was *it* – that I didn't make it. He said that he was trying to get back to me but "there were a lot of people coming at me and you were gone. I had no idea what happened to you." It was a relief. Then a co-worker said "God knows what the shape of our building is – we don't even know if it's standing." It was complete destruction down there and I hadn't realised it. I started to think about where our building was and where everything else was. Then I thought *I may not have a job to go back to.*

'At about 12.30, one o'clock in the morning I picked up the phone to dial my boyfriend at the firehouse just to see if there was any news about when we might expect to hear from him, and there was a knock on my door. My room-mate answered the door and there was my boyfriend standing in his firemen clothes covered in debris and it was like him returning from a war scene. It *was* from a war – and an amazing reunion to see the other person after such a horrible, horrible day. I said, "how did you get here?" and he said, "there was a truck going uptown and I asked if I could get a ride.

All I knew was that I needed to see you because I knew you were hurt" – we'd had one minute on the phone together earlier on. I wish somebody could have taken a picture of me hobbling towards him and him just covered with debris . . .

'We were allowed back the following Monday to get a file or two. I went to Rhode Island for five days to see my family and our office re-opened temporarily in a hotel in midtown but we couldn't really do a whole lot of work there. We were not allowed back into the building until October 3. Our office got some debris and dust in it but it was all cleaned up. You looked at my window sill, however, and there were pieces of glass and paper from the World Trade Center. I also found charred documents and a piece of carpet.

'I definitely think my boyfriend and I have coped differently with the aftermath – although probably in many ways the same way. Obviously he does a lot of talking with the guys in the firehouse. I think most of his dealing with the emotions is through that and with that. He lost a lot of friends, over fifty guys that he knew closely. He plays on a 'pick-up' hockey league with the fire department – not an official FDNY team, but a group of guys from their house played another group of guys from another house. The guys that played on his right and on his left – on his line, I guess you'd call it – both perished. He was lucky in the sense that everyone he was working with got out. It was a twist of fate that they were OK.

'That's why I say sometimes someone was looking down and it's not your time yet. One of the companies – there were two companies in his house – was heading into the Trade Center and they pulled up. Someone said, "hey, move that truck, you can't just leave it here because we need to get other vehicles through." They went to move the truck, the building came down and they were OK. Another group heard the building was coming down and ran. They ran *that* way, the Chief ran *this* way – and he died. I'm absolutely thankful for the men and women who do put themselves on the line to protect the freedom of this country.

'It has certainly brought us a lot closer together. I don't hang up the phone on him or leave him without saying "I love you". You don't know that tomorrow he won't be here or I won't be here. You just don't know. That is a realisation I have every day when I get up and go to work, that I might not return home or he might not return home or someone from my family or a friend might not be there tomorrow. That's how my life has changed. You just don't take it for granted. It makes you live harder: live every moment.

'What has happened is that I moved in with him. There were a number of reasons, including the safety of being there. I feel a little safer, you know.'

On November 3 Mangalo ran in the New York City Marathon for Windows of Hope, a charity helping families who lost relatives working in food services throughout the World Trade Center.

'I thought I wouldn't do the marathon and then I thought *you've got to move on, you've got to survive, you've got to be part of it*, so I said I'd raise some money. Prior to September 11 I was training really hard to do a specific time. That all went down the drain but the realisation that I was there and able to run was a huge thing in itself. I set out to do it and I did it faster than I thought I was going to do it. An amazing day. New York was so united, it was emotional, it was the most incredible feeling running through the streets, people cheering, firemen and policemen everywhere cheering you. It was great for the city, we moved on, we're not going to let them do this to us. I raised a couple of thousand dollars. My boyfriend ran as well and got a flag and ran across the finish line with the flag. We didn't run together – he's a very fast runner! I am so happy I did it. Afterwards, I felt I could run another marathon.'

On September 10 if I had shown you a blank map, could you have found Afghanistan?

'No, I don't think [I could] have picked it out on that, but I will say I've always been very interested in the occupation of the Taliban and, way before 9/11, I'd read a lot of stories about the women. I've always been interested in the treatment of – and the plight of – the women there. I did a lot of reading because I was so distraught about it.

'Prior to September 11 I guess I truly didn't believe that people have evil in them. I felt that people's circumstances in their lives created that, and I always wanted to take that into account any time there was a bomb or anything. I didn't expect them to act in society the way I act – but these people were purely evil. It was pure evil what was done, coldly calculated, against innocent people who had done nothing and who only wanted to live their lives.

'The people flying the plane [into the second tower] even banked it so that it would cause maximum damage. Reading all that, well, every time I read a little more it made me feel angry and I tried to think of the worst torture possible for those who were responsible. A friend of mine at work felt the same way, although we still didn't believe in the death penalty. I wanted them in the middle of Times Square and I wanted people to torture them daily, but not use guns on them.

'It's not just for the Trade Center or the embassy bombings,[4] it's for what they did to women in Afghanistan for many, many years. Maybe we should get the women of Afghanistan to deal with that. I was fascinated by it, but why hadn't the UN or anyone else done anything about these human rights violations for years and years? I couldn't believe that we allowed women to be treated that way.

'I have often wondered whether the Taliban's strategy was to diminish women to the point where the men of their own society, including their own sons, would separate themselves from women – distance themselves and dedicate their lives to Islam rather than being into a family, and seeing the happiness of family life and the importance of family. You look at the fighting soldiers, they are all young kids, teenagers, just boys. Now they can't rely on their mother, they can't have their mom, the mother is not important. They are being told: you can dominate women, you don't need to love your mother, you don't need to respect her, she's a non-person.

The Insurance Attorney

Maybe this is their strategy – to separate the men and make them dedicate themselves. Then you can create these monsters.'

If there were more women leaders would there be less war?

'Absolutely. Women are talkers, rarely do you ever see women have fist fights and there is a proverb: women deal with it through words. I just don't believe it is in our nature to be violent, to strike out. A man's reaction – and I don't know if it's the way they've been brought up or if you see it in the little boys – is always to lash out. Most women think about families and that's a big goal in your life.

'You may not feel that way at 18 or 21 but, as you get older, you learn the importance. Most women put a lot of stress on raising their children and that's a huge part of their lives. Women are going to be more deterred risking their own flesh and blood in a war because they know the bond a woman has with her children, and those children are soldiers who might get killed.'

Later, I invited Ms Mangalo to read these words and reflect on them if she wished. This is what she said: 'I feel I am men bashing. I also don't want it to sound like all that women think about is their families and babies. I just think women are less likely to take the military approach, but they have in the past – and will do so – if it is to protect their people. I think most women would tell you that if they needed to resort to violence to protect their children, family or friends they would do so. I would do so.'

What would you have done after 11 September?

'I am not sure I would have handled things much differently. I would have first secured the country. As soon as possible I'd have had a news conference to calm people down, but be very truthful about the situation. Then, once I felt the country was stabilized, I would have immediately got all the leaders of the Arab world together to discuss what we could do to handle this problem. I would make sure I had the majority of the Arab world behind me, and the other major world leaders. I think it was wise that Bush waited before he took action. I am unsure what has been accomplished, although one good thing is that Afghanistan has been freed from the Taliban. I do hope the US and the rest of the world gives the country the financial support and other resources it needs to put it back together. Otherwise, economic desperation and poverty could bring the country right back to where it was.

'People act out of desperation. We see that with the Palestinians. The people see no sign of hope and, therefore, they don't value their lives or those of others around them. They are desperate for a better life.'

SILENCES AND OTHER VOICES

In spring 2002 the BBC broadcast a programme in their *Correspondent* series entitled *Silent Scream*. It began with a RAWA worker, 'Danish' – face covered up to the nose for, presumably, security reasons – saying 'nobody thought about the rights of Afghan women. The Afghan woman is not a human being, she is the woman who has lost everything and then she became prostitute, or widow, or beggar on the streets. In Afghanistan that means that you are nothing. So for me, Afghan woman, she is not alive. She is like a dead moving body.'

The words are spoken over film of women in their bright blue burqas, with nothing visible except the mesh in the hood for seeing and breathing. They move, in what always seems somehow a slow shuffle, like silent creatures from another age and another dimension. A woman, squatted on her haunches, begs. She is showing her hands. Another, oblivious of the camera so close to her, turns and smoothes the burqa down with a hand. Another advances along a railway line holding a child in both arms, the child wearing a little jerkin of the colours of the rainbow and what looks like a heavy woollen hat. To hold the child she must expose her hands.

The burqa is central to this book because it symbolises the separation of the two worlds which met on 9/11: one western, rich, seeing itself enlightened, legislating for women's equality; the other

The Insurance Attorney

eastern, poor, seeing itself persecuted and, in its extreme religious form, granting women fewer rights than – as someone said – animals. Of course these descriptions are so generalised as to be near caricatures, but we can at least work with and around them.

To a westerner, the burqa *shows* how the east is still in the Middle Ages but, like Ground Zero, the burqa has its own different levels.

Tahmeena Faryal has said of the Taliban: 'Their thinking is men cannot be controlled and what is the answer to that? Burqa! I guess the good point about this is that they accept men cannot be controlled and they cannot control themselves, and that's why women have to be covered, and are not laughing, and are not wearing colourful clothes – but that's what these men don't say.'

Jennifer Middleton, the New York attorney whose working day revolves around gender issues, reflects on Ms Faryal's words.

'It's not that the men can't control themselves, it's that they don't *want* to control themselves so they put up all kinds of signs and signals, like the burqas, to reinforce this idea that they can't control themselves. That means, to them, if they do lose control it's excusable. If women really imposed on men a requirement to control themselves they could, but, because we allow some degree of latitude – boys will be boys – they don't trust themselves and they don't trust women. *Because* they don't trust themselves and they get that idea reinforced, it becomes OK to cross those boundaries.'

An American reporter called Tasgola Karla Bruner was assigned to Afghanistan by *The Atlanta Journal-Constitution* and went through all the normal western emotions about how could women tolerate the burqa which, she interpreted, was a form of punishment on *them* for what she described as male lust.

Ms Bruner, however, discovered the burqa's advantages when she donned one herself. She could cross the Afghan-Pakistan border unhindered and she found the border guards and men on both sides treated her with absolute respect. She used it whenever an interviewee didn't want to be seen talking to a westerner like her.

And whenever she wore it she was no longer a sex object. She recounted how, once, instead of the burqa she'd worn other clothing and immediately became a sex object again, with one of Hamid Karzai's bodyguards talking dirty and saying he'd been offered money so men could take her off for sex. She understood then when so many women retain the burqa. They're frightened.

The burqa is an intensely physical thing.

Margaret Owen of the Empowerment for Widows describes wearing it as 'horrible because you can't breathe. You have this tiny little grill in front of your eyes like a few squares, so you can't see either side. Also it's terribly stuffy. I suppose a lot of other people had worn it because it was smelly and nasty and awful. On the other hand it was a protection.'

Christina Lamb of the *Sunday Telegraph* 'wore a burqa years ago on one of the trips into Afghanistan and I hated it because I felt you could only see the world in little snapshots. You feel like you're speaking and no one is taking any notice of you. You can't make yourself be heard. You are just nothing – and it's extremely ugly. In the hot weather, which is most of the year, it's very, very hot and sweaty. It's also hard to walk because the sun blinds you. It's a very, very horrible garment. It was extremely frustrating becoming nobody. I was in a bus full of people when we went to Afghanistan and I was in the burqa. I wanted to say something but nobody was taking any notice of me. It makes you realise how much you use expressions and gestures. All that had stopped.

'I asked Afghan women how they recognised each other when they wore the burqa, because your whole personality seems to be subsumed into it. I have a fairly characteristic walk, I move lopingly – quite fast – and I have one leg longer than the other. People often laugh at my walk but once you are in a burqa all that disappears. The only way it has a benefit is if you want to do things very secretly – nobody sees what you're doing. I never worked out how women did recognise each other. They were allowed to speak in the street but not to laugh. It seems girls can go around without one until puberty. Thirteen, fourteen – that's the age they go into purdah.'[5]

You're now facing a complete generation of men who have never seen a woman except their mother. They don't know what they look like, any more than you could know what other women look like.

'But they would have seen women at home, they'd have seen relations. Nobody hasn't actually seen a woman.'

All right, beyond that nothing: all women would be a mystery.

'No, because women would have come to the house, and what goes on inside the house is different to what is going on in the street. And don't forget a lot of them marry their cousins, anyway.'

If a friend came to the house, she'd be able to take it off?

'Yes, in many houses but not every house.'

But to take an example, a 19-year-old growing up under the Taliban, how many women's faces would he have seen? And what has this done to his mind?

'I'm not sure that that's the main point. What has happened is people of that age have grown up to think that a woman is something which shouldn't be seen: seeing a woman is the quick way to eternal damnation. They have been given a certain view of women.'

How did they reconcile that with their mums?

'I remember talking to a woman in a refugee camp in Pakistan whose son had gone to one of the Madrassahs. She couldn't hug her son from the age of when he started at the Madrassah and he was about seven. So he would never have known from the age of seven onwards a woman's contact, and would have been taught that women are some kind of strange creature. Also – and it might sound callous – people grow up much more quickly there.'

Lamb quoted Zena Karamzade, a student who went to the underground Sewing Classes in Herat, as saying: 'If we did go out we had to be accompanied and wear a burqa, which is like being

The Women's War

imprisoned in a closed space. With the carbon dioxide you breathe out and not enough oxygen coming in, after a while your lungs feel like exploding.'

And Dr Sima Samar, Afghanistan's first minister for women's affairs, said in February 2002: 'The burqa is a symbol of oppression but it is not the biggest issue by any means. First, women should be counted as human beings, not property.'

I want to contrast this with the experiences of three interviewees in the book who are Roman Catholic. They weren't chosen for that reason because, as I've said, I had no idea until I met them that they were, and even if I'd known it would have made no difference.

Renée Mangalo, the defence attorney: 'I would say at the moment that I felt I was going to die, somehow I knew in my heart that this is not how it is intended to be. This is not the moment. I feel like I'm here for whatever reason, there is a destiny for me and I knew this was not how it was going to end.'

Now reviewing the fate of the people in the Twin Towers, how do you feel about that?

'I do in some ways feel that when it's your time to go it's your time to go. There are too many stories of friends who were supposed to be there . . .'

Why would your God have allowed all that to happen?

'For whatever reason He takes people from this earth. There is a reason. I don't know what it is but I do believe we are put here for a reason – for a period of time – and we don't have control of when it's going to be taken away from us.'

Why did it have to be fire and innocent people jumping? What God would do that?

'I don't know, I don't know. I can't justify that but I don't think that's His doing, I think that's people's doing. I'm very uncomfortable talking about religion. I have been wearing my cross since 9/11. I got it for Christmas and I wanted to wear, maybe because of my superstition, my belief.

'I have always said that God doesn't give you anything you can't handle.'

Dianne Kenna, who worked next door to the Twin Towers: 'I was bred a Catholic, I was a Catholic in school and high school but I don't go to church regularly. It's not as driving a force in my life as it might have been. Obviously it must be internally inherent in me because at that moment [of crisis] that's exactly what I felt and what I was reaching out to: my faith. Did it reinforce it? I don't know, but it reminded me of it. A re-birth to it – maybe.'

Terri Tobin of the NYPD, whose astonishing story began this book, should have the words to end it.

Apart from anything else, did the events of 9/11 shake your faith?

'No. I think they reinforced it. Part of it to me personally is that miracle after miracle happened – just one of them the fact that Joe Dunne grabbed me and said "put on an Emergency Services Unit helmet". The helmet that we normally wear is sturdy but not necessarily that sturdy . . .'

It seems to me there were no miracles there at all. It was purely chance – that's how chance would play itself out. Some people happened to be in the wrong place and some didn't. Why wasn't God looking after the ones in the wrong place?

'I don't think we will ever know the answer to those questions – perhaps not until we die, anyway.'

Notes

Introduction

1 Columbia University's Lamont-Doherty Earth Observatory, some 21 miles north of New York City, has calculated the times of the impacts on the Twin Trade Towers (*New York Times*, 12 March 2002). The first plane crashed into the north tower at 8:46.26 and the second plane into the south tower at 9:02.54. The calculations were based on the 17 seconds it took the seismic waves from the impacts to travel to the observatory and had a possible error factor of two or three seconds but not more. The south tower collapsed at 9:59.04 (56 minutes after impact) and the north tower at 10:28.31 (102 minutes).

2 The World Trade Center was a whole complex comprising seven buildings over 16 acres with the Twin Towers as the centrepiece. It contained financial buildings, subway stations, the train to New Jersey, a Marriott hotel, shopping malls and a plaza. 1 World Trade Center was known as the north tower and 2 World Trade Center the south tower. These were the ones hit.

3 BBC South Asia analysis (December 2000).

4 Frontline, PBS (public broadcasting) of Virginia.

Chapter One

1 Lt Tobin did this in preparation for our interview 'because it might help you'. It did that, all right. More, because the lieutenant has some experience of the written word (in-house magazines and so on) it was what we call clean copy. You can put it straight in, and I did.

2 The Twin Trade Towers complex was very close to the Hudson River. See the map on page x.

Notes

3   Triage is one of those curious words which is well known throughout the United States but perhaps less so in Britain. It means a place where injuries can be assessed on the basis of immediate need. As Tobin says 'you are treated very quickly but not extensively. It's patching people up.'

4   In March 2002, to mark six months after the attack, CBS screened a documentary called *9/11* made by French brothers Gedeon and Jules Naudet. They had spent some weeks filming the progress of a probationary firefighter and this took one of them inside the north tower. It was the only film of that in existence and captured brave men suddenly trapped in chaos and incomprehension. Many aspects of the film were unbearably poignant, but the worst moments were the thudding of the bodies of those who had jumped. Next day the *New York Daily News* filled the whole of its front page with the headline INSIDE HELL on a black background with, below, the photograph of a helmeted firefighter, face coated in ash. It captured the mood of the whole city.

5   There is a system of national monuments, memorials and parks (Statue of Liberty, Ellis Island, Yellowstone for example) and National Park Rangers work there, environmental specialists who give talks to visitors, some about the history of the park.

6   CAT scan is an X-ray machine – a tube which rotates round a patient taking pictures as it goes. These are then reconstructed by a computer into a whole.

7   Rockaway is a suburban area near Kennedy Airport.

8   That Tobin was a Catholic I did not know (it would have made no difference). As it happened, two other interviewees were also Catholics (which again I did not know). Because of the intense nature of Roman Catholicism, I was curious about the reaction of all three to *9/11*. I have grouped them in *Silences and Other Voices* at the end of chapter eleven.

Chapter Two

1   The predominant ethnic group in Afghanistan.
2   Meena (known just as that) was born in Kabul and, university educated, formed RAWA in 1977. She was invited to the French

Notes

Socialist Party Congress in 1981 and when she appeared and cheering began the Soviet delegate walked out. She was assassinated (RAWA's word) at Quetta, Pakistan.

3   Ruhollah Musavi Khomeini, known throughout the world by his position of Ayatollah, was exiled to France and returned to Iran when the Shah was deposed. He led Iran back towards a strict interpretation of Islam.

4   The two Buddist statues, enormous and hewn from a rockface in the Bamiyan Province in the third and fifth centuries, were designated a world cultural heritage site by UNESCO. They were blown up by the Taliban in March 2001.

5   Mullah Omar, friend and protector of bin Laden, was 'commander of the faithful' under the Taliban, a powerful title. A recluse who was never interviewed by western journalists and virtually unseen even by Afghans, he is thought to have escaped the American-led fighting on a motorbike.

6   *Afghan Women Challenge the Fundamentalists*, published by RAWA.

7   http://www.rawa.org

8   UNESCO Mission report, 5–8 March 2002.

Chapter Three

1   A freshman is a student in the first year of college.

2   Choosing your major course of study.

3   Strictly a student at a preparatory school who'd wear blazers, trousers of a certain colour, ties, button-down long-sleeve shirts – preppy here implying a certain kind of (uninteresting) conventionality.

4   Rugby shirt. Dave played Rugby and Marian spent her 21st birthday in the traditional Rugby-playing way: sitting beside him in hospital.

5   Brownstone building – self explanatory except implying a certain age and solidity.

6   Dave worked for Ladder 122, a designation for the firefighters in a firehouse who man the ladders. However, on 9/11 he was with the Special Operations Command. Their function is described in the text.

7   Rudolph Giuliani was Mayor at the time.

8   The FDNY Commissioner.

9   The FDNY Deputy Commissioner, a woman.

Notes

Chapter Four

1. The Swedish Committee for Afghanistan, 24D, Chinar Road, University Town, P.O. Box 689, Peshawar, Pakistan. Website www.sak.a.se/
Donations to: Swedish Committee for Afghanistan Information Unit. Account number: 113-15-6038-7001.
Bank: Standard Chartered Grindlays Bank Ltd., Peshawar Branch.
2. Between Kabul and Peshawar.
3. North of Kabul and bordering Pakistan.
4. A hand-made silk sari.
5. Non-governmental Organisations.
6. Women have had acid thrown in the faces by their husbands in remote, fundamentalist areas of Pakistan and, as it seems, the husbands feel they have a perfect right to do this. This had moved to Afghanistan because the Reuters news agency reported in April 2002 that, in Kandahar, an 'unidentified man' threw acid on a woman teacher. This followed the circulation of hand-written pamphlets, evidently from an unknown Islamic group, warning men not to send their daughters to school or their wives to work.

Chapter Five

1. The *New York Times* carried, as a regular feature, obituaries on *every* victim.
2. The sense of guilt at having survived recurred like a tangible theme throughout the interview, and I have not edited out the repetitions because they express Kenna's thoughts with absolute accuracy.
3. A sports and leisure centre at the West Side Highway.
4. Tri-state: New York, New Jersey and Connecticut.
5. The coffee shop which was in a mall next to – and attached to – Kenna's building.
6. Someone working regularly for a newspaper but not on the staff.
7. A primary election is when several candidates from the same party are running for the same office, in this case Mayor of New York. So Bloomberg was facing another Republican he had to overcome before he went on to face his Democrat opponent.

Notes

8 Check in – what reporters and photographers do as a reflex action when they're working out of the office.
9 FDR Drive runs down the eastern shoreline of Manhattan, as the West Side Highway runs down the west – see map on page x.

Chapter Six

1 Lamb won the Foreign Reporter of the Year at the UK Press Awards in March 2002 and also the Foreign Press Association Awards December 2001.
2 Benazir Bhutto became Prime Minister of Pakistan but lost that post amid corruption allegations.
3 Stringer – as Marilynn K. Yee had done for UPI long before she joined the *New York Times*.
4 Mujahideen, the Afghan warriors who fought the Soviet Union.
5 The Soviet Union's war in Afghanistan was regarded as part of the Cold War, with the United States arming the Mujahideen.
6 Estoril, a resort near Lisbon.
7 Canary Wharf is part of London's Docklands development – an immense (by British standards) office block.
8 Yvonne Ridley, 43-year-old journalist working for the *Daily* and *Sunday Express*, London, got into Afghanistan illegally wearing a burqa and was seized. She had two guides with her. She was eventually released without trial and deported to Pakistan.
9 Pashtuns are the dominant ethnic and linguistic group in Afghanistan. Most of them speak a language called Pashtu.
10 Hamid Karzai, a Pashtun and senior politician, well educated and westernised.
11 An American journalist, Don Oberdorfer, wrote in his book *The Turn: How the Cold War Came to an End* (Jonathan Cape, London, 1991): 'In early March 1989, only a few weeks after the withdrawal of the last Soviet troops, close to eight thousand Afghan guerrillas from several disparate tribal groups laid seige to the eastern city of Jalalabad in what became the biggest battle of the Afghan War. The siege was mounted under pressure from the Pakistani intelligence agency, which distributed the U.S. and Arab aid to the Mujahideen tribesmen . . .

Notes

In the short run, at least, Jalalabad [was] saved by emergency Soviet military aid, a resolute defence by Afghan government troops who were fighting for their lives, and the failure of the various guerrilla groups, who were unaccustomed to conventional warfare, to develop effective coordination or a competent battle plan.'

12 Tandy: an early lap-top computer which journalists could carry round with them, put their stories into and send them down phone lines to their newspapers. They had limited memory capacity and one reporter (not Ms Lamb) beat his to pieces when he discovered his machine had erased what memory it had, destroying all his work.
13 The documentary – *Correspondent* – was broadcast by the BBC in spring 2002.
14 Jihad, a word often taken in the west to mean holy war. Its true meaning is broader and less intimidating: a task.
15 Religious schools.
16 Merlin provides healthcare for women and children in crises around the world. Donations can be sent to them at 5–13 Trinity Street, Borough, London, SE1 1DB, England or go online at www.merlin.org.uk

Chapter Seven

1 Stairwell, strictly the shaft in which a staircase is built but used to mean stairs.
2 JP Morgan, a leading world financial company.
3 Cantor Fitzgerald's offices were on floors 101, 103–5 of the north tower. They lost more than 700 employees.
4 You can contact Debbie Barrett's group through the web site, which does not contain any confidential information. www.fiancesof911.com
Ms Barrett says, 'hit the Contact Us button and it will allow you to write a note.'
5 A service in New York to try and help identify the victims using relatives' DNA.
6 The 75–25 split in favour of men seems explicable because most of the employees – traders, businessmen, executives – would be male. The women would tend to be receptionists, waitresses and secretaries. This is my opinion. Ms Middleton commented thus: 'This seems like a sexist

Notes

assumption to me. After all, the secretaries always get in earlier than their bosses, so wouldn't that mean more women died? [The first attack at 8.46, the second at 9.02.] It may be an inaccurate assumption . . . but it is true that many of the very high-level people weren't in yet, in part perhaps explaining why the average age of decedents [a US legal term for deceased] was so low.'

7 Special Master Ken Feinberg, the lawyer named to oversee the Federal Fund for Victims' Compensation.

Chapter Eight

1 Cryptology: making and breaking codes.
2 Turn over: a military term for passing on information to other members of an office or team.
3 A rank: Yeoman Chief.
4 911 is the US emergency phone number, in the way 999 is in Britain.
5 Escambia, where the Allegers were living, is the most western county of Florida, bordering Alabama.
6 Intravenous drip.
7 Prep. Alleger explains it means 'stabilise medical condition, place on backboard and strap person down for transport to medical facility or ambulance'.
8 United Flight 93, a mere 80 miles from Washington, came down in Pennsylvania – as it would seem, the passengers stormed the hijackers and the beginning of that – 'Let's roll' – heard over a mobile phone became almost a national anthem. The man who spoke those words was called Todd Beamer. His widow Lisa gave birth to a daughter Morgan Kay four months later.
9 DPS, Defense Protective Services, the Pentagon security force.
10 Condition of spaces: the condition of the offices people were coming out of.
11 Flatbed carts are used for hauling large or bulky items – and it's easier to move a person safely on one.
12 The water, the Potomac River which flows nearby.
13 A litter is a portable, collapsible stretcher.
14 Field Injector – a type of syringe.

Notes

15 The Dilorenzo Medical Clinic is inside the Pentagon – it's a satellite clinic of the Army Hospital Walter Reed.
16 The US Marshals service protects the federal courts and ensures effective operation of the judicial system.
17 In fact, the car bomb was a rumour.

Chapter Nine

1 Rwanda, a central African state where genocide was carried out during a tribal civil war.
2 Cambodia (with Vietnam and Laos) had been part of French Indo-China.
3 A group of aid workers – from the Antioch Community Church, Waco and two Germans – who were arrested in Afghanistan for distributing Bibles. They were imprisoned but escaped when the Taliban fled.
4 Ahmed Shah Massoud, 48-year-old leader of the deposed Afghan government and fierce opponent of the Taliban, was killed by two suicide bombers on 9 September.
5 Mazar-I-Sharif, the town in the north.
6 Muslim law, which is controversial and of which almost no westerner knows anything.
7 Faizabad, Afghanistan, not to be confused with Faisalabad, Pakistan.
8 International Committee of the Red Cross.
9 Straw, British Foreign secretary.
10 The Loya Jirga is, according to the UN, a 'tribal council which is set to play a central role in Afghanistan's political transition.' [April 15 2002]. This first stage would involve Afghans in about 300 districts selecting potential candidates to 'form a pool from which 1,500 members will be selected in a second stage of elections after 20 May'.

Anders Fange, of the UN Assistance Mission in Afghanistan, said that although women were entitled to present themselves as candidates, 'relatively few would feel confident doing this'. He explained that 160 seats have been reserved for women, the equivalent of 11 per cent of the seats – and this would 'put Afghanistan ahead of all Muslim countries'.
11 The EWD web site is www.oneworld.org/empoweringwidows

Notes

12 Israeli Prime Minister during the Yom Kippur War, who said of Israel's opponents: 'We haven't hit them hard enough yet.'
13 Indira Gandhi, Indian Prime Minister who could conceal her hardness with a certain gentility.
14 The Red Crescent, part of the International Federation of the Red Cross.

Chapter Ten

1 Ex-King Muhammad Zahir Shah, deposed in a coup in 1973.
2 Pashtu and Dari are the two official languages, but there are many others and bilingual people are common.
3 UN talks, involving a broad spread of Afghan leaders, were held in Bonn, Germany. They led to a decision to set up an Interim Authority which would assume power on 22 December 2001.
4 The west is little better. The restricted role of women is mirrored in their treatment in the Protestant Church of England (where the question of women bishops is highly contentious) and the Roman Catholic church (where the idea of women priests at all is regarded as something too cataclysmic to be even discussed).
5 Chadour, a long black veil worn also in Iran and Iraq.
6 Chadari is the Afghan expression for the burqa, a word of Pakistani origin.
7 The World Food Programme, the front line UN aid organisation against hunger, aiming to feed 9 million Afghans.
8 The currency of Afghanistan: the afghani. To calculate the value of an afghani is a tricky business (literally). At one point before Kabul fell a bundle of notes *weighing* one lb (0.4kg) was worth $1.

Chapter Eleven

1 Gatorade, a sports drink that helps athletes stay hydrated.
2 The documentary *9/11* broadcast on CBS in March 2002.
3 The 110-storey building in Chicago.
4 The 1998 bombings of the US embassies in Kenya and Tanzania.
5 Purdah: used in certain Muslim (and Hindu) countries to literally curtain off women from strangers.